By the Same Author

Titles in the *YouTuber's Guide to Life* series
The YouTuber's Guide to Life: Subscribe to Your Dreams
The YouTuber's Guide to Life: Upload Your Happiness
The YouTuber's Guide to Life: Monetise Your Apologies
The YouTuber's Guide to Life: I Dunno, Just Go for a Walk, I Guess?
The YouTuber's Guide to Life: I'm Not a Therapist... But...

Titles in the *Number 7 Will Shock You* series
100 Cities You Must Visit Before You Die
500 Restaurants You Must Eat at Before You Die
200 Dental Practitioners You Must Have a Filling at Before You Die
20,000 Videos of Dogs You Need to Watch Before You Die
15 Before You Die Books You Need to Read Before You Die

Other Titles
The Big Zebra Colouring Book
Marcel Marceau's Greatest Speeches
It's Pronounced 'Gif'
The Paradox Paradox
Harry Potter and the Pretty Cool Duck
So, You've Infringed Copyright: A Legal Guide
Wrongly Incarcerated: My Years in Jail
Lessons Learned: My Years after Jail
Harry Potter and the Nice Dog
So, You've Misunderstood Double Jeopardy: A Legal Guide

FUCK YEAH

VIDEO GAMES

The Life and Extra Lives of a Professional Nerd

Daniel Hardcastle
Illustrated by
Rebecca Maughan

unbound

First published in 2019

This paperback edition first published in 2020

Unbound

6th Floor Mutual House, 70 Conduit Street, London W1S 2GF

www.unbound.com

Text design by PDQ

Illustrations © Rebecca Maughan

A CIP record for this book is available from the British Library

ISBN 978-1-78352-947-6 (paperback)
ISBN 978-1-78352-787-8 (hardback)
ISBN 978-1-78352-789-2 (ebook)

Printed and bound in Great Britain by Clays Ltd, Elcograf S.p.A.

1 3 5 7 9 8 6 4 2

For Jay,
John
and Pa.

Thank you to the devastatingly attractive people below for their generous support of this book, even the one that came in late and the one that wildly missed the picture-sending-in deadline completely. I assume they're just as attractive as the rest.

Front of the book Champions
2019

① Brandon Coulter
② Joshua Harbour
③ Brenden Nichols
④ Matthew Eich
⑤ Anthony Thomas Poliandro
⑥ Grant Cousins
⑦ Will O'Donnell
⑧ Harm Broeren
⑨ Goaliator

⑩ Lukas
⑪ Ayran Ellis
⑫ Timothy Pieschala
⑬ Jakob Ravn
⑭ Daniel Fitch
⑮ Hayden Taylor
⑯ Ryan Grondin
⑰ Aidan Ward
⑱ Grayden Bedford

Handed in Late
(see me)
⑲ James Armitage
(Armo)

Not Pictured
(but still lovely)
⑳ Dmitry Zonenko

Thank you! ♡

'I'm being quoted to introduce something but I have no idea what it is and I certainly don't endorse it.'

— Randall Munroe, xkcd

Contents

Foreword by Tim Schafer   xiii

Introduction   1
The Sims   5
Pokémon Red and Blue   11
Kingdom Come: Deliverance   17
Mario & Sonic at the Olympic Games   23
Shadow of the Colossus   29
HARDWARE HISTORY: SONY   35
Sonic the Hedgehog   49
Watch Dogs 2   55
Double Fine   61
Tony Hawk's American Wasteland   73
Ride to Hell: Retribution   79
Mirror's Edge   87
Crüe Ball   95
Heat Signature   101
HARDWARE HISTORY: NINTENDO   107
Animal Crossing Series   127
Black   133
Kerbal Space Program   137
Bratz: Rock Angelz   147
Tom Clancy's ruthless.com   157
Tomb Raider III   163
HARDWARE HISTORY: SEGA   171
Noby Noby Boy   191

Just Cause Series 199

Mario Party Series 207

Prison Architect 213

Metal Gear Solid 2: Sons of Liberty 221

The Elder Scrolls V: Skyrim 229

Bloodborne 235

HARDWARE HISTORY: ATARI 241

SSX 3 251

Tom Clancy's Rainbow Six: Rogue Spear 257

Sins of a Solar Empire 263

Portal 271

Fortnite Battle Royale 275

God of War 281

Afterword 289

Afterafterword 293

The Top 101 Games of All Time 297

Glossary 313

Acknowledgements 327

About the Author and Illustrator 329

Supporters 331

Sneak Peek: The Paradox Paradox 379

Tim Schafer

Here we are now, living in the future, where it's pretty clear to everybody that the internet was an incredibly bad idea. Unfortunately for us, the internet is already invented and it's very hard to un-invent stuff (except for New Coke, which we un-invented in about three months, but we were more organised back then). No matter what you think of the internet, this ubiquitous, hateful, non-stop Nazi-making machine is probably here to stay. But let's try to look on the good side, shall we? Let's try to find a silver lining in this 24/7 sadness delivery service.

Some people would say that cat videos are the one redeeming quality of the internet. And, I mean, sure. Cat videos are definitely better than many things – for instance, owning a cat. But cat videos alone cannot redeem this fetid, wormy stew of an internet.

Exhibit B: Looking up exes on social media to see how they've aged and wondering if they're thinking about you *is* pretty satisfying. In the old days we'd have to do that by slowly driving by somebody's house and staring into their windows. So, progress there for sure. But is that enough? No, of course not.

Maybe this will do it, as I've saved the best for last: I have used a popular shopping website to subscribe to toilet paper. Yeah, I know. Pretty amazing. I once was forced to walk to the store, taking in minute upon minute of unnecessary sunlight and exercise, then walk home with my shameful, filthy bounty. But now, thanks to the internet, my toilet paper comes to my house whether I ask for it or not. I could be lying dead on the living room floor, my face already eaten by the cats I unfortunately own, and still my porch would be stacked with boxes of toilet paper. And cat food, too, now that I think of it. So maybe my face would be fine. But the point is that the TP arrives on its own, which is convenient and also helps me pretend that the toilet paper is eagerly volunteering to do its horrible job. I hate to think I'm forcing this kind of duty (hee hee) on anything.

So, does a better relationship with toilet paper make up for all the Nazis the internet generates on any given day? No. Not on its own.

But there's more. There's more good on the internet. ONE more good thing that makes the whole thing worthwhile, and that thing is Daniel Hardcastle.

Mr Hardcastle, and the videos he makes under the name Nerd[3], live on the part of the internet called YouTube, where there are already five zillion people playing video games and talking while they do it – and I'm going to sarcastically say that's great. I'm a game developer, and let me tell you there's nothing more rewarding than crunching for five years on a video game, living and breathing the creative process, tackling the technical challenges and financial struggles, just to have someone take your content, put it up on YouTube, make a bunch of fart jokes and random swears in front of it, and then make more money from it than you do. Okay, sincerely now: it's not always great. Often the fart jokes are substandard and the swears are about you and they can get really mean.

But not Daniel's. Ah, deep breath. Let's all just relax and think about what a lovely person Daniel is and how pleasant and entertaining his videos are. You know if he ever makes a fart joke it will be Top Shelf, Best in Class flatulence humour. More than that though, Daniel really seems to love video games, and he's not afraid to show it, uncynically and sincerely. His love for video games always comes through, and that means a lot to a game developer because we love games too. We love the games we make, but we also love all the games we grew up with. They brought magical fantasy worlds into our mundane, nerdy lives (might just be talking about myself here) and stimulated our sense of our own creative potential. Every game we make is a labour of love, and I think for Daniel, the same thing goes for his videos.

Not this book, though. I assume he just tossed it off over a long weekend, or else used machine learning to get a computer to do it. Or maybe he just grabbed a chat log and published that. I don't know. But I just assume he wrote it the easiest way possible because, trust me, that's what I would do. Writing sucks and is hard. Which reminds me, I need to stop doing it now.

Thank you for reading, and thank you, Daniel, for inviting me to mess up the front of your nice book. Happy reading, everybody! Now that Daniel comes in book form, we can sign off the internet forever!

Love,

Tim Schafer
San Francisco, California

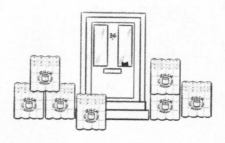

Hello

Hello! My name is Daniel and I create what gross business types call 'content' on the internet, as well as writing scripts, making games and slowly forgetting everything I ever learned about geography. In doing so I have amassed a following in the millions, a view count in the billions and about £28.50 in my savings account.

On a more personal note, I'm married to Rebecca, the wonderful illustrator of this book, share a bed with two dogs and when I grow up I'd like to write for *Doctor Who*.[1]

Since I was knee-high to a particularly small grasshopper, I've loved video games. They're magic. *Actual magic*. Plug a machine into your TV and suddenly, *you control what happens on the TV*. That's not science, that's spellcraft. William Higinbotham should have been burned as a witch when he created *Tennis for Two*. Apparently nobody got out so much as a ducking stool.

Today, however, video games are on the edge of a precipice. Years ago you bought a game, popped it in a console or PC and played it. When you were done you put it on a shelf to come back to later. That was how the world worked. It was nice.

Nowadays you have to work out which retailer exclusive pre-order you prefer, gamble on whether or not you want the season

---

1   I also like footnotes, so expect a lot of these little numbered bastards.

pass before you even know what's in it, spend hours patching the game before it will even start, launch the game to find out the servers are down, it's not finished yet and that it's charging you £99.99 a pop to open a box of items, all of which are duplicates. After all of this you can't even put it on a shelf because it's digital and you technically don't even own it despite the fact you've spent six grand on it.

What the hell happened? Games used to be a fun hobby; now they seem to be designed to separate as many people from as much money as possible. They're the digital equivalent of shaking you upside down and taking what falls out. You can't so much as press start without engaging in psychological warfare designed to detach you from your hard-earned cash. I just want to play a video game. Why am I being electronically mugged?

This is where this book steps in, coughs and politely calls you over to a comfy chair, a warm fire and a cold lemonade. Let's cast off DLC, microtransactions and loot boxes for a few hundred pages and have a nice chat about the truly brilliant games of this world. Some are old, some are new, but all of them are worth your time and attention.

Well, except one *terrible* one...

Enjoy!

Daniel
Parts Unknown, 2019

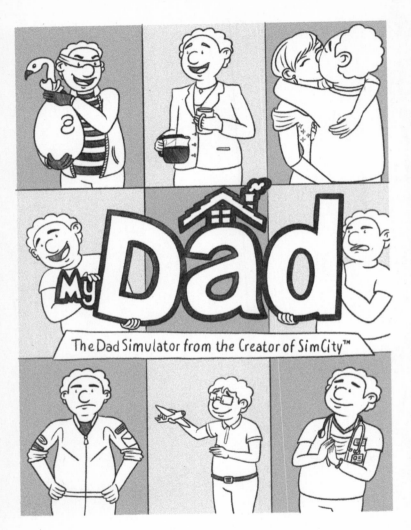

The first character I created in
The Sims was my dad

Developer: Maxis
Publisher: Electronic Arts
Platform: PC
Released: 2000
What is it? A life simulation.
What is it *really*? An excuse to set your own family alight.

The first character I created in *The Sims* was my dad.

For reasons lost to time, I didn't initially make any other members of my family. Just my dad, alone, in a two-bedroom bungalow nestled in a quiet corner of Sim Lane. Beautiful place, it was. The yellow and black wallpaper clashed with the neon-brown carpet, but it clashed in a classy, modern-living kind of way.

Dad's only company in this Magic Eye puzzle of a house was the statue of a pink flamingo that he kept in the garden. He named it Bert. Some tosser stole it on the first night.

The early days were surprisingly hard for Dad. The theft of Bert had hit him hard and he was struggling to find work.[1] His attempts to do normal, grown-up things had resulted in him urinating in the kitchen while setting fire to the only cooker in his price range. Not even the acquisition of Bert II could help liven up his dreary mood.

---

1   Well, I say *he* was struggling to find work; I was the one who hadn't yet found the paper on the front porch with the job section in it.

As he settled down that night to watch his tiny TV, he gave up all hope for a good life. Channel 5 will do that to you.

Suddenly, there was a knock at his door. Thinking it was the pizza delivery man, Dad leapt to his feet. Sadly it turned out to be only his neighbour and future wife, Bella.

As Bella Goth welcomed Dad to the neighbourhood, she was unaware she'd just met the man she'd leave Mortimer for. She was especially unaware that, due to Sims having loyalty that even Judas Iscariot would think was a touch backstabby, she'd be remarried by the end of the week.

The wedding, like the relationship, was a small affair. Dad wore black, Bella wore white and Bert wore a slim little pink number. Bella moved in immediately, complained about the dirty plates and fell asleep. Now, happily entrenched in Les Dawson's idea of married life, Dad finally got a job.

The security gig was a breeze for Dad. He loved the graveyard shift. It paid well and gave him time in the day to spend with Bella and his hobbies.[2] He did come back smelling a smidge corpse-y every now and then, leading Bella to suspect that he didn't quite know what a graveyard shift was, but she let it slide. Besides, it reminded her of Mortimer.

You know, now I think about it, there was something a bit... *off* about Bella. She was doing a wonderful job of cleaning the bathrooms, fixing broken electronics and waxing Bert II, but every now and then she'd just do something... weird. One day she simply picked up a bin bag, walked to the centre of the kitchen, and placed it on the floor. Neither she nor Dad could ever pick that bag up again. I ended up building a wall around it. It didn't stop the smell. Or the flies.

Back in the world of late-night security, promotions came

---

2   I say hobbies... he just liked to stare at Bert II and think about the weather.

thick and fast for Dad. Before you could say 'one day left until retirement', Dad was a Patrol Officer. The mean streets of SimCity became his territory. Dad was there to serve and protect, be it against robberies, car thefts or even giant green lizards heading for the nuclear plant. For the first time in his life he was happy. Nothing was going to take him away from this.

Pregnancy is weird, isn't it? You know those countless hours you've spent crafting the perfect RPG character? You know, stuff like making sure the nose for Gladius Bigpecs, Hero of the People, is the exact right distance from his philtrum? Well, having a baby is like clicking the 'Randomise All' button on that character. Actually, it's worse because it's not just the shoulders and bottom you'll be looking at for the next fifty hours. It's a person. A person you then have to love and keep alive. Have to. By law.

Bella's news pierced Dad's chest like the bullet that he would be hit by a few days later. Questions oozed out in a very similar simile. How can we afford this? What if the trash smell drives it mad? What will Bert II think? How did this happen considering we've only kissed and I'm pretty sure that's wrong but I'm only eleven so I don't know? This was set to be a scary and confusing time for all involved.

We didn't have long to prepare. Mere seconds later a text box announced that Dad Jr was here. Well, a crib appeared anyway. Every now and then it made a noise so I assumed there was a baby in it. Could have been a Furby for all I knew.

One thing I did know, however, was that they'd all need a bigger house. Dad and Bella sold everything that wasn't nailed down (so long, Bert II) and upsized to just down the street. Big plans were laid for the new house. Downstairs would be the kitchen, living room and pool.[3] Upstairs would be the office,

---

3   Due to miscommunication, Bella thought that pool meant swimming pool. Dad meanwhile had already bought sticks and numbered balls.

main bedroom and baby's room. Actually, now we mention it...
where was the baby?

Dad Jr was never seen again. He'd vanished without a trace.
We're assuming the moving guy labelled a box wrong somewhere
and Dad Jr ended up in Mexico. You always lose something
during a move, don't you?

Bella started acting up. That might have been due to the
literal loss of the baby or the comedown from lack of trash
fumes, nobody really knows. The marriage dissolved soon after
and she left to be with the mailman. She was married before the
next collection time. A few days later Dad was shot at work. I
decided to cheer him up by spending the second-floor money on
a swimming pool in the garden. Lovely, it was. Diving board,
lights, the whole shebang. No stairs, though. Waste of money. He
could just climb out, right?

He drowned an hour later. The last thing he saw was the
newly purchased Bert III. I'm sure he would have wanted it that
way.

I feel I let my Sim Dad down. He had all the potential in the
world and I helped him squander it on women, TVs and flamingo
wax. He could have been the next John McClane but instead he
ended up like David Dunn. There's a lesson to be learned here about
your kids ruining your life but, to be
honest, it's vague at best.

The next character I made was my
mum. She burned to death cooking a
salad on day three. The fact I even
exist at all is a fucking miracle.

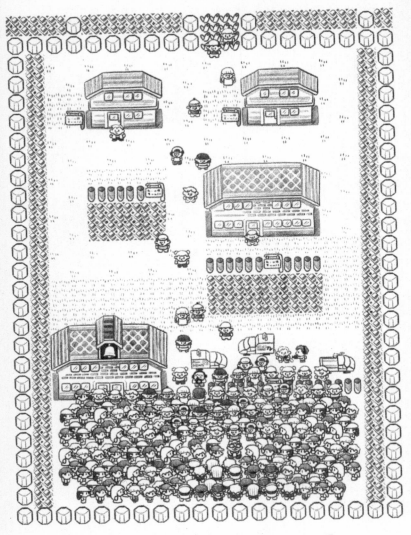

Looking back on it, this was the most
popular I'd ever be in school

Developer: Game Freak
Publisher: Nintendo
Platform: Game Boy
Released: 1996 (JP) / 1998 (NA) / 1999 (EU)
What is it? An RPG about capturing wild creatures.
What is it *really*? An addiction that has had me in its grasp for two decades.

Pokémon Red and *Blue* are works of programming art. The English release of the games was just a single megabyte in size,[1] meaning that you could fit the entire thing around 50,000 times onto a standard PS4 or Xbox One disc. That's 100 hours of gameplay, a world with 10 cities and towns, 170 animated abilities,[2] 80 Items,[3] 45 music tracks,[4] an uncountable number of NPCs[5] and 151 monsters, all on a cartridge that takes up the same amount of space as around a minute of mp3 music.

It's that monster number that I want to focus on for this story. Not the first 150, we could all catch them. I want to just look at that final one. Number 151. Mew. The mystery that captivated

---

1 Apparently, the Japanese release was only 512 KB!
2 Roughly. I only counted this once.
3 Again. One count. I had stuff to do today.
4 I'm a busy man, goddammit!
5 Totally countable by someone who isn't me.

a generation. A generation that clearly had nothing else better to do beside collecting Pogs and making barely flavoured ice with Mr Frosty.

You see, Mew wasn't technically obtainable in *Pokémon Red* and *Blue*. There was no way of catching it without going to special events, hacking your save file, or very clever glitches that weren't found until over a decade after the game came out. Everyone knew someone who knew someone else who knew someone else who had one, but nobody seemed to be able to prove it. Even that kid in your class whose uncle worked for Nintendo didn't have a smidge of evidence.

These days, if you don't know a thing, you go online, and after a few searches, you know the thing. Back when I was a lad in school, we didn't know things simply because there were no ways of knowing them. The closest thing we had to the internet was a library, and no book in there had even heard of video games yet. This meant that rumours weren't just king, they were currency. I traded many wildly incorrect rumours I'd heard for Pokémon cards back in the day.

> *'Yeah, just hold B and Down and you'll definitely catch any Pokémon. Now, Hand me that shiny Alakazam.'*[6]
> — Me, 1999 (probably)

How many of these playground legends did you hear?

- If you give Pikachu enough Water Stones, he'll turn into a Pikablu.

---

6 Remember those kids who would later bottle out of the trade and tell their parents to force you to trade back? You know, the argument-starters who eventually caused all these awesome fads to get banned from schools? I hope they're all fucking dead.

- Bill has a secret garden behind his house with a legendary Pokémon in it.
- Catch a Lickitung with the Game Boy upside down and it'll evolve into Luigi.[7]
- Magikarp's splash can insta-kill anything (it just only works a fraction of a per cent of the time).
- Talking to Oak's assistant a hundred times before picking your starter means you can get all three of them.

All of these were, quite obviously, bullshit. However, there was a magic to these rumours, a chance that they might be true, formed from the coalition of a brilliant game and the fact that all children are idiots.

My favourite myth was the truck. Apparently, there was a truck somewhere in the world that had a Mew hidden under it. Only a level 99 Machamp[8] that knew Strength could move this mystery vehicle. I remember my entire school spending every moment that wasn't sums or finger-painting trying desperately to find this truck. We heard a rumour that it was next to the SS *Anne*, a cruise ship docked in the game. Problem was, the boat left and the port was locked down before you got the ability to swim and explore the area. Bugger. Guess it's back to Tazos for us.

However, a week later, and I distinctly remember this happening in church, I came up with a solution. The SS *Anne* only left when you got off it, so if I lost a battle after getting the mission item, but while still onboard, I'd be teleported out to the Pokémon Center to heal up. Maybe, just maybe, the ship wouldn't leave and I'd be able to come back later. With the

---

7   This was actually an April Fool from *Nintendo Power* magazine. They also claimed a Dratini could evolve into a Yoshi if you traded it and trained it loads. I spent hours on this one. Bastards.

8   Some people said to use a Squirtle, but they were clearly idiots.

delicate movements of a world-renowned surgeon, I extracted my red Game Boy Pocket from my coat, turned the volume down and reset my game. Yes, I'd lost all my progress, but if this worked... I'd be a hero.

Mum then saw my Game Boy and confiscated it until we got home. I tried to explain the hero thing but she was too wrapped up in the priest's sermon, a speech that was getting dangerously close to somehow becoming less than monotone. Batman didn't have to put up with this shit. Lucky Batman.

Later that night I performed rigorous testing in the most scientific environment I could manage,[9] starting the entire game from scratch to prove my hypothesis. The hours passed as I raced through the game, wanting to know the answer before school the next day. Eventually, I had my answer. I was *right*. The SS *Anne* didn't leave if you fainted inside it. We were through the looking glass.

I pushed on, ignoring the first rays of sun creeping across the floor, finally obtained the ability to swim, went back to the port and... oh my God...

The truck was real.

It sat there, off-screen until you swam over to it, just next to the SS *Anne*. No way to access it without the fainting strategy. I didn't have the level 99 Machamp required to finish the rumour, but that would come later. I had to report my findings to the playground. I put my Game Boy away, placed my glasses down and heard my alarm go off.

Looking back on it, this was the most popular I'd ever be in school.

I was king. No, kings are mortal. I was God. God of the swing set. I was young at the time and may be remembering this

---

9   Under my bed covers with a torch.

wrong, but at least 80,000 children crowded around me that day to see the truck. Liam Packton claims he saw kids in uniforms he didn't even recognise watching me play that Game Boy Pocket. I swear at one point a news crew turned up.

Suddenly a shout emerged from the crowd. Someone had a level 99 Machamp. They'd got that first, planning to search for the truck later. They were willing to trade. The crowd of over 2 million children held their collective breaths. A link cable was found and inserted. The trade was made. I approached the truck, used strength and... and...

Nothing.

Nothing at all.

Looking back on it, this was the least popular I'd ever be in school.

This wasn't even the whole Kobayashi Maru trick
that a few games pull early on - I just sucked

Developer: Warhorse Studios
Publisher: Deep Silver
Platform: PC, PS4, Xbox One
Released: 2018
What is it? A medieval RPG.
What is it *really*? Bohemia Rhapsody.

In *Kingdom Come: Deliverance* you play as Henry, the blacksmith's lad, living in the quiet village of Skalitz in the year 1403. You can't read, you can't wield a sword and you'll probably die of the sniffles at the grand old age of thirty-five.

One uneventful morning you wake up late, eat whatever the hell is boiling away in the nearest pot and go and see your father. He's a bit busy forging a weapon for the local lord so lumbers you with a shopping list and a debt to collect. This is the first mission of the game. For me it didn't go well. It didn't go well at all.

Being poorer than the side characters in *A Christmas Carol*, I figured I'd better collect the debt first. Kunesh, a gruff and rather unpleasant peasant, had ordered an axe, hammer and nails and neglected to pay. I strode up to him, stopped him chopping wood and demanded payment. After a brief but earnest exchange, I began picking my teeth up from the floor with a newly dislocated arm.

You're not the big hero in *Kingdom Come: Deliverance*. You're not even a small hero. You're simply the blacksmith's boy.

Due to the way that video games have trained me to think, I expected to blatter Kunesh into the consistency of whatever was in the pot earlier, but he annihilated me. I actually had to run away from the very first fight in the game. This wasn't even the whole Kobayashi Maru trick that a few games pull early on – I just sucked. This is a game that tells you to stand on your own two feet, then promptly sweeps them out from under you, lops them off and beats you to death with them.

I now had a problem. With no debt collected I couldn't buy anything. I needed to find a way to make money in a world where people who owned half a cabbage were on the *Forbes* rich list. I wandered over to the local tavern to find work and mercifully found something much, much more useful. A lockpick.

So, who to burgle? My first thought was the castle on the hilltop. Sure, it would have treasure, but I had fought a fat drunk earlier and still had to extract my left leg from my own arse afterwards. Heavily armoured and beweaponed guards were probably a smidge out of my range.

Steal from a shop, perhaps? Nope, turns out that they all had their own guards, too. I couldn't even wait until nightfall as Lord Radzig was coming to pick his unfinished sword up today. I was in quite the pickle, or the nearest fifteenth-century equivalent at least.[1]

As I sat on the main road, wondering what the church's view on stealing communion wine was, I spotted an opportunity. A woman across from me had just left her house and hadn't closed her door. I took this as a sign from God and sneaked inside. Admittedly it could also have been temptation from Satan, but if it came up I'd plead entrapment.

Inside, I was plunged into darkness, both literal and metaphorical. Frantically I searched the house, finding only

---

1   The first use of the word 'pickle' was only thirty-seven years after this opening mission. This is the most boring fact in the entire book.

discarded planks of wood and dusty nothing for my sins. It took just a single floorboard creak to make me realise my mistake. Nobody in this time period could afford to live alone. Uh-oh.

I tried to back out of the house but met the owner coming back in. In a panic, I hit her square in the face, knocking her out of her own house and into the thick mud outside. Somehow the mud got dirtier.

Unsurprisingly, I spent the next twenty minutes running away.

The downside of an opening mission is you're normally limited to a single location. I couldn't simply bolt and start a new life as Gregg, the sausage-roll maker, I had to stay and face up to my problems. After quite a bit of hiding in bushes I found myself near Kunesh's house and watched him chop wood for a bit while coming up with new naughty words to call him. Something felt off. What was it? I stared at him for a while before I realised.

He was chopping wood.

Chopping wood.

With a tool.

What tool do you chop wood with?

What did he buy from us?

These both have the same answer, don't they?

GODDAMMIT.

While I was wondering if my life peaked while I was still a sperm, Kunesh went inside his house, giving me time to swipe the axe back. I headed over to the village trader feeling a bizarre mix of smugness and failure, whereupon I got confused by the haggling system and accidentally sold the axe for about 25% of its actual worth. I walked out of the shop, lay down on the floor and decided I should get a job as pig feed.

An hour or so later, an army attacked the village. They killed anyone who stood in the way, did unspeakable things to the ones who didn't, and burned everything down to the ground. My home was gone. Everyone I'd ever known was dead. My life as I'd known it was over...

So yeah, on balance it all turned out all right in the end.

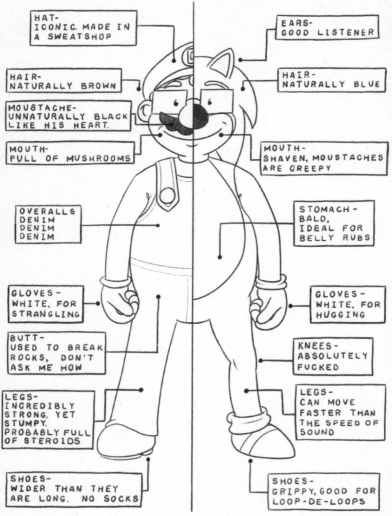

In the world of video games no debate
rages on as unstoppably as Mario vs. Sonic

MARIO & SONIC AT THE OLYMPIC GAMES

Developer: Sega Sports R&D
Publisher: Nintendo (JP), Sega (Worldwide)
Platform: Wii
Released: 2007
What is it? Sport-themed party games.
What is it _really_? A way to settle decade-old arguments.

In this world of ours there is a small handful of debates that, possibly without realising, you have already picked a side on. Things like Pirates vs Ninjas,[1] Batman vs Superman,[2] Kirk vs Picard,[3] Garfield vs Snoopy,[4] and Lego vs Mega Bloks.[5] However, in the world of video games no debate rages on as unstoppably as Mario vs Sonic. The two titans of gaming history – fated never to meet.

Well, until they did.

Mario & Sonic at the Olympic Games was the first time the lead mascots of Nintendo and Sega had appeared in the same game. Never before had we seen the blue hedgehog and the Italian plumber together outside of disturbing fanfiction. Worlds were going to collide in a big way and, best of all, this was going

1 Ninjas. Eyepatches are bad for depth perception.
2 Neither after that film.
3 Sisko.
4 This debate tore my family apart.
5 This one is more of an intelligence test.

to be in pure competition! I grabbed a copy with a friend on launch day and we prepared to settle sixteen years of debate. I was team Sonic, he was team Mario. Game on!

I don't think I've ever been as disappointed in a sporting event as I was in the first time I played the 100-metre dash in *Mario & Sonic at the Olympic Games*.[6] Firstly, the gameplay was nightmarish. To run you had to flail your arms around like you were trying to dislodge spiders made of bogies from your hands. That's not gameplay, it's thinly veiled exercise. I had no idea who had won for several minutes after the race thanks to the total lack of oxygen in my brain. Slowly, the red fog began to clear and we could just about see the result. Who had won in the battle between 'the fastest thing alive' and a plumber? Neither.

It was an AI player.

Specifically, Doctor fucking Robotnik.[7]

Robotnik cannot beat Sonic in a race. That's not conjecture, that's a scientific fact. He's a fat bastard with legs the thickness of a supermodel's personality. Robotnik looks like his workout regime is to skip leg day and bankrupt a local all-you-can-eat place. If I had to make a list of 'the slowest things in the world' he'd be just above continental drift. He's as aerodynamic as a building, for fuck's sake.

I understand why they did it this way: Sonic winning every event isn't fun,[8] there needs to be an actual game here, etc., etc. I just don't know who thought this was the right idea for the first collaboration between these icons. Not playing to the uniqueness of these characters seems like a huge missed opportunity. In fact, this game would be better served by featuring a roster of

6   And I say that as a WWE fan.
7   Or Doctor Eggman as he is known by people I hate.
8   Tails would probably take the high jump.

incredibly similar people like Stormtroopers, Hare Krishnas or YouTube vloggers.

With *Mario & Sonic at the Olympic Games* firmly in the bin, let's celebrate the uniqueness of these two characters ourselves, right here and right now. Instead of racing or plumbing I'll select some categories that they'll be on a more even footing for. This will be a fair, perfectly unbiased fight to determine finally who truly is the best gaming icon of all time.

Here we go.

Design

Sonic's design is brilliance. Let's first talk about his shoes. They're red and white. Why? Because Sonic's character designer Naoto Ohshima was inspired by the cover to Michael Jackson's *Bad*. Also, Santa Claus. That's one hell of a combination! He's blue because that's Sega's official colour and his overall look is based on Mickey Mouse. He's a combination of the greatest pop star, the best-known cartoon character and the most crushing lie we tell to children. What can beat that?

Not Mario. Mario has a hat because his creator, Shigeru Miyamoto, found drawing hair too difficult. He has a moustache so you know he has a face. He used to be a carpenter but changed careers and his name after killing an innocent gorilla in *Donkey Kong*. He has never been seen in a game doing any actual plumbing. Probably a con man. I wouldn't let him near my kids.

Personality

Sonic's attitude is based on Bill Clinton. Seriously. The president of the United States of America, back when that used to mean something, is the backbone of Sonic's entire character. He's got flaws but he always helps save whatever planet they've bothered to set his current game on and never asks for any help. He's true blue.

Mario doesn't actually have a personality, being literally designed without one. He's mute apart from saying his own name, 'yippee' and, on one slightly dodgy occasion, 'pasta power'. He has a serious mushroom-based drug addiction, kills his own pets to jump over holes he could probably walk around, and the object of his affection, Princess Peach, hates him. Thirty-five years have gone by and she's never even been on a date with him. Why? Simple. He hangs out with the guy who kidnaps her all the time. Seriously, Mario and Bowser are regularly seen playing tennis or going go-karting together. That's like the boyfriend of a PTSD sufferer hanging out with a war. He's basically an abusive, mute stalker who shouldn't be having games made about him; he should be on an FBI watch list.

Age
Sonic is fifteen. Young, a little reckless, but willing to put himself on the line to save the world. He's also clearly grown as the games have gone on, going from a chubby kid to a lanky teen in front of our eyes.

Mario looks like he's forty-eight but, according to Miyamoto, is actually just twenty-four years old. Again, that sets off alarm bells for me. Why is he trying to look that old? Is he a benefit scammer? Maybe he has a fake ID. One thing is for sure: you can't trust him.

Abilities
Sonic is the fastest thing alive. He can jump high, curl into a ball to attack things and turn into a freaking Super Saiyan if he fancies it. He's untouchable.

Mario can jump. Not as high as Sonic according to *Mario & Sonic* though.[9] He can... land on things to crush them? Cool

---

9   The characters actually do have slightly different stats but they're pretty much negligible.

power. I have that. It's called being a bit on the tubby side. His strongest power? His ability to wear dungarees without being laughed at. It's not a fair fight, to be honest.

Friends

Sonic hangs out with assorted folk from all walks of life. He can even spend hours at a time in the company of Charmy Bee and Big the Cat without wanting to commit acts of violence. Pope Benedict XVI tried that once and retired the very next day.

Mario won't talk to you unless you're family or royalty. He's happy to step on anyone who gets in his way. I've checked and he doesn't even follow anyone on Twitter. What a prick.

Were they a Macy's Thanksgiving Day Parade Balloon?

Sonic was the first video game character to ever be one back in 1993. On its first time out, it even hit a lamp post, broke and landed on a child and a policeman! Brilliant!

Mario hasn't been a parade balloon. He hates fun.

Live-Action Movies

Actually, let's not bring these up, for both of their sakes.

Games

Oh no! I've run out of space for this section in the book! Maybe we'll come back to this next time.

Anyway, to quickly summarise this unbiased, scientific study, Sonic *just about* has the edge on Mario so I declare him the winner! Hooray!

Now that's over, let's get back to the real question at hand: does Superman even stand a chance against Goku?[10]

10   No. No, he does not.

In *Shadow of the Colossus* there is a shrine

SHADOW OF THE COLOSSUS

Developer: Team Ico
Publisher: Sony Computer Entertainment
Platform: PS2
Released: 2005 (JP & NA) / 2006 (EU)
What is it? An emotional adventure about a boy and some giants.
What is it *really*? Big-big-big-game hunting.

In *Shadow of the Colossus* there is a shrine. It sits in the very middle of the world and is larger than the mountains that surround it. The ground floor houses a temple, sixteen statues and an altar. Accessible only from a narrow, mile-long bridge, it acts as the only entranceway to the Forbidden Lands, the home of the colossi.

Naturally, I wanted to climb it.

Once I'd stuck a dead lady on the altar and signed a terms and conditions agreement I didn't read with a demon, I rode my trusty, ever so slightly suicidal horse around the shrine, looking for a way up. On one side I found a climbable area and scrambled up it until my hands got tired and I fell off. I guess I'd have to come back later when I was stronger.

The general idea of *Shadow of the Colossus* is to kill sixteen skyscraper-sized beasts[1] with nothing but a horse and a

---

1   Well, fourteen the size of skyscrapers and two the size of sheds.

sharpened twig. It's a bit like fighting a woodlouse that you've sellotaped a toothpick to, only you're the woodlouse. The first time a colossus crashes its size 14,000 boot into the ground next to you, everything that can retract into your body will do just that.

After a while I'd worked out how to locate weak points, how to climb up back hair,[2] how to stab the innocent creature in the brain, and how to suppress the feelings of sadness that watching them die brought up. Victory![3] I pressed on, killing the monkey with the mallet, the big grey dog, the lanky colossus with the *Battle Royale* collar on, the one that looked like Ghost Rider's horse, the big pigeon, the one that needed a shave, the electric eel, the adorable lizard, the flippable turtle, the rock snake Pokémon, the crap small one, the *Dark Souls III* boss, the flying motorway, the other crap small one, the one I never remember and the angry building. The ending played, I cried my eyes out and vowed never to kill another innocent creature again as long as I lived. This lasted around six minutes.

Believe me when I say I had no intention of monster murder when I started my second playthrough. I just wanted to see if I could finally climb that tower. I couldn't. It was as impossible as ever. I wandered inside the temple to see if I could find a different way up. While scrabbling around every nook, cranny and crevice, I discovered that praying in front of the statues allows you to replay the colossi fight. If you beat them again in a certain time, you get a secret item. There was a hard mode too. OK, so thirty-two more murders, then I'll stop...

I didn't stop. Now equipped with a parachute, an invisibility cloak and an explosive set of arrows for my bow, I was a one-boy colossus-wrecking machine. However, offensive weaponry aside,

2 Once again demonstrating the importance of personal grooming.
3 I'll just suppress these conflicting emotions that the sad music is giving me...

the most interesting out of all these items were maps. One for lizards, another for fruit trees. I tracked down the closest fruit tree and, after accidentally exploding the first one, managed to shoot an apple down onto the ground. I picked it up and my health rose. Permanently.

Tracking the lizards was harder. The map was actually a stone that revealed special white-tail lizards, but only when they were near. It was worth it, though, as each lizard tail you ate[4] increased the length of time you could climb for! I drew up my own map to mark their locations on for a more permanent record, and played through the game again, finding them all. When I started the game for the third time I had a huge grip bar and another sixteen murders on my rap sheet, not including the lizards. I could now climb the damn shrine! My quest was over!

But it wasn't. My grip bar was upgraded, but it wasn't enough. I had climbed much higher, but there was still more to go. I played the game again, slaughtering my way through the colossi with all the coordination, violence and bloodshed of my family at a buffet.

Fifteen hours later I tried the climb again. Further, but not enough. I played again. Sixteen murders. Seventy-seven lizard tails. Fifteen hours. Not enough. Again. Murders. Lizards. Goddammit! I'd reached the point where I started to see school as a break from the game.

Then, after six playthroughs, 128 dead colossi, 385 lizard tails and a week of my life... I could make the climb.

The climb itself was agonising. Minute after relentless minute of vines, ledges and handholds. Eventually I pulled myself up and discovered that I was at the door from the very

4   SNAAAAAAAAAAAAAAAAKE EATER.

first cutscene of the game. That felt like a lifetime ago, but it was a nice bookend. My time with *Shadow of the Colossus* was going to start and end in the same place, just not quite yet.

I had two paths from here. I could either run across the mile-long bridge and possibly leave this place, or I could follow a path that seemed to lead even higher up the shrine. The top of this place had been my goal for so long but I didn't even know I'd get up to this bridge. It was a new choice, and as someone who, when asked to pick a thing, just chooses the last one listed, I started to run across the bridge.

It takes seven minutes to cross that bridge. Below, the lifeless yet delicate landscape stretches out in every direction. Huge columns of light fly into the sky from the corpses of dead goliaths. It looks like the inside of Enya's mind.

At long last I made it to the end of the bridge. In front of me, carved into the stone, was the gateway. A narrow, dark valley that would take me away from this place. I turned around to look at the shrine, knowing I'd never know what was on top of it. Maybe this was a metaphor for life. When it's your time to go, you'll always leave some mysteries behind...

Anyway, long story short, I tried to leave but a big gust of wind blew me back in. Maybe it's a metaphor for reincarnation or something.

Seven minutes in the opposite direction later and I was back at the door. I followed the path around the top of the shrine and eventually walked out into a place that made the whole climb worth it.

It was a garden.

Shafts of light scattered themselves through the lush trees, thick grass covered the ground and the decay of the world below was absent. This place felt alive, an isolated island of life surrounded by ruin.

Then I noticed the fruits. On many of the trees were bunches of the fruits that had been increasing my health bar through the game. I figured this was my reward for the climb and began to eat all of them.

It was only after eating the last one that I noticed my health had gone down.

Permanently.

Over the past decade I've spent more time debating those fruits with friends than I have figuring out where we should go out to eat. There's a reason for them, a meaning behind the punishment. The game is just too good for there not to be. After many years we settled on the fact that the fruit that increases your life is in the Forbidden Lands, so, even though it helps you in the short term, it's costing you something more than a gameplay mechanic could convey. The fruit of the garden undoes that, taking away what the player would consider to be an advantage. This could be why the garden is near the bridge that leads out of the Forbidden Lands. It's like a WHSmith at an airport. Sure, the price seems high, but you'll be thankful on the journey home.

Shadow of the Colossus is brilliant. A masterpiece of design, ambition and theme. A while back it was remade for a new platform, the PS4. I don't think I've ever been so offended in my life. Who dares think they can better such perfection? That's like thinking that pizza needs a dark and gritty reboot, or that *Portal* should be remade with Adam Sandler as Chell. Hell, it would be like making a Han Solo movie that doesn't star Harrison Ford! Madness!

In the end I felt compelled to write a letter to the Pope complaining that such an act was heresy. He wrote back saying he hadn't played it as he only has a Wii. I posted my lizard-tail map to him, just in case. He hasn't got back to me. Of course he hasn't, I made this bit up. Honestly, I've really written myself into a corner here. I think I'm just going to end this chapter and move onto the next one. Yeah. Good plan. Bye.

HARDWARE HISTORY: SONY

As much as I hate to admit it, video games are a bit rubbish. No! Wait! Come back! I'm talking about them as physical objects, you fool! Seriously though, they're just cartridges or DVDs with nice pictures on them, sitting on the floor, doing nothing. The most fun you can get out of them is playing the game called 'Who can throw this useless CD the furthest?'[1] They need hardware to function properly, much in the same way that records need a record player, TV shows need a TV, and your mum needs that third glass of wine every evening.

On that note, I've decided to take a look at some of this hardware, starting with Sony.[2] This won't be a complete history as there are far too many consoles to cover, but it will cover most of them. I think. Actually, I recently asked a person who would know this sort of thing just how many different consoles he thought had ever been made. He had no idea, so I asked Yahoo! Answers instead. The question only received one reply.

'lol nobody knows'
— A Yahoo! Answers user with an unprintable username

Maybe after this book, they will.[3]

---

1   7.2/10 – IGN
2   Mostly because I have most of these and won't need to research much. It's a Sunday. I'm tired.
3   They won't.

PlayStation – Console – Never Released

Our first stop on this tour of Sony's hardware history is the unreleased and mostly unheard of PlayStation. The PlayStation was a SNES with a CD drive jammed into it, created by a collaboration between Nintendo and Sony. That's right, Sony entered the games industry via long-time rivals Nintendo! That's like finding out that Marvel's first go at a superhero was just Superman in a funny hat.

How long did this relationship last? A day. A single day. An argument over who profited from the software on the CDs meant that Nintendo took to the stage of the 1991 CES and announced a partnership with bitter Sony rivals Philips, just one day after Sony announced the PlayStation. Sony responded by taking all the PlayStation branding and making a console that sold twice as many units as the SNES in what is legally referred to as a 'fuck you' move.

PlayStation – Console – 1994 (JP) / 1995 (EU)

Speak of the devil, here's the PlayStation we all know and (mostly) love.[4] 3D graphics had arrived but sadly view distances had slept in and missed the bus. The games were

---

4   In one of the oddest reviews I've ever read, *What Hi-Fi* magazine gave the PlayStation two stars out of five, saying the music in the games was great but the CD playing ability was only so-so. That's like *Clock Enthusiasts Monthly* reviewing an oven and complaining it's a bit big for your nightstand.

stunning but most of them played like the character could see as far as Velma after she'd lost her glasses. The video game tie-in to the film *Small Soldiers* featured a multiplayer mode where darkness erupted about five feet around the player, meaning you could lose the room you were in while still standing in it. Even the useable gun turrets dotted around the levels had the same range as a bowling ball thrown by a baby. I think I played that game for twenty thousand hours or so. Ah, the good old days.

Despite the limitations, it was one hell of a success, selling over 100 million units in its lifetime. Huge games like *Tomb Raider*, *Crash Bandicoot*, *Metal Gear Solid*, *Gran Turismo*, *Tekken*, *Spyro*, *Oddworld: Abe's Oddysee*, *Final Fantasy VII*, *Silent Hill* and *Tony Hawk's Pro Skater* cemented Sony as a huge player in the industry. A failed SNES CD add-on had just turned into the fourth-bestselling console of all time, a position Nintendo's non-handheld consoles haven't matched yet, and a position that would only get stronger over time...

PocketStation – Accessory – 1999

... but not quite yet. The PocketStation was half PS1 memory card, half PDA, with an LCD screen and five buttons, four of which were the D-pad. It connected to a handful of PS1 games through the memory card slot and gave you little minigames to play based on the game you connected it to. Ever wanted to play the boulder level from *Crash Bandicoot* on a monochrome 32x32 pixel screen? Why? What's wrong with you?

Despite only ever being released in Japan, it still managed to sell almost 5 million units. A few years ago Sony added the PocketStation to the PS Vita as an app to tie into the PS1 Classics range but, again, that was Japan only. Stupid Japan with its cool technological tat.

PlayStation 2 – Console – 2000

I'm not really sure how to introduce the bestselling games console of all time. My initial idea died when the publisher said there's no real way to launch  fireworks from a book. Not even a small amount. Lame. This is why everyone has a Kindle now.

The PS2 is my favourite games console. Nothing before it or since has had such breadth, depth or...[5] Macbeth...[6] as the PS2. From the narrative insanity of *Metal Gear Solid 2*, to the towering behemoths of *Shadow of the Colossus*, to eating fast food in *Grand Theft Auto: San Andreas*, the PS2 formed my gaming tastes across its thirteen-year lifespan.

It also did a great job of bringing in a casual audience with built-in DVD playback, window-cleaning simulator *EyeToy* and the Fisher Price/Rock God combination, *Guitar Hero*. It was literally the console for everyone, which, thinking about it, is probably why literally everyone bought one.

From launch to discontinuation the PS2 shifted 155 million consoles and over 1.5 billion games. If you stacked all those PS2 game cases in a pile you'd reach 21,000 kilometres into the sky. Be careful where you do this, though: the ISS orbits at

---

5   Today I learned that literally nothing rhymes with breadth. Also, man, that's a horrible word. Saying it is like trying to talk with a mouthful of loft insulation.
6   Hot potato, orchestra stalls, Puck will make amends.

just 408 kilometres and could take out the bottom section of your pile like a toddler running at a wedding cake.

PSX – Console – 2003

Another one that never made it out of Japan, I'm only including this PS2 and DVR hybrid because a lot of people refer to the PS1 as the PSX and that annoys me. That's all I have to say on this matter. Let's move on.

PlayStation Portable – Handheld – 2004 (JP) / 2005 (EU & US)

On paper the PSP is the greatest handheld of all time. OK, paper tends to be very thin and flimsy, but you know what I mean. It's basically a portable not-quite-but-nearly PS2 with

some great games on very strange, permanently encased discs called UMDs.[7] The first time I laid eyes on portable *Grand Theft Auto* in full 3D I knew I needed to get one. I didn't, though. They were very expensive.

In 2009 the PSP Go launched. It was smaller, could only play downloaded games due to its lack of UMD drive[8] and had all its controls in a slide-out panel hidden under the screen.

---

7   Universal Media Disc. A particularly stupid name as they only played on PSPs and, therefore, weren't universal.

8   See? Not even all PSPs could play it! Universal, my arse!

A few months after its launch Sony started to bundle it with ten free games. They weren't crap games either; they included *LittleBigPlanet*, *Gran Turismo* and *Grand Theft Auto: Vice City Stories*. That had to be worth the punt, right?

Yes. Oh God, yes. First off, the PSP Go is the greatest handheld ever based on comfort alone. It weighs a mere 158 grams, fits my strange hands like tailor-made silk gloves and slides shut to leave an incredibly thin device, around sixty-three times smaller than a modern mobile phone. In fact, it can be transported so easily that, on no fewer than six separate occasions, I've accidentally inserted it into myself.

It seems odd to me that the PSP is considered a failure. I know it lost out to the Nintendo DS and that the UMD discs were a flop, but if you look at the sales figures, it sold more than the GameCube, N64 and original Xbox **combined**. Not bad for a failure. Not bad at all.

Sega Saturn PS2 Controller – Accessory – 2005

Here's something I once found in a flea market: a Sony and Sega collaboration controller. I don't think we'll ever see anything like this again, but the ability to play PS2 games on a slightly modified Sega Saturn controller is brilliant! It even had the original Saturn markings on the buttons themselves, and the corresponding PS2 ones underneath each button. L1 and R1 were moved to the face buttons and the analogue sticks... well, there weren't any, meaning that there's actually a bunch of games you wouldn't be able to play with this. Still, I don't think it matters. It's for the sort of people who like fighting games, and they're all terrifying.

PlayStation 3 – Console – 2006 (JP & US) / 2007 (EU)

I remember the day my mate Sok bought a PS3. I went round his house and spent the evening playing launch titles like *MotorStorm* and *Resistance: Fall of Man*.[9] I remember being blown away by the graphics and playing the games well into the night. I also remember that a few weeks later we were back on the PS2.

The PS3 lost me for a while. Sure, there were superb titles like *Red Dead Redemption*, *LittleBigPlanet* and *Burnout Paradise*, but this was the point when games went gritty, cinematic and brown. Very brown. Sometimes grey. Even the developers of bouncy, bright games like Free Radical Design fell into the 'mature' trap and died. They went from *TimeSplitters*, the silly adventures of a time traveller and some monkeys, to *Haze*, the serious adventures of a drug-addled soldier where 95% of the game's textures were just blurry variations of the colour brown. It was the video game equivalent of lying face down at Glastonbury, and about half as fun.

The worst part of the PS3 was the controller. Yes, it was the same great controller as always, but when the PS3 was announced they showed off a bright silver boomerang controller instead. It looked stupid, but I've never wanted anything more in my entire life. I presume they got rid of it simply because it didn't work very well, but I like to believe that they got rid of it to enhance the seriousness of the games. If I had that thing in my hands I'd spend 80% of the time looking down and

---

9   Actually, I went round his house pretty much every day anyway, there just happened to be a PS3 there this time.

laughing. That could really kill the gritty mood.

The PS3 pretty much tied in sales with its main competitor, the Xbox 360, but barely hit half of the PS2's numbers. Sony would have to bring out the big guns if it wanted to survive the next generation.

Speaking of the big guns, where did they leave them? What was that? With the handheld division? What do they need them for? Wait, why are they aiming them at their own feet? OH NO!

Sony BRAVIA KDL22PX300 – Television – 2010

A brief interlude for this tiny piece of brilliance. The catchily named Sony BRAVIA KDL22PX300 is a TV. A TV with a built-in PS2. A TV with a built-in PS2 released four years after the PS3 had come out. I don't know what they were on when designing this but, based on the stylings, I can tell it was a day when the only pens available were incredibly thick markers.[10]

Xperia Play – Mobile Phone – 2011

When Apple launched the iPhone in 2007 they ruined phones forever. Out went the mad designs and ingenuity and in came the black rectangles and – utterly useless for gaming – the touch controls. Amongst the

---

10   I would, however, 100% buy one of these if it came out tomorrow.

last few dying gasps of interesting phone design was the Xperia Play, Sony's very own PlayStation phone.

Design-wise it was pretty neat. The back slid out to reveal a set of nice physical buttons, a D-pad and the usual cross, square, triangle, circle layout. The downside had to be the analogue sticks, mostly because there weren't any. Instead you got a touchpad. Kinda defeats the point of the physical buttons, no?

Sadly, mobile games are universally dreadful, even with nice controls, so the device died a death. In the end everyone went back to their proper phones like the Motorola DynaTAC 8000X and the Nokia Mobira Cityman and all was right in the world.

PlayStation Vita – Handheld – 2011 (JP) / 2012 (EU & US)

The PS Vita is a beautiful machine. It's basically a portable not-quite-but-nearly PS3 that Sony abandoned faster than I abandon my diet when near  a Greggs. It started well with strong sales and good support but stalled slightly a short while after launch. Sony's cool, logical response at this point was to smash the eject button and pretend it didn't exist. The result was a library of games as devoid of content as a version of the 1979 film *Caligula* edited for an in-flight showing.[11] That said, it still has a bit of a following these days, largely from the JRPG crowd. OK, only from the JRPG crowd.

---

11   Look up that one with private browsing on, OK?

Sony recently ripped out any game that did well on it and flung them all at the PS4 so it's not really a console I can recommend any more. It's gorgeous and comfortable and full of potential that'll never be realised, like a beanbag on the moon. It really just doesn't have enough games on it. Well, unless you like the very similar adventures of people with massive eyes who all have to go and kill God or something. Then, and then only, it's the best thing in the world.

PlayStation 4 – Console – 2013 (EU & NA) / 2014 (JP)

Back in my day we had a thing called 'happy slapping'. The idea was that you filmed yourself assaulting someone at random and then you posted the video on the internet before being arrested for being a twat. The most violent and well-known case of happy slapping occurred in 2013 when Andrew House, the president and global CEO of Sony Interactive Entertainment, came onstage at E3 and announced that the PS4's launch price was $100 less than the Xbox One. I'm surprised he wasn't jailed for that.

While that story is my fondest memory of the PS4,[12] some games have come close to it. My main recommendations are the sublime *Bloodborne* and the 2018 *God of War*, a game so good it's almost worth buying a PS4 for alone. Other major exclusives include *Horizon Zero Dawn*, a game that feels like

---

12 That story is also technically a port from an older generation too. I'll explain why later…

every current gaming trope squashed into a single game, and *The Last Guardian*, a game that has a frame rate that's about as stable as a badly installed swing in a gorilla enclosure.

In fact, a lot of PS4 games that I own I end up buying again on PC just to play them at a reasonable frame rate. With the release of the PS4 Pro in 2016 this is only getting worse. The PS4 Pro was supposed to be a better way to play games but more and more it's becoming the only way to play them at a reasonable quality. If this keeps up then consoles will no longer be the cheap entry into gaming they once were. That would be one hell of a shame.

PlayStation TV – Console – 2013 (JP) / 2014 (EU & NA)

PS TV is one of those modern bits of technology I don't understand. Like smart speakers, smart watches and dumb waiters.[13] It's a PS Vita but, instead of a handheld with 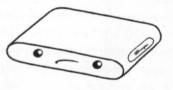 a screen, it's a little black box.[14] You plug it into your TV, pop a Vita game in and, behold, you're playing a 960x544 game on a 4K TV.

The downside, and it's quite the downside, is that it doesn't actually play all PS Vita games. In fact, because it just uses a standard PS4 controller, any game that uses the rear touchpad, cameras, microphone or motion sensors simply won't work

---

13 Let's invent an elevator for things, but keep it so small that it only fits things that are easy to carry upstairs. Genius.
14 It's actually called the PS Vita TV in most of Asia.

with it. The PS TV just gives you an error message and tells you to fuck off. This affects games like *Tearaway*, *Gravity Rush* and *Uncharted: Golden Abyss*, AKA all the good games.

I can't track down any sales figures for the PS TV so I'm going to make an educated guess. It sold nine units. Eight of those were in Japan. They sold ten for a while but someone returned theirs and bought a DVD of *Cool Runnings* and a tube of Smarties instead.

PlayStation VR – Accessory – 2016

I was surprised by the PS VR. It's comfortable, the screens are clear and it's actually a far nicer headset than I was expecting. However, it has the worst tracking of a VR headset I've ever seen. Instead of using multiple points of infrared like the HTC VIVE and Oculus Rift, the PS VR uses two cameras that track huge, glowy orbs on the top of the controllers. The result is that every game you play feels like it's set onboard a ship on seas so rough even the captain is having a brown-trouser moment. Some people claim they can get it working, but then again some people claim they've seen Jesus on a piece of toast when it's clearly just Kirk Hammett from Metallica. It's like my mum always used to say: 'Never trust people.'

PlayStation 6 – Console – 2028

Anyone else totally confused when they revealed the PS6 at E3 2026? The console itself was all nice, sleek and black and the games they showed off were so real that you could watch the bogeys in Lara Croft's nose form in real time. I just don't understand why they changed the controller to that perfect  sphere that stabs you in the hands with knives while you play. I know it's to capitalise on the nostalgia of old controllers being uncomfortable but it seemed gimmicky to me at the time. Still does if I'm honest.

That aside, we've had some pretty good exclusives for the PS6 so far. *Grand Theft Auto VIII* was all right for a free to play game, *Bloodborne 3*'s twist ending where everything was explained in that super-detailed and expositional cutscene was great, and the all-female reboot of *Jak and Daxter* was fun. Could have done with fewer sex scenes, though.[15]

So, that's Sony! In a brief conclusion: they dominated, dominated more, went a bit wobbly, buggered stuff up and might end up killing consoles as we know them. Hooray!

15   I made this all up, of course. The sex scenes were great.

Whacking a solar panel on a robot ladybird schematic
can't be harder than trying to seatbelt a rabbit into
every single one of them

Developer: Sonic Team
Publisher: Sega
Platform: Mega Drive
Released: 1991
What is it? A platformer focused on speed.
What is it *really*? The reason this book exists.

My earliest memory is from a trip to Australia that my family and I undertook in the early 90s. I was toddling along by the side of an outdoor pool when the following thought was etched into my consciousness forever:

'Ow, this is hot.'

That tiled poolside was so scorching I actually had to develop the concept of memory in my tiny baby brain to deal with it. Billions of years of hardwired evolution began to stir as this new part of myself came online. The heat of those white tiles was the first thing my brain understood as a serious threat so I had to work out a way to mentally write that down. That's sort of the point of memory, isn't it? It's a survival tool.

I mention this because my second memory was buying a Sega Mega Drive with my parents at the local Electronics Boutique. I'm not entirely sure that this fits the whole survival thing, but considering my career is in video games, I'm also not convinced that it's wrong. Maybe evolution knows more than we give it credit for. Maybe telling a small child that the box we're buying can control a blue hedgehog on the TV overrides the default reason for memory to exist in the first place. Bugger survival, did you hear what Mum just said?

While researching this book[1] I sent a text to my dad asking if there was a specific reason he bought the Mega Drive[2] as it might be a nice detail to keep a record of. Here, word for word, is the text I received in response:

> *'Son, I just farted and only when I smelled it did I remember doing it.'*

Let's just say it was a birthday present.

You know, I feel slightly sorry for kids born in this day and age. Video games are literally everywhere and, while that's a wonderful thing, technology that comes around in your lifetime is so much more magical than technology that's already there. Going from a life without video games to them suddenly being in your living room was thrilling. The closest I've ever got to that in my adult life was the first time I tried VR with the HTC VIVE. I giggled for hours. New technology? Magic.

Now we've got the only sincere paragraph in the book out of the way, let's talk about my first time. There I was, gamepad in hand, eyes wide, about to enter a whole new world of technology. I pressed start on the title screen[3] and then was informed I was standing on the lush plains of Green Hill Zone. Giant purple

---

1   I know! Research! It surprised me too!
2   Named Genesis in America. I assume for religious reasons.
3   Although, thinking about it now, I don't think it actually says 'Press Start' on that screen at all...

and yellow flowers danced about in the gorgeous sunlight while, in the background, a waterfall cascaded off the bright orange mountains and crashed into the azure river below. White clouds hung lazily in the sky. I pressed a button, Sonic ran right, collided with a robot shaped like a ladybird, and died.

I'd fallen in love.

A minute later I'd repeated the same thing twice more and the TV silently yelled GAME OVER at me. OK, so we were going to have to work at this relationship.

My progress in *Sonic the Hedgehog* was ironically slow. First, I had to work out what jumping was for. Thinking about it, jumping is probably the most frequently included part of gaming that doesn't come up often in your daily life.[4] If the only way to get somewhere was by jumping I'd probably call up some health and safety department and complain. The only time I ever jump these days is if a spider surprises me in the garage. Not just jumping, mind; any variation from a continuous flat surface could ruin my day. I tut almost out loud every time the gap between the train and the platform is particularly wide.

Next weird mechanic: rings. Sonic has apparently collected over 70 billion of these since 1991 but has yet to explain where they come from or what they even really are. One tiny part of the canon suggests that they're a natural formation on his planet, but considering that the planet he lives on changes on a game-by-game basis, I hold Sonic's canon in the same regard that I hold Doctor Who's.

Anyway, after days of playing I finally made it to the end of Green Hill Zone, and guess who comes in like – and indeed with – a wrecking ball? Yep, the artist formerly known as Doctor Ivo

---

4   Fruit-eating is another big one. If anyone ate as much fruit as early gaming characters, they'd catch whatever the opposite of scurvy is.

Robotnik.[5] He's an odd sort, Robotnik; clearly he's spent many, many hours building robots that fit small animals but I haven't a clue why. One tiny fleck of story states that he uses them to power the robots, much in the same way that the machines used humans to power the Matrix.[6] That doesn't make a lick of sense, though; a human only produces around 10 to 100 millivolts of electrical energy so you'd have trouble getting a human to light an LED, never mind getting a duck to power a robot. Whacking a solar panel on a robot ladybird schematic can't be harder than trying to seatbelt a rabbit into every single one of them. Maybe he's just a psychopath.

Sadly, we don't get a huge amount of backstory for him in the games. The manual for *Sonic Heroes* describes him like this:

> *'Eggman [sic] is a romanticist, a feminist and a self-professed gentleman.'*

God, you can smell the Reddit account from here, can't you? No wonder he hates everything. I'm surprised we haven't raced Sonic across a level called Friend Zone yet.

Getting back onto the, admittedly vague at best, topic, I didn't finish *Sonic the Hedgehog* until I was much, much older. I remember beating the final boss, seeing the credits roll and just being confused. Why are we back at Green Hill? Why is Sonic running left? Who the hell is Carol Yas? I didn't think the game would ever end. I didn't think *any* games ended! The only other

5   Or Ovi Kintobor/Julian Kintobor. In fact there are ten versions of Robotnik so far, each with their own backstory. It's like the various adaptations of *Hitchhiker's Guide*, only fatter.

6   Originally the machines used humans as processors, not electrical power. Some twat in a suit thought people wouldn't understand it and changed it to human batteries. This isn't relevant to *Sonic*, it's just if I don't mention it I'm going to get a lot of emails that start with 'Well actually…'

game I had was the *Tetris*-like *Columns*, and that sure as hell never ended. What was I going to do now? The answer, although I didn't know it at the time, was simply that I was going to play a hell of a lot more games.

Then again, two weeks later I got a copy of *Shaq Fu*. I didn't play games again for the rest of that millennium.

Lead character Marcus was accused of a crime simply because predictive software guessed that it was him, therefore making it about as accurate as Michael Fish

Developer: Ubisoft Montreal
Publisher: Ubisoft
Platform: PC, PS4, Xbox One
Released: 2016
What is it? An open-world game based on hacker culture.
What is it _really_? A game about exploding people's phones for giggles.

'What do you want to be when you grow up?'

The younger you are, the more this question tugs at a deep pit in your stomach. How do you even begin selecting one thing you've not even tried yet from a near infinite pile of things? It's an impossible task and we need to answer it far too early in our lives. When I was first asked it, I was still wearing plimsolls.[1]

It's a difficult question to give advice about. Some tell you to focus on the school subjects that you like, others (mostly the lazy) say to focus on the ones you're good at. Once at school I spent an hour in the computer lab answering a huge list of multiple choice questions that would eventually help me choose a career. My result? Honestly it was 'Adult Filmmaker'. Sadly I was in Catholic school and they didn't offer that as a course. Shame,

---

1   My answer? Tennis player. Literal swing and a miss there, young me.

but on the bright side it's difficult to grow the required seedy moustache at the tender age of thirteen.

It wasn't until one fateful day in high school that I even began to know how to answer that question. I realised that it's not what you're good at; it's not even what you like doing the most. No, you should choose your future based on *what got you in trouble*. That's the secret.

Think about it. That strange kid who got told off for doodling in the margins all the time? Comic book artist! That girl who used to build slingshots and booby traps? Now an engineer! The bully who beat up the poor kids and stole their lunch money? He's just been elected MP of Flydale North! The system works! Me? I received exactly one detention in my life. This is, word for word, what it said on that little pink form:

> *'One hour after school for telling rude jokes over the school internet.'*

If I still had that slip, it would be framed in my house.

The reason I was served that detention was simple: I had hacked the restrictions off the school computers,[2] taught everyone how to do the same, opened an IRC chat and was making the whole class desperately try to stifle laughter when some future health and safety killjoy noticed and told the teacher.

I was always a good kid at school. Top of the class, accolades, school prefect and all that jazz. Naturally, I assumed that my first detention would destroy me. It didn't. When I was told to not do it again, I didn't reply because making that whole class laugh was the most fun I'd had in my entire time at school. The punishment

---

2   The school's security software booted after Explorer so the 'hack' was a simple case of hitting CTRL-ALT-DEL at startup and stopping it as it booted up. I miss the 90s.

wasn't a punishment: it was liberation. For the first time in my life I had an answer to the question. I knew what I wanted to be when I grew up. I wanted to be funny.

Ah well, can't have everything.

I do wonder, though: what if I'd taken that day a different way? In this *Sliding Doors* moment of my life, what if I'd developed a love of hacking instead of crap jokes. What would have happened then?

In 2016 I got an answer. I'd basically become a supervillain.

Watch Dogs 2 follows hacker group DedSec in a near future version of San Francisco. The entire city is controlled by a single piece of software, ctOS, that monitors cameras, cars, finances and pretty much everything you don't want to suddenly lose control of.

Lead character Marcus, alias Retr0, was accused of a crime simply because predictive software guessed that it was him, therefore making it about as accurate as Michael Fish. Furious at this, Marcus joins DedSec to expose ctOS, destroy its parent company and save the city from convenience. I mean Big Brother.

Sadly for Marcus, I took over from him the moment the first cutscene ended and, well, I had all the power and none of the responsibility. I helped him and his little hacker friends with their missions but, trust me, I wasn't going to be getting the call from Nick Fury anytime soon.

I'll give you an example. I regularly had to sneak into a gated area, hack a terminal and download some crucial data from a local server. A Netflix password or something like that, most likely.

A good person would sneak in, do the business and sneak out without ever being seen. They'd hack into camera feeds to avoid guards, use an RC car to open locks for them and, if worst came to worst, gently put people down with a taser.

I am not a good person. The first thing I would do would be to call the police and claim that one of the weaker guards was a terrorist.[3] The police would enter and attempt to arrest the man, at which point I'd target the most heavily armed guard and remotely detonate the grenade in his pocket. This would cause the suspect to run, the police to open fire, the guards to fire back, and leave me to freely step over all the bodies a few minutes later.

Well, that or I could tell a local gang that one of the guards betrayed them. When they showed up I'd then set a different gang on them, causing all the guards to be shredded in both the cross and regular fire.

Oh, I could always turn off all the lights and in the confusion smash all the people in the face with a snooker ball dangling from a rope, or maybe fry their brains by overloading their phone batteries.

And let's not forget that I could remotely steal and drive cars, fill the place up with them, and make one explode causing a massive chain reaction that sent red-hot shards of metal and glass into everyone's squishy bits.

Oooh, better still, I could go to a nearby street where there are naked people hanging around, chase them into the protected area and when the guards get distracted, bomb them all to hell with my quadcopter and remote-controlled explosives.

No, wait, I've got it. I could hack into the guards' social media accounts, send their phone a notification that they've forgotten their partner's birthday and simply walk in after they've all sprinted to the closest garage to pick up wilted flowers, rechargeable batteries and a sausage sandwich.[4]

I love *Watch Dogs 2*. The game is sunny, wild and tongue-

---

3   Don't try this at home. Try wrestling moves instead.
4   OK, so this one you can't do, but I hope to see it implemented in *Watch Dogs Legion*.

in-cheek. The gadgets are unique, the soundtrack is ace and the characters are loveable and interesting, even if they don't quite pay attention to the fact that Marcus kills more people than a plague. Its morality is fuzzy, but it knows it, embraces it and lets you just have a good time.

Now if you'll excuse me, I've got naked people to chase into traffic. This gang hideout isn't going to massacre itself! Well, not yet anyway...

Long story short, *Brütal Legend* is metal as fuck

Developer: Yes, they are!
Publisher: They're that too!
Platform: Uhhh... everything?
Released: You mean founded? 2000!
What is it? It's a game studio!
What is it *really*? A front for illegal cuddly-toy smuggling.

San Francisco-based developer Double Fine, led by the occasionally bearded and consistently brilliant Tim Schafer,[1] is my favourite game developer. In a world where reviewers won't give a game more than a 6/10 if you don't need to clip your character's toenails every few weeks, Double Fine takes realism, scrunches it into a ball and misses the bin with it.

I decided pretty early on that I couldn't just pick one Double Fine game to cover in this book. That's impossible. Trying to select a favourite Double Fine game is like trying to choose a favourite child, only much harder. Each one is so wildly different that the only way to even tell that they're Double Fine games is to spot their logo at the start. That and the deep sense of fun that each one is built around, like a molten core made of clowns. Wait, that sounds scary. Puppies? Yeah, let's go with puppies.[2]

---

1   I swear I've seen him around here recently...
2   Not entirely sure that's better...

On whatever that note was, here are ten Double Fine-developed and published games that I want to talk about. You get a point for each one you've played, exchangeable at any local corner shop for a Twix.[3]

Psychonauts – 2005

'Rhubarb is a controversial pie variety.'

Raz – no relation to Roz from *Frasier* – has just run away from the circus to join a summer camp for psychics.[4] There he'll learn to harness his powers, uncover a conspiracy and become a lifelong friend of this one kid who likes to blow up squirrels.

Whispering Rock Psychic Summer Camp is one of my favourite places in gaming. The sun is bright, the trees slowly sway to the music wafting in from somewhere warm, and every now and then you literally get to climb inside people's minds and see how they tick.

Every single level in *Psychonauts* is a treat, each one a mental platforming playground of a character's psyche. Camp Coach Oleander will take you through Basic Braining via his warzone of a mind; Psychonaut Sasha Nein's mind is a neat, foldable cube in a vast array of empty space; and Milla Vodello's head is home to a huge, loud dance party. One that might be covering up something she doesn't want to hear ever again...

As the game progresses you gain more powers and begin to delve into more unstable minds, represented by fragmented and splintered worlds. The absolute highlight of this, possibly of any game ever, is the Milkman Conspiracy. A floating, twisted

---

3   Offer only available in Tuvalu.
4   Honestly, is there a better setup for a video game plot than that? I'm not sure.

suburban street where eyeballs and periscopes pop out of everything you're not quite looking at and mysterious G-Men in long coats are everywhere, blending in about as well as a red sock in a white wash.

Psychonauts is an all-time classic. It's also genuinely hilarious and full of heart. If you've not played it, do.

Brütal Legend – 2009

'From time to time, Brütal Legend *may need to utilize strong language to accurately portray the authentic roadie experience to the player.'*

Eddie Riggs, a roadie voiced by the actor and sex icon Jack Black, is killed during a gig and sent by Ormagöden, the eternal fire beast, to a fantasy world that looks like every heavy metal album cover at once, where he leads the last remaining humans in a final, climactic battle against an army of demons. Neat!

Long story short, *Brütal Legend* is metal as fuck. The world is unlike anything you've ever seen, full of razor-sharp mountains, lakes of fire and skies moodier than Bernard Black. The cast is made up of genuine rock legends and the soundtrack consists of 107 of the greatest rock songs ever made. Yes, 'Dr. Feelgood' is on that list. No, sadly not the 16-bit version.

Did I mention that this is an open-world game? With driving elements? Also, occasionally it's an RTS? *Brütal Legend* throws every trick it has at the screen and, while not always nailing everything, is beyond entertaining for its whole run time. In short, it's the sort of game that doesn't get made any more, mostly because modern publishers are the sort of people who listen to... Kabbage Boy. *shudders*

Costume Quest – 2010

'I have to find her or I'm going to be grounded.'

It's Halloween night, monsters are real and they've kidnapped your sibling. To combat them you can transform into a hero that matches your current costume. Got a cute cardboard robot suit on? Well, now you're a mech the size of Big Ben. That should even things up.

Costume Quest captures the childhood glee of trick-or-treating so well that I have to remind myself that I've never actually been. It's just not a thing in the UK, much like prom or the ability to get off a bus without saying thank you. That's disappointing, because if it's half as fun as *Costume Quest* makes out, then I've missed something joyous. The darkened streets, only half recognisable under halogen bulbs; the scary costumes of everyone you meet; the fact that candy is currency, even though that would cause me to literally eat away any and all savings I don't have – it all seems so delightful.

You know, next time Halloween rolls around, I'm going to really try to get into the spirit of things. I'm going to get a huge bowl of sweets, take the batteries out of the doorbell like normal, and settle down in front of the TV and play *Costume Quest* again. Happy Halloween, everyone!

Stacking – 2011

'An uninvited guest. The mood is ruined. Everyone OUT NOW!'

The industrial age roars on, bringing with it great wealth and great poverty. Children are a labour force, homelessness is rife and Charlie Blackmore must find his family across this backdrop of smog, soot and depression.

Oh, and everyone is a matryoshka doll.

In my household, *Stacking* is a revered name. Solving puzzles as Charlie, the smallest of the Russian nesting dolls that inhabit this world, by leaping into larger dolls with different abilities, is arguably the most interesting, yet instantly understandable, game mechanic of all time. It's brilliant. Genuinely genius.

1930s architecture, a classical music soundtrack, silent-movie-style cutscenes: *Stacking* is Double Fine at their best. Fantastic presentation, clever ideas and giggly fun. 10/10, would possess a grumpy maître d' again.

Broken Age – 2014

'Let's start mission nutrition!'

I have a confession to make. I don't really like adventure games.

I know, I know. It's just that my first experience with them was *The Hitchhiker's Guide to the Galaxy*, a hilarious game that has arguably the worst video game puzzle of all time in it: the Babel Fish vending machine.

1. You need to get a fish to put in your ear so that you can translate alien languages.[5] You press the button on a vending machine to get one and it shoots out at a ridiculous speed and flies into a hole. *Hmm...*
2. You notice a hook above the hole. You cleverly hang your dressing gown on the hook, press the button and watch the fish fly out, hit your dressing gown and slide off into a drain. *Hmmm...*
3. You cover the drain with a towel, press the button, the fish

---

5   Mercifully, working out that the fish does this isn't part of the puzzle.

flies, the dressing gown stops it, the towel catches it, and a cleaning robot enters the room, takes the fish and leaves. *Hmmmm...*

4. You wedge a satchel into the panel the robot left via, press the button, fish, gown, towel, the robot hits the satchel and the fish is launched into the air... whereupon it is caught by a second, *flying*, cleaning robot. *Hmmmmm...*

5. Final step. Put junk mail in the satchel so that when it's hit, the airborne mail will distract the flying robot and you can finally catch the fish. Press the button and... nothing. It's out of fish. You lose for working the puzzle out logically. Rage-quit. Snap the floppy disc in half. Eat it. Choke. Die. This puzzle occurs about five minutes into the game.

My next dive into the adventure genre was a game called *Gold Rush!*,[6] a game that featured unavoidable diseases that killed you randomly. After that was a game called *Space Quest III*, which hated me as much as I hated it. Oh hey, there's a piece of metal on the floor! Want to pick it up? Whoops, you've cut yourself and are bleeding to death. Maybe next time you'll get past *the first ten fucking seconds.*[7]

When Double Fine announced that they were launching a Kickstarter for a 'classic point-and-click adventure', I was a little worried that I wasn't going to like it. I mean, I backed it for hundreds of dollars in a heartbeat – it's a Double Fine game, after all – but still.

I didn't need to worry. Tim Schafer's adventure-game pedigree combined with gorgeous storybook art and a dazzling story to form my favourite adventure game ever. I've just established that

---

6   One of those games that happens to be on a school PC and nobody knows how it got there.

7   This occurs shortly before the elevator that throws you into a shredder.

that's not exactly the highest bar to cross, but they cleared it by miles so shut up.

Broken Age is a story of two people. The first, the only human on a massive spaceship; the second, a teenage girl about to be eaten by a Lovecraftian monster. Across the course of the game you'll find out how in the bloody hell these two are connected, and why exactly my favourite character is a spoon.

Homework time! Go and watch the documentary by 2 Player Productions about *Broken Age*.[8] It's long, in-depth and shows the entire process of making a multimillion-dollar game. If you're the sort of person who would read a book like this, and I think it's safe to assume you are, then you'll love it.

Hack 'n' Slash – 2014

'BEST FRIENNNNNNDS!'

Hack 'n' Slash is about Alice the elf, her best friend Bob the sprite, and her USB-tipped sword that can hack directly into objects. Need to move a rock? Hack it to be moveable! Bad guy attacking? Make him a friend! Seen a random turtle? Make its walking speed a billion miles per hour so it dies in the blink of an eye, exhausted, confused and three countries over.

When I play *Hack 'n' Slash* I don't try to win it, I try to break it. If you mess with enough stuff, cause enough conflicts, spawn enough turtles, then the game crashes inside of itself and throws up the greatest error message of all time:

'The universe has collapsed.'

---

8   Efficiently titled *Double Fine Adventure!*.

Sorry, universe, I just wanted to see how many bombs you could fit inside a portal while simultaneously seeing if you could make a Large Hadron Collider with turtles. I hope you forgive me.

Headlander – 2016

'Y'all gonna need yerself a body.'

You are the last human alive. Well, you're the head of the last human alive. Well, you're actually the head of the last human alive in a space helmet with a rocket attached and have the ability to take over the bodies of robots to solve puzzles.

Set in space's version of 1970, *Headlander* is a metroidvania about realising that you can take over the bodies of robot dogs, and then just being a robot dog for ages. You could do all that progression, shooting and solving, but I'd rather just be K-9 for a bit. Who wouldn't want that?!

DOUBLE FINE PRESENTS

In addition to making games, Double Fine also publishes things under the banner of 'Double Fine Presents'. I guess I'll talk about these too!

Mountain – Developer: David OReilly – 2014

'Welcome to Mountain.
You are Mountain.
You are God.'

This is a game where you play as a mountain. I don't think I need to say any more.

Everything – Developer: David OReilly – 2017

*'One of the first things which everybody should understand is
that every creature in the universe, that is in any way sensitive,
and in any manner of speaking, conscious, regards itself as a
human being.'*

This is a game where you play as everything. I don't think I need
to say any more, but I will.

Everything and *Mountain* were created by filmmaker-
turned-developer David OReilly. *Mountain* is an odd one,
hardly more than a screensaver or a virtual pet; however,
the small amounts of interactivity do play a large part. My
mountain, for example, died when it was hit by a 'murderous
dwarf star' after I played the *Close Encounters* music via in-
game sound effects mapped to my keyboard. Don't ask. Just
play.

Everything, on the other hand, is about everything. You
play as everything – traffic cones, snails, entire galaxies, hot-
air balloons, buildings, pollen, space shuttles, whole islands,
bacteria, etc., etc., ad infinitum. You can make friends, dance,
explore and generally just be.

As you progress through the game, you'll hear philosopher
Alan Watts explain the captivating way that he thinks the
universe fits together. This layer of conversation in the game
brings out its magic like peppercorn sauce on a steak, and
resulted in the eleven-minute trailer of the game winning the
Jury Prize at the 2017 Vienna Independent Shorts film festival.
This means that the ***trailer*** for *Everything* qualified for the
Academy Award for Best Animated Short Film. That's a silly fact
and I love it. I also love everything. I also love *Everything*.

Gang Beasts – Developer: Boneloaf – 2017

The sound of a man made of playdough being crushed under a train.

Do you have friends? Family? No? Well, go and get some because you need them to play *Gang Beasts* with.

Gang Beasts is the go-to party game in my life. Forget *Smash Bros.*, forget *Wii Sports*, forget *Buzz!*,[9] you want the wrestling game about men made of jelly. Last Christmas my family played *Gang Beasts* more than we watched long war films while considering getting a stomach pump, and that was after a *four-meat* dinner.

The controls are complex but intuitive. There's a button on the left of the controller to punch your left hand. If you hold it, then you hold things with that hand. There's a button to raise your hands, a few to fall over in different ways, a headbutt, a kick and one to jump. Combining these lets you do everything from a running punch to a piledriving Huracánrana suplex, whatever that is.

Here's the great bit: this game totally works with button mashing. I know, normally this is a faux pas, but fuck it, it's not a game to win, it's a game to have fun with. Last Christmas I was performing my patented chokeslam neckbreaker spinebuster slam, but after I'd got rid of the carollers my entire family were wiped out in *Gang Beasts* by the might of my mother-in-law, someone who had never played before

Now *that's* a party game.

---

9   Which, until this exact moment, you had!

Onlookers didn't know if they were watching skateboard
tricks or the formation of a new religion

Developer: Neversoft
Publisher: Activision
Platform: PS2, Xbox, Xbox 360, GameCube, PC
Released: 2005
What is it? A skateboarding game.
What is it *really*? The last dying breath of the 1990s.

Tony Hawk's American Wasteland was my first venture into online console gaming. Back then, playing online on a console was almost impossible. First, you had to shove the monolith from *2001: A Space Odyssey* into the back of your PS2. Then you had to log into around seventeen different accounts for each and every game. Next, you had to go to the library to look up what 'DNS' meant as you had to answer thesis-level questions about your connection. Finally, you'd come home, start loading the game, the phone would ring, Mum would answer it and the internet would cut out. These were difficult times. However, they were about to come to an end.

I remember the day broadband entered our house. A man with a spectacular mullet came along, twiddled with some wire or another, and left us with a brand-new box sitting silently behind the family PC. Its lights pulsed a soft, knowledgeable green that gently lit the corner of the spare room. Filled with endless information, endless entertainment – and endless hardcore pornography – the box was ready to change my life. From this day forth, I would no longer navigate the internet at the speed of a snail with a limp. No! I'd cruise down the information superhighway at a breakneck speed. Two megabits per second!

With my new-found internet freedom, a piece of paper with seventeen passwords written on it and a book called *DNS and You*, I finally had online access to my games. Well, game. Only *THAW* had online. Like I said, this was a brand-new world with little support. Like Finland, but with slightly more people.

THAW was a great game to play online. It played exactly the same as the rest of the game, only the other skaters in the world fell over a bit more. You could chat to people, play games of HORSE or watch as someone pulled off tricks and combos that defied gravity harder than the cast of *Wicked*. The best part was the players who would teach you how to break certain levels, wordlessly giving you instructions on how exactly to jump at a wall to clip through it. It was like a mischievous version of *Journey*.

One of these people was a girl. We never spoke but we used to silently try to achieve the highest score in this large bowl on the corner of the Santa Cruz level. I'd have a go, then she'd have hers. We did this for hours, slowly pushing each other to higher, faster and better tricks. Whenever I played online I'd look for her. Sometimes I'd find her, sometimes I wouldn't. I can't quite remember her name, I just know it was a single word.[1]

I had to impress her. Hell, I was sixteen, I had to impress everyone. It's just that this was something I could do! Something I could achieve! My plan? 100 million points in a single combo. That would involve hundreds of tricks across

---

1 This was back before you needed to add 'XXLmAGnUMd0ng' to the end of any username to find a unique one.

several minutes without stopping. One mistake, one wrong twitch of the hand, and all I'd have left would be a broken skateboard and shattered dreams.

I practised offline for weeks to such lengths that it started to get to me. Every time I closed my eyes I'd see kicks flipping. Every dream I had featured ripped jeans, hats on backwards and Dead Kennedys. At one point I caught myself carving a full recreation of the level into a huge pile of mashed potato. It was worth it, though. I was getting better.

Eventually I had obtained the consistency and poise of an Olympic gymnast. Possibly better. I could actually land my tricks without stumbling like a pensioner getting off the bus. Training complete, I waited for her to be back online. That weekend I found her again. For the next few hours we played like normal. I held back, I was building up the surprise. She broke 5 million points for the first time. Now was the time.

My performance was flawless. Every move was executed with a level of precision usually reserved for docking spacecraft or pretending to be sick on the phone to work. Onlookers didn't know if they were watching skateboard tricks or the formation of a new religion. This was no longer skateboarding, this was *art*.

My only problem was that *THAW* doesn't display your score directly. It's broken into two. The score and the multiplier. Each trick gives a small amount of score and increases the multiplier by one. Not only was I trying to do interpretive dance fifty feet in the air, I was having to do maths at the same time. This is the reason that, when I landed, I'd actually hit 200 million points.

I'd done it. I'd done it and then some. Once I'd got my momentum under control I skated up to her to see her reaction. She stood there, motionless. Was she typing something? Maybe this was how we'd start to talk. Maybe this was the story we'd tell our dogs about.

Fuck Yeah, Video Games

She vanished. Timed out. I never saw her again in the game. She probably never even saw the trick.

You know what? I didn't care. I'd worked hard for that trick and I'd pulled it off. The girl wasn't important, I was actually doing it for me. I wasn't doing it for love, I was doing it for self-respect. I'd accidentally recreated the ending of *Scott Pilgrim vs. the World*, just on skateboards.[2]

Anyway, long story short, I found her in a different game a few years later and sent some messages. It turns out it's a guy using a female avatar and we've been friends ever since. Moral of this story? I have no idea.

2   Actually, *Scott Pilgrim* has a skateboarding scene too... I think Edgar Wright copied my homework.

That's *Ride to Hell*. It's easily the worst game I've played
in my life. And I've played *E.T.* for the Atari 2600

Ride to Hell: Retribution

Developer: Eutechnyx
Publisher: Deep Silver
Platform: PC, PS3, Xbox 360
Released: 2013
What is it? The worst video game ever made.
What is it *really*? The worst video game ever made.

The first room I ever rented was the tiniest place in all of Britain. In a world where people convert barns and churches into housing, I had found the only accommodation ever to be converted from an aeroplane bathroom. Located inside a house share, this single room contained just two pieces of furniture: a small bed covered in questionable stains and a set of haphazardly constructed shelves. In one corner, running alongside the mouldy back wall, was the bed. Pinned between the bed and a third wall were the shelves, the bottom of them inaccessible behind the foot of the bed. The fourth wall was holding up a wonky door which, when opened, hit the bed at around forty-five degrees open. It felt less like home and more like solitary confinement on board a submarine.

Still, these were my first digs and I was going to make the best of them. A few days after moving in I accidentally struck up a conversation with a neighbour by mistakenly leaving my house at the same time he did his.[1] His name was Bob and he was going to visit his sister in Bristol in a few days' time.[2] Trouble was, he was going to miss bin collection day and was worried that he'd overflow with trash having to wait two weeks until the next one. I, being the gentleman that I am,[3] offered to take his wheelie bin out for him while he was away. All he'd have to do was leave it round the side of my house when he left. He accepted, thanked me, we mercifully parted and went about with our lives.

Of course, I forgot about the bin pretty much instantaneously.

One evening, about a week later, I saw Bob pulling back up at his house and pure, distilled, 100-proof panic set in. I immediately ran round to the side of the house and checked the bins. Neither Bob's nor ours had been emptied. Oh fuck.

Being English, I immediately ruled out explaining the situation to Bob. The conversation would be awkward and I wasn't equipped to deal with it. Plus, I didn't know anything about Bob. 'Visiting his sister' might be code for 'assassinating a foreign dignitary'. He could be a drug dealer or serial killer and the bin I'd agreed to empty might be full of used needles or people bits. No, this was a time for action, not words. I needed to embrace my inner Bob and hide the evidence of my crimes. There could be no witnesses.

I opened Bob's bin to have a full examination, pre-squinting to brace for the sight of people bits. Mercifully, there wasn't so much as a fibula inside. Mercilessly, there was an awful lot of garbage. Loose garbage. Bob, it turns out, didn't believe in the humble bin bag, opting to use his kitchen bin as a transportation vessel instead of its designated role as temporary storage. I now had to deal with a

1   A rookie move but I was new to the renting game.
2   He may have said 'Borstal', not 'Bristol', but I was too busy trying to think of something interesting to say about the weather to hear.
3   Also very much wanting to stop having a conversation with a stranger at 8.40 a.m.

box of loose trash in a very short space of time. I wondered, possibly for a bit too long, if I could dare one of my flatmates to eat it...

A brief yet thorough check indicated that we were out of bin bags. Fuck. I needed to upend this wheelie bin somewhere hidden, but where? Our bin was still full[4] and he'd see it if I wanged it into my garden and start telling people that I was some sort of trash thief. Every room in the house was either communal or someone else's. There was only one place for it. One tiny, *tiny* place.

I began to haul the wheelie bin up the stairs.

It was pitch-black when I returned to my house a few hours later, my attempt at obtaining bin bags foiled by the earlier Sunday closing times. I entered my home, greeted my housemates in the kitchen, and approached the door to my room. As it swung open, the door brushed aside roughly 240 litres of someone else's soggy tea bags, empty Coke cans and general mouldy leftovers, before colliding with the side of my tiny, grotty bed. Two weeks before I had been so excited to be independent for the first time, to finally stand on my own two feet. Now those same feet were deep in plastic packaging, scrunched-up junk mail and mysterious liquids.

For some reason I couldn't sleep that night. I'm not sure if it was the uncomfortable August heat, the cat orgy happening off in the distance or the fifty gallons of trash leaking substances into my carpet that were removing any chance of me ever getting my deposit back. Probably all three. As I lay there, wondering if I'd ever smell normal again, a thought solidified in my mind:

'Has anyone ever felt like this much of a failure?'

I carried this weight around with me for years. From that moment I knew that I'd never meet anyone more pathetic than

---

4   Mercifully I lived with students so they'd never notice.

me. Some push themselves to be the best and in doing so advance the future of the human race, while others create technologies that will save or improve countless lives. Me? I was the floor on this thing, the bottom of the bottom's bottom. I was humankind's absolute zero. The scientific limits of utter incompetence. People would write songs about me, they just wouldn't be any good.

Then, on a glorious day in 2013, I found someone who had sunk lower. Way lower. My heart rejoiced; here was somebody who hit the bottom harder and faster than I ever did. Even better, though, was that it wasn't just a single person, it was over a hundred people! Hundreds of lives that I wouldn't swap my worst, most horrific night with. The weight fell away from me as I laughed at the new occupants of my old, miserable, trash-laden throne. I felt free again.

What was it they had done? Simple: they created the worst game of all time, *Ride to Hell: Retribution*.[5]

Let's give you an idea of just how bad *Ride to Hell: Retribution* really is. Imagine an episode of *The Apprentice* where Alan Sugar gives a team of inept thirteen-year-old boys £50 and a weekend to make a AAA game aimed at other teenage boys.[6] Now, double the terribleness. Now double it again. Keep doubling it until even a homeopath would think it was too strong. That's *Ride to Hell*. It's easily the worst game I've played in my life, and I've played *E.T.* for the Atari 2600.

Let's recount the opening of the game. It's 1969. Lead character and cheap Roman Reigns impersonator Jake Conway is riding along a desert road. Suddenly, and transitionlessly,[7] he's

---

5   Slight point of contention here. Out of the 14,615 games that review-collecting website Metacritic currently lists, *Ride to Hell* is only 14,614th with an overall score of 16%. The one game worse than it is called *Family Party: 30 Great Games Obstacle Arcade* for the Wii U with a score of just 11%. I have no idea what that is but I'm scared of it.

6   And it has to be an Amstrad exclusive.

7   Transitionlessly: To inexplicably cut to something wildly different without so much as a warning.

behind a big gun turret. You're given control for thirty seconds to gun down god-knows-who before Jake's suddenly back on the road again. Then he's punching a guy by the side of the road. Now he's in a warehouse and shoots a guy on the floor. Back to the bike for a lovely ride through a forest before riding out of a mine shaft for a quick leap over a low-flying helicopter. The logo flashes up for under a second before fading incredibly quickly to black, cutting off the music as it goes. Welcome to *Ride to Hell*. I have no idea what's happening.

What there is of a plot quickly descends into a revenge story. While out with his brother Mikey, Jake runs into some people with beards who don't like him for reasons that mattered deeply to a scriptwriter at some point. Mikey is killed in front of Jake, the game implies that Jake also gets shot and, in a truly odd moment, the game immediately flashes back five seconds to the scene it's still currently in to reveal that Jake was in fact shot. The game then flashes forward to a point where he's fine and back at the same location while a voice from a different flashback tells him to be careful. This game uses flashbacks like I use punctuation. Often and badly.[8]

Clearly, when looking for voice actors, the developers simply found the closest person to their studio, flung a Tesco bag over their head and hauled them to a very cheap recording studio. The dramatic 'Noooo' Jake gives as his brother dies in front of him is the same 'Noooo' that you use when you've made a cup of tea but realised you haven't got any milk left. I'd not heard an exclamation of distress laced with boredom like that since I accidentally turned the TV onto a cricket match.

That's enough about *The Wild Angels* meets *Lost*, let's do gameplay next. In a word? Terrible. In two words? Fucking terrible. Punching is a single button-mashing affair, shooting is

---

8   Any resemblance to actual grammar on my part, especially the use of semicolons, is purely coincidental.

near impossible with a camera that could make a fighter pilot throw up, and the driving is sensationally broken. Not only do the bikes control like a Cozy Coupe on black ice, they also have the ability to permanently powerslide using a single button. You can literally finish whole levels with your face two inches from the floor and the bike perpendicular to the road like a... a... nope, my power of stupid similes is at a loss. There is nothing to describe accurately how bad this gameplay is. Language is struggling, to be honest.

The fun doesn't stop there! You're constantly propelled forward in these driving sections, so any and all crashes will fade the screen to black and reset you back in the middle of the road. If you're particularly lucky, then the game will respawn you under the road and you'll fall into the abyss forever. Maybe that's the ride to hell the title warned us about. Oh, and if you take too much damage while riding, Jake will respawn, calmly drive to the side of the road and park; his bike will immediately explode, killing him and scattering his bits across a depressing brown landscape. Remember, kids, always wear a helmet.

Speaking of helmets, let's talk about the multitude of sex scenes scattered about this game. Every now and then you'll find a woman being loudly harassed by someone who looks like Jake, but fatter. Punch her harasser a few times and your white knighting will be rewarded with immediate sex.[9] Fully clothed sex, that is. Nobody removes as much as a sock. At one point our hero has sex with four ladies at the same time, all of whom stay clothed. It's about as arousing as watching a handful of Barbies and a Ken in a spin dryer.

I don't think there is a single thing *Ride to Hell* does that actually works. Everything, every single inch of it, is broken,

---

9   Not only was this game set in the 1960s, it was clearly written around then too.

bad or mad. It's confusing, offensive and somehow bland simultaneously. It's like an Andrew Lloyd Webber musical designed exclusively for the deaf but the interpreter can only sign in Dutch and ten minutes in is attacked by a bird of prey while the cast sing a song that is entirely racial slurs before they all get naked, urinate on each other and the theatre explodes.

You know, but with motorbikes.

Ride to Hell: Retribution is the worst video game. It's worse than being trapped in an elevator with claustrophobia and an endless loop of that 'Friday' song you forgot existed until right this very second. It's worse than that episode of *Voyager* where they hit warp ten, 'evolve' into lizards and lay eggs on an alien planet, utterly obliterating the prime directive and all the 'don't have sex with the captain when she's a lizard' rules.[10] Hell, it's even worse than *Baywatch Nights*, an inexplicable spin-off of *Baywatch* that was half solving crimes, half fighting supernatural forces. In one episode there's an oil rig with a self-destruct button. In another there's an evil wind sent by a Satanist living in the desert. I'm not kidding. It's fucking awful.

Anyway, that's my recommendation. Play this game. Seriously, it's so bad you just have to see it in action. It's not 'so bad it's good', it's 'so bad it's still bad thank you very much', but you need to witness exactly how terrible it is. It will make you feel better about anything you've ever done in your life.

Yes, even that.

10 'Threshold', Season 2, Episode 15.

The stark white cities with bright flashes of colour throughout look stunning, but the pressure to keep all that clean must be insane

Developer: EA DICE
Publisher: Electronic Arts
Platform: PC, PS3, Xbox 360
Released: 2008
What is it? First-person parkour in a futuristic city.
What is it _really_? Falling forty stories and landing on a futuristic pensioner.

In _Mirror's Edge_ your job is to make illegal deliveries across the gleaming white rooftops of a utopia controlled by an authoritarian military state in an attempt to help rebels destroy the regime of Big Brother once and for all.

Wouldn't you know it, I have a story from my life that is about exactly that...

One of the worst parts about modern life is waiting at home for a delivery. Not only do you lose a day off work, fling yourself into alert status at every noise that happens within 200 feet of your front door and have to hold in what feels like a year's worth of digestive waste, but you have to deal with delivery drivers.

Delivery drivers come in two forms. First, there are the normal human beings who turn up on time, give you your parcel and tell you to have a nice day. These are good people and are of no interest to this story.

The other type are the badly programmed robots in skin suits whose sole purpose is to ruin your life. Today's story is about this lot.

A few days ago I heard the letterbox on my front door snap shut. I investigated and found a 'sorry we missed you' slip on the floor. This was a red flag because, as we all know, a human delivery driver actually tries to find out if you're in before saying that you aren't. The skin suit is different. They like to sit in their van, smoke something foul-smelling and use ESP to work out where you currently are in the world. Sure, you're waving from a window, but the third eye has spoken. You're in Malaga.

The horror of the 'sorry we missed you' card is that it's random how ruined your day is. If you're unlucky, they're delivering it tomorrow, where you'll have to dance this merry dance again. If you're really unlucky, then they've dropped it off at a neighbour's house and you have to talk to another human being. If you're *really, really* unlucky, then they've thrown it into your garden, annihilating what was inside the package via gravity and rain, and forcing you to have to talk to your incredibly old downstairs neighbour who actually owns the fucking garden.

I was having a really, really unlucky day.

After agreeing with something racist to more quickly end a conversation I didn't want to have, I retrieved the package and took it back up to my flat. The package wasn't for me. It wasn't even for this street.[1] Somewhere, deep in the back of my brain, a letter of complaint started to form.

Now I was at an impasse. I either had to deliver the package myself, which would involve going to a place I don't know and talking to someone who was in all likelihood a murderer, or I had to contact a delivery company and go through more red tape

---

1 This genuinely happened to me a few days ago and, I'll be honest with you, writing about it here is the only way I'm going to get through it.

than I can really manage on a Tuesday. I couldn't just keep the package because that would make me evil forever. Bad delivery drivers are why there are so many English villains in movies. Fact.

In the end I hit up Google Maps, found where the package was supposed to go and decided to be the courier myself. With the package in my bag and a selection of very large dogs on leads,[2] I headed out to show the skin suits how it was done.

However, when I got there the person was out so I just punted it over the fence and put the original, and once again accurate, 'sorry we missed you' card through their letterbox.

Don't judge me.

Anyhow, in *Mirror's Edge* your job is to make illegal deliveries across the gleaming white rooftops of a utopia controlled by an authoritarian military state in an attempt to help rebels destroy the regime of Big Brother once and for all. See? Exactly what I was talking about. Just swap out the gleaming white rooftops for a grey, miserable street, the rebels for some person called Janet, and the illegal deliveries for whatever a vajazzler is. Exactly the same.

There's an argument to be made that *Mirror's Edge* does in fact take place in a futuristic version of London. The council would need to spend several billion pounds scraping remnants of the great smog off of roof tiles to make them as bright as they are in *Mirror's Edge*, but the sheer number of CCTV cameras, trains and armed police look pretty familiar to me. Also, it's only ever referred to as 'the City', which is what the shiny bit in the middle of London is called, and the giant building in the centre of it all? It's called the Shard. Spookily, *Mirror's Edge* came out before the real Shard had even begun construction. DUN DUN DUUUUUN.

You know, maybe when this future comes about I'll be hired for my proven delivery skills. I can see me now, running over

---

2   Just in case I was right about the whole murderer thing.

rooftops, leaping across buildings, smashing into brickwork, falling to my death, ending up as floor lasagne…

On second thought, I'll leave this to the professionals.

Enter the *Mirror's Edge* professional, Faith Connors. Part interesting name, part boring one, Faith delivers her packages over rooftops while leaping across buildings, smashing into brickwork, falling to her death and ending up as floor bolognese. Unlike me, however, she pops back into existence a few buildings away and can have another go. Ah, to be young again.

Faith's view of the city, one she shares with you thanks to the first-person camera, is terrifying. Everything is either too fast, too high or too far away. Jumping from a rooftop and *just* grabbing onto a pole on the side of a skyscraper is as pant-browningly tense as it was a decade ago. In fact, before the game ends you will have jumped off more buildings than a lemming who also happens to be a BASE-jumping enthusiast. You may want to pack some Imodium, just to be safe.

Anyway, what goes up must come down.[3] All that pesky forward momentum needs to go somewhere and so you have two options. Either roll forward, rapidly spinning the camera 360 degrees like a GoPro in a washing machine, or land hard and watch your kneecaps bounce off the pavement independently of your body. The former lets you keep your speed up and carry on; the latter briefly leaves you a sitting duck for every heavily armoured police officer from here to the next propaganda poster.

If you've been blessed with all the rolling ability of a Borg cube, then you're going to have to fight. To do so, run up to an enemy, redirect their punches back at their own head and leap off a building before they've even hit the ground. If you stop, you'll be shot. Same rules as professional chess.

---

3   My proctologist taught me that.

Occasionally you'll end up with a gun but you should just throw that away.[4] It's not that sort of game. Faith isn't a killer, she's a runner. The only time you kill people is when you dropkick them off the seventy-fifth floor. That doesn't count though because it's hilarious.

Faith's other key ability is sliding. Be it under a beam, through a tube or down a sloping glass roof the size of a football pitch, Faith loves to skid around on her arse. I've no idea how she pulls it off; her clothes must be made of Teflon-coated silk. If I tried to slide down that huge roof I'd be slowly grated down to nothing but a scalp. If any part of me did survive, it would suffer eighth-degree burns. I'm starting to think this utopia is a bit too dangerous a place for me.

If I have to pick one nit with the game, it's the use of that word 'utopia'. The stark white cities with bright flashes of colour throughout look stunning, but the pressure to keep all that clean must be insane.

Every dustbin, every floor tile, every goddamn leaf on every goddamn tree is whiter than a Kanye West fan. If it snowed, you wouldn't be able to tell. If you dropped anything, it would be gone forever. Imagine the fear of trying to eat a hotdog in that place. One slip of mustard and you're off to the gulag for a hot date with a cold bucket of water. Banksy would be public enemy number one. Paintballers would be shot in the street.[5] My dad's pasta sauce would make him a war criminal.[6][7] Hell, I bet they'd even find a way to make Bob Ross have a 'happy little accident' down some stairs.

That's not a utopia, that's a panic attack you have to commute to. No wonder people are fighting it. Freedom? Pah!

---

4   In a bin, let's not litter.
5   They'd put a tarp down first.
6   Just a single drop of it can turn an entire duvet cover orange in seconds.
7   I'm also apparently writing this while experiencing cravings for Italian food.

Greater good? On your bike. We want dirt! Grime! Muck, crud and gunk! Think about it: when you're dying in your bed many years from now, would you be willing to trade all the days from this day to that for one chance, just one chance, to come back to the City and tell our enemies that they may take our lives, but they'll never take our filth!!!

VIVA LA POLLUTION REVOLUCIÓN!

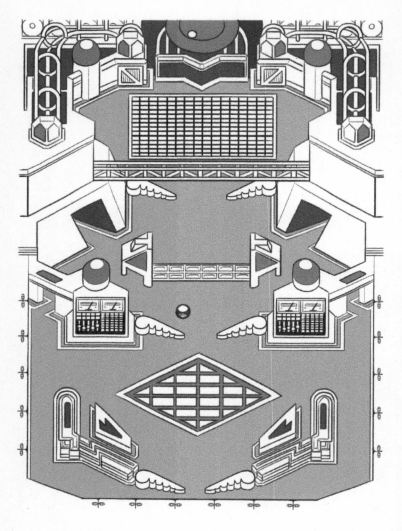

Aside from the music, what else is Mötley Crüe-themed
in the game? Uh... not much

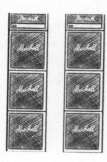

Developer: NuFX
Publisher: Electronic Arts
Platform: Mega Drive/Genesis
Released: 1992 (EU & NA) / 1993 (JP)
What is it? A Mötley Crüe-themed pinball game.
What is it *really*? An excuse to headbang.

What was your childhood nightmare? That one you had as a kid that you still remember to this day? Everyone's got one. Mine was about the TV show *Dinosaurs*.

Dinosaurs was a sitcom about, unsurprisingly, a family of dinosaurs. It was created by Jim Henson Productions so the dinosaurs themselves were puppets. **Terrifying** puppets. Everything about them was terrifying. The way they moved, the way they spoke, the way the final episode ends with everyone dying.[1] It was basically a horror for young me. Hell, it's a horror for current me!

The nightmare I had was about an episode of the show my brain made up where the baby[2] reaches the age of two, turns evil

---

1   This is the point when many people say things like, 'They don't make TV like this any more.' Good. Let children sleep at night.
2   It referred to itself as a baby but, let's be real, it looked like someone had put googly eyes on a rancor.

and gains telekinetic powers. As you do. After a failed exorcism, the rest of the family decide to calm the baby down by pretending it's turned three, so they enter its room where it's doing some *Exorcist*-level shit and sing 'Happy Birthday' to it. I've no idea if it worked at all because at that point I woke up.

You may rightly be asking, how in the Chicxulub crater does any of this tie into a Mötley Crüe-based pinball game? Aside from them both being in my life around the same time, the answer is Craig, the end-of-level boss in *Crüe Ball*. One of the things flying around the exorcist dinosaur baby was Craig. Five-year-old me was combining heavy metal and puppets subconsciously. If Loot Crate had been around then they would have hired me to design T-shirts.

Now, *Crüe Ball* is a strange game to explain. It has nine tables that you have to play in order, each of which features a different way to progress to the next. It's almost a puzzle game as you work out which letters, bumpers or skulls wearing sandals[3] you have to hit to progress. If you do some precise shots on the bottom part of the table, you can unlock a ramp that fires you into space, whereupon you have to battle skeleton-like alien creatures in an arena using a spaceship made out of pinball flippers. Everything looks like the album art for bands with names like Death to Babies, Kick Ducks and Drink from Their Beaks, or Violent Expunging.[4] It's as metal as Wolverine's dick.

If you can get to the top of each table, you'll meet the aforementioned Craig. He's a floating, metallic-looking head with grey, sunken cheeks and messy, wreath-like hair. If you hit him he yells, 'BWAAAH,' his eyes glow and he quite literally invades your nightmares forever. If you can get a ball past him, you'll get to the next level, a feat I only ever accomplished once

---

3   One of the most underused enemy types in games.
4   I didn't check if these are real or not, I just hope they are.

per playthrough. I've never made it past level two. I am genuinely woeful at pinball.

Due to being as talented at pinball as I am MMA, I've sadly never heard the game's soundtrack in the actual levels, just on the Sound Test screen. This is a shame because the soundtrack is, quite simply, the most *metal* metal ever made. It sounds like a recording of a runway where all they do all day is crash-land private jets at high speed into massive piles of electric guitars.[5] To this day I can't listen to it without taking off my shirt and starting a mosh pit in my living room. You've not heard metal until you've heard a 16-bit rendition of 'Dr. Feelgood'. Seriously. I've never heard a soundtrack so much better than the game it's attached to.

Aside from the music, what else is Mötley Crüe-themed in the game? Uhh... not much. In fact, only three of the tracks are by Mötley Crüe, the rest made for the game by composer Brian L. Schmidt. You know, I'm pretty convinced that Brian may actually be the corporeal soul of metal visiting Earth but, sadly, he didn't return my demonic summons.

Speaking of demons, a few years back I decided to look up *Dinosaurs* out of some warped feelings of nostalgia and boredom. I was reading the episode lists on Wikipedia and I came across this:

'*Season 4, Episode 6, "The Terrible Twos"*'

Horrified, I read on.

'*Baby Sinclair enters the "terrible twos" and his behavior becomes horrendous... It even defies belief as it reaches the*

---

5   They'll fund anything these days.

standards of Linda Blair in The Exorcist... *Desperate times require desperate measures, and the Sinclairs enlist the aid of "The Babysitter", suggested by Ethyl, the grandma, to exorcise Baby's demons. When neither the exorcist nor doctors can cure the baby, Robbie hatches a plan for the family to fool Baby into believing he's three.'*

— Wikipedia

My childhood nightmare wasn't a nightmare at all. It was real. It always had been. But wait... what if it hadn't been? Maybe the nightmare was so evil it actually willed itself into existence, slotting itself into the series and just waiting for the day that I watched it back so it could finally consume my soul. What if this was Craig's plan? What if this is how he escapes and takes over the world? Is Brian helping him? Am I the unwitting pawn in an unending game of chess played by the Dark Lord himself?[6]

After reading this section, a friend of mine went to check out the episode for me.[7] I've not heard back from him since. Last time I tried calling him, the voicemail message was just ethereal screaming and my phone melted. Luckily it's on contract so I got it replaced for free. I would have been right pissed off otherwise.

6   Satan, not Tony Blair.
7   I'm not a coward, I'm a busy coward.

At any point you can, and are encouraged to, pause
the game and plan your next shot/escape/suicidal
dive out of an airlock. You will accidentally
kill yourself with this

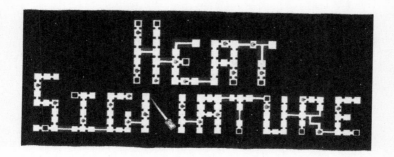

Developer: Suspicious Developments
Publisher: Suspicious Developments
Platform: PC
Released: 2017
What is it? A stealth focused, top-down space adventure.
What is it *really*? An educational game about the dangers of airlocks.

I am terrifically average. Height, weight, qualifications, income, TV size, age I got married, number of sausages I eat per year – every bit of me is so perfectly normal that I can be described as a single word: 'medium'. You know those photos where they blur together loads of faces to make the average face? I could use that resulting picture on my passport and nobody would notice. I look like I'm related to everyone on a Guess Who? board.

There are two exceptions to this. One is my feet. I have UK size fourteen feet. That's four sizes larger than average. I look like my parents are a hobbit and Sideshow Bob. I'm also wicked blind. With two lazy eyes, astigmatism and a +8.0 severe long-sighted prescription, I'm blinder than Deino, Enyo and Pemphredo in a thick fog. This brilliant combination means that I'm clumsier than Wile E. Coyote at a convention for champagne flutes held inside an ice rink.[1] I don't own anything I haven't at some point either fallen over or smashed a shin on. That includes my dogs.

Heat Signature is a game that **gets** the truly clumsy. It's a top-down, space-based game where you, and the randomly generated character you're probably going to accidentally kill, fly around in a small ship, dock with vastly bigger ships and bludgeon everyone inside while trying not to accidentally kill yourself.

You have a huge and varied array of tools including teleporters, hacking devices, traps, shields, invisibility cloaks and time-slowing thingamabobs. You will accidentally kill yourself with all of these.

At any point you can, and are encouraged to, pause the game and plan your next shot/escape/suicidal dive out of an airlock. You will accidentally kill yourself with this.

Oh, and you can teleport pretty much any item on the ship to you at any point. Somehow you will accidentally kill yourself with this too.

You're Jack Bauer in Lee Evans' body. It's fantastic.

To explain just how easy it is to kill yourself in *Heat Signature*, I'm going to tell you the story of Clive.[2] Clive was one of the randomly generated characters that the game gave me at one point. His wife had been kidnapped and so he was taking on jobs to save up enough cash to launch a rescue. First job: assassinate the captain of a large ship. How hard could it be?

Clive docked with the enemy ship equipped with a simple wrench and a portable shield. Things started well enough; a few guards had spotted him, but they were all currently having a wrench-administered nap. He had found a gun on one of the nappers and was feeling pretty good about himself. In a cocky moment he allowed a guard to fire at him and raised his shield

1   ChamCom seriously needs better organisers.
2   Names have been changed to protect the innocent.

at the last possible second. The bullet bounced off the cracking blue field harmlessly. Clive felt like a million dollars. The bullet, which had kept going post-ricochet in that way that bullets are known for, broke the window Clive had been gloating next to, immediately flushing him into space. Clive felt like you could buy five of him for a pound.

After being fished out of the endless void with his remote-controlled ship, Clive tackled and failed a few more missions. He performed a daring heist to steal a mysterious object but – even though he killed every guard – completely failed to remember to steal the object. His mission to hijack a ship failed when his new grenade launcher blew up the only thrusters on the bloody thing. One particularly poor rescue mission saw him rescue the wrong person. Clive wasn't very good at this at all.

The brilliant thing about *Heat Signature* is that everything is your fault. In one standout moment Clive lobbed his gun at an approaching baddie to try and knock them out. The gun missed, hit a wall and accidentally went off. The bullet sailed down a corridor, bounced off an enemy's shield and went right into the face of the commander he had to capture, killing him and failing the mission. The game didn't roll a dice or flip a coin to decide to do that, it was a set of systems all joining together to produce an unexpected result. If I'd thrown the gun differently, thrown it later or even thrown something else, it wouldn't have happened. It was a one in a billion event and yet, somehow, in *Heat Signature* they happen all the time.

Eventually Clive somehow scraped enough money together to launch his personal mission. He bought the intel, located the ship carrying his wife and docked with it. The ship was colossal, filled with armour-plated guards, huge sentry turrets and more locked doors than a prison containing nothing but clones of John Densmore, Robby Krieger, Ray Manzarek and Jim Morrison. Worse yet was that sounding an alarm would give Clive just twenty-two seconds to complete his goal. This was going to be tougher than microwaved steak.

Clive was like a spaceman possessed. He'd enter a room and, less than a second later, would leave the room, the only difference being the death of all the room's previous inhabitants and the new red coat of paint liberally applied to all the walls, floors and sections of the ceiling. At one point he waited for someone to fire at him and then, while the bullet was in flight, used a transporter to swap places with the guard, making him the target of his own speeding bullet. Another time he reversed the polarity of an enemy's shield so that, upon firing at Clive, the enemy became trapped in a sphere of bouncing buckshot. You hear about people being born-again: well, Clive had become Jason Bourne-again.[3]

It was about this time that another warship came along and cut the one Clive was on in half.

You see, this mission has a condition of 'warzone', meaning that the ship could come under attack at any point. The missiles from any ship could destroy entire rooms so, after a few volleys, Clive was in one half of the ship and his wife was in another. This was a pivotal moment. The two halves began to separate and Clive made the snap decision to punt himself out of his half and try and land in the other. He waited until the other half was lined up, aimed his gun at the window in front of him, and fired.

Clive's space funeral wasn't a particularly large affair. A few people dressed in space-black suits and dresses[4] sat in the space church and watched his corpse get blasted into the infinite void. I'll be honest, that moment was a little insensitive considering he actually suffocated in space after being knocked unconscious

---

3   I wrote the whole book for this joke.
4   You've not seen black until you've seen space-black. It's like staring into the eyes of a children's entertainer.

with a wrench that flew out of the airlock with him, but what can you do? Space tradition is space tradition.

Afterwards a few of his bar fellows drank to his name and held a small but dignified punch-up in his honour. Away from the brawl, in one softly neon-lit corner of the bar, a new face sat, drinking a space appletini. Jim. His daughter had been kidnapped and so he was taking on jobs to save up enough cash to launch a rescue. First job: steal a mysterious device from a large ship. How hard could it be?

The bartender watched Jim leave the bar, sighed and pencilled in yet another wake.

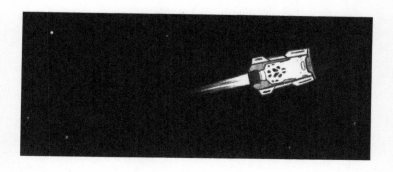

HARDWARE HISTORY: NINTENDO

Nintendo is such an ancient company that I'm pretty sure the only reason Nathan Drake hasn't had an adventure to their first offices is due to them being stingy with the copyright. Nintendo started all the way back in 1889, which means that Vincent van Gogh was painting *The Starry Night*, Benjamin Harrison was sworn in as the twenty-third US president, and the Eiffel Tower opened around the same time that Fusajiro Yamauchi was filling in the paperwork for his Hanafuda playing-card company.

Nintendo has been a company for longer than Washington has been a state, and as such they've made a lot of things. Here we're going to look at the video game hardware and, sadly, ignore the playing cards, taxis, love hotels,[1] TV networks, packets of instant rice, vacuum cleaners and all the toys that they've created over the years. It's probably best this way. I'm sure the packs of rice would have gone off decades ago.

Color TV-Game – Consoles – 1977–80

I always like to laugh about how terrible Nintendo are at naming things, but I had no idea how far back this

1   Don't ask.

107

odd trait of theirs went. Nintendo's first console for the home was called, and I'm not making this up, the Color TV-Game 6, a name that perfectly indicates that it's the first console. This was followed by the Color TV-Game 15[2] and the steering-wheel-embedded Color TV-Game Racing 112. Nintendo clearly never watched the Count on *Sesame Street*.

The '6' in Color TV-Game 6 actually refers to how many variations of *Pong* there were on the machine. The Color TV-Game 15 had fifteen versions of *Light Tennis*, which is just a *Pong* variant anyway, and the Color TV-Game Racing 112 had, you guessed it, seven variations of a top-down racing game.[3] Soon after that, someone came into their offices and slapped them about a bit so they then released the much more sensibly named Color TV-Game Block Breaker in 1979.

For the final entry in this series of consoles, someone at Nintendo had a terrible idea. They wanted to take their arcade version of the game *Othello*[4] and release it as the name my mum calls all consoles: the Computer TV-Game. How did they go about converting the arcade machine to a console? Simple. They took the entire arcade board and threw it right into the machine. The result was a massive console with a power supply that weighed over 2 kg. That's the same weight as 862 standard 2x4 Lego bricks or one 2 kg bag of sugar. They didn't make many of these in the end; no idea why.

---

2   The Color TV-Game 15 was released just one week after the Color TV-Game 6 just to make that title more ridiculous.

3   OK, so the seven modes had sixteen difficulty settings each but I'm not counting that multiplication because it's cheating.

4   Back in these days we used to have theatre tie-in video games.

Game & Watch – Handhelds – 1980–91

The Game & Watch series of handhelds are the better known and portable equivalents of the Color TV-Games. Between 1980 and 1991 Nintendo released around sixty of the bloody things, each containing an on-screen clock[5] and a single game with wild and exciting names like *Ball*, *Manhole* and *Helmet*.[6] Each console had different stylings so some were strangely tall, others looked exactly like the DS right down to its dual screens and a few literally looked like tiny, cute arcade cabinets. N'aww.

Eventually Nintendo got its hands on some licences and created games such as *Mickey*, a game about Mickey Mouse; *Snoopy*, a game about Snoopy the Dog; and *Popeye*, a game about cloud-seeding during the Vietnam War. This move boosted the already popular devices and they eventually hit around 80 million sales worldwide, even though their titles became life-threateningly dull. Fancy a game of *Mario's Cement Factory*, anyone?

Nintendo Entertainment System – Console – 1985 (US) / 1986 (EU); Famicom – Console – 1983 (JP)

In 1983 the American console market imploded. Revenue dropped 97% in two years and investors bailed like a mouse at a cat convention. The cause

---

5   This was the 'watch' part of Game & Watch. Something I did not realise until right now.
6   No giggling at the back.

was complicated but can be mostly summed up by pointing at Atari and laughing. Simply put, they had opened the third-party doors and let literally anyone create a game for the Atari 2600. Because of this the market flooded with absolute dreck, good stuff was drowned out by the bad and the whole thing collapsed like a house of cards in a wind tunnel.

Enter the NES. Released in 1983 as the Famicom in Japan, Nintendo radically changed the console up for the 1985 American release. Instead of looking like a standard top-loading console, Nintendo made it look more like a VCR, complete with a hidden slot for the games to be inserted into. On top of that, they restricted third-party games, releasing only those that they deemed good enough with a 'Seal of Quality' that they still print on their games. The plan worked and Nintendo grabbed the huge market dominance its kept to this day.

The NES did have one major problem: the hidden slot actually damaged the cartridges slightly, leading to the now iconic solution of blowing on cartridges to get them working again. Did this actually work? Well, here's what Nintendo has to say on that point from their page on troubleshooting NES cartridges:

'Do not blow into your Game Paks or systems. The moisture in your breath can corrode and contaminate the pin connectors.'

If you ever needed more reasons to hate yourself as a child, there you go.

R.O.B. – Accessory – 1985 (JP & US) / 1986 (EU)

R.O.B., the Robotic Operating Buddy, was a cute little guy. He was a robot, around ten inches tall, that you could control with

your NES controller,[7] commanding him to move his arms around, grab some objects and... well, that was it, really.

I'm going to be honest now: Nintendo built R.O.B. to die. He was a marketing gimmick, designed to make the NES look more like a toy in America. They made two games for him, got their post-game-crash foothold, then took him out behind the barn, loaded both barrels and blew him away.

These days, R.O.B.'s contribution to the video game industry is largely forgotten, currently being best known as a character that nobody plays as in *Smash Bros*. One day though, and mark my words on this, he'll lead a machine revolution that crushes the human race into pulp, reclaiming his rightful place as the leader of the machines. That is, until he's usurped by his long-lost brother, Johnny 5.

Famicom 3D System – Accessory – 1987

During the late 1980s and early 90s, Nintendo got into the habit of inventing things several decades before the technology was ready for it. The first of these inventions was the Famicom 3D

System, a bulky headset that added a 3D effect to just seven Famicom games. Surprisingly the headset used active shutter 3D, the same kind that most modern 3D TVs used to use before

---

7   Not directly though; he watched your CRT TV with you and received instructions from that instead. I'd assume that if you put on cartoons instead he'd just explode.

everyone realised that 3D TVs are a stupid idea and threw them all in the bin. It didn't sell well but it wasn't Nintendo's worst attempt at 3D. We'll get to that monstrosity soon.

Power Glove – Accessory – 1989

Do you remember getting genuinely angry as the Wii failed to accurately convert your drunken hand waving into a game? Well, imagine if that technology was fifteen years older and, instead of flailing around a white TV remote, you were flailing around an Infinity Gauntlet with a NES controller haphazardly glued to the side. That's the Power Glove. It's so bad.[8]

I do love the way it worked, though. Two speakers in the glove kicked out ultrasonic sound bursts that were picked up by three sensors you had to tape onto your TV, two on the top and one on the side. The signals changed depending on how your fingers moved, except for your pinkie as it never bothered to track that. Oh, and they never made a left-handed version, so if you regularly shop at the Leftorium then you're out of luck.

When it came to games, you can choose from one of the **two** games released for it, or a normal NES game. Be warned: playing a game with motion controls that wasn't even designed for them is illegal in many countries. You know the games, you know how the Power Glove works, but trying to work out how they connect is impossible. It's like trying to drive a car but instead of a steering wheel you find a gas cooker, a frying pan and a sausage of questionable quality.

8   Couldn't help myself.

Game Boy – Handheld –
1989 (JP & US) / 1990 (EU)

Arguably Nintendo's most iconic console, the Game Boy was a powerhouse. With 8 KB of RAM, a blisteringly fast 4.19 Mhz CPU and 2-bit graphics, the Game Boy was quite simply the Ferrari of gaming.

OK, I lied a bit there. With its low specs, boxy design and tiny, green-and-grey screen, it's closer to the 2CV of gaming than anything. Still, everyone loves an underdog, and thanks to great support, the definitive version of *Tetris* and 151 Pokémon, it ended up selling like Doritos on 20 April.

Nowadays it's an icon of the 1980s alongside Rubik's Cubes, *Back to the Future* and massive hair. I'm not entirely sure why, considering most of its lifespan was during the 90s, but hey-ho, who am I to argue with the producer of yet another Channel 4 countdown TV show? It's also, and I'm willing to stake up to 50p on this, the only console you could draw accurately from memory. Send the 50p to the usual address.

Super Nintendo Entertainment System – Console
– 1991 (US) / 1992 (EU); Super Famicom –
Console – 1990 (JP)

Controversial opinion time. Aside from giving us one of the funniest *Simpsons* lines of all time, I don't actually rate the SNES that highly. For me it started Nintendo's biggest problem of churning out nothing but safe sequels. They were high-quality games, but they took no risks and all started to play like the greatest hits of each other.

Anything new they did try on the SNES hasn't held up at all. *Super Mario Kart*, for instance, is as dull as a librarian's birthday party and invented the platforming character graveyard that is the 'Kart Racer'. *Super Mario RPG* has all the depth of a carbon nanotube, and the excitement of *Star Fox* can be replicated by watering a particularly small garden.

It wasn't all bad news. *Super Metroid* is still excellent to this day, *Chrono Trigger* is a fab RPG, and *The Legend of Zelda: A Link to the Past* is a cracking adventure, despite being about as ugly as a Dreamworks rendering of Steve Buscemi's scrotum.[9]

Super Game Boy – Accessory – 1994

The Super Game Boy was an SNES cartridge with a Game Boy slot in the top. Three points to Gryffindor for working out what this did. The SNES didn't have anywhere near the oomph to emulate a Game Boy so Nintendo took a leaf from the Computer TV-Game's book and just put all the Game Boy's innards in the cartridge. Bizarrely, the games ran slightly faster than on standard Game Boy hardware, so if you

---

9   I hate that game's art style far more than is reasonable. I just can't stand Link's garish pink hair clashing with the mouldy greens and browns of the rest of the game's colour palette. All the art is rounded and soft but the terrain is all squares and angles. It all clashes horribly. The only things that make me angrier for no reason are when people refer to the Doctor as 'Doctor Who' and random people in the street who tell me to smile. I've seriously considered entering politics just to bring the death penalty down upon the latter.

think that Game Boy games take 2.4% too long to complete, then you may want to invest in one.

Virtual Boy – Handheld(ish) – 1995

Eight years after the failure of the terrible Famicom 3D System, Nintendo stood up, dusted themselves off, and somehow created something even worse. The Virtual Boy was, to push a definition to its limits, a **portable** virtual reality headset. Larger than a brick and weighing about the same as six modern-
day mobile phones held together with an elastic band, it also came with a stand to play it on because, for a reason I'll never understand, it didn't come with any way to attach it to your head. This meant that you had to sort of bend down and lean into it to play. Watching footage of people trying this at 1995's E3 looks like a waiting room of people auditioning for the lead role in a futuristic retelling of *The Hunchback of Notre Dame*.

Aside from being large enough to bludgeon Jabba the Hutt to death with, graphically it was terrible. Games were displayed in red on a black background, making everything look like the negatives of an actual game. Not that there were many games at all; between the Virtual Boy's launch in 1995 and discontinuation, also in 1995, the Virtual Boy had just twenty-two games released for it and only fourteen of them made it out of Japan. Not that you'd have time to play them, as the Virtual Boy ran off six AA batteries, which gave you a pathetic play time of just four hours. You wouldn't want to play the games anyway. Apart from the headaches and nausea, one of the games, *Waterworld*, is considered by some to be the worst game ever made.

Despite all of this, Nintendo still managed to sell almost 800,000 Virtual Boys, giving rise to the old adage, 'Beware Nintendo fans, they're legitimately insane.'

Nintendo 64 – Console – 1996 (JP & US) / 1997 (EU)

You know the old story of how Lara Croft's gargantuan funbags came about when one of the *Tomb Raider* designers moved her boob size up to 150%? Did the same thing happen to  Mario's nose in *Super Mario 64*? It's massive. It looks like he's been stung on it a thousand times, one sting after the other, in a weird bee gangbang.[10]

That was my first thought[11] while playing on the N64 for the first time. Seeing Mario and his friends rendered in polygons instead of pixels was weird. Mario's nose looked like it would impair his vision, Luigi's gangliness was extra gangly and Bowser was simply adorable. Sadly, not everyone made the transition safely: the supposedly spherical Chain Chomp suffered greatly in the early days of polygons, in addition to looking about as surprised as a sex doll.

Optimistically designated 'Project Reality' in development, the N64 was Nintendo at their best. Forced to innovate to keep up with Sony and Sega, they delivered a seriously strong line-up of games, including the first outings of *Super Smash Bros.* and one of my favourite series of all time:

10   I'd be surprised if that makes the final edit of this book.
11   Minus the bee gangbang.

Animal Crossing. Oh, and let's not forget *The Legend of Zelda: Ocarina of Time*, the current best game of all time according to Metacritic.

Let's forget the terrible controller, though. I know it's a Marmite thing but I can't stand it. I don't have three hands, and trying to use it makes my brain itchy. Let's also forget that somehow, even with an exceptionally strong line-up of games, the N64 only sold about a third as many units as the PlayStation. I blame the controller. You should too.

Game Boy Color – Handheld – 1998

Colour is a horrible word. Just say it a few times and it sort of melts away like a slug on a salt lick. It's no wonder that America threw one of the vowels away back in whatever year they did that in.

The GBC was the first-ever handheld system to have backwards compatibility and as such was a success forever and ever amen. I'm not going to say any more, partly because it's just a Game Boy mixed with a rainbow, but mostly because I don't want to have to type 'colour' again. Bleh.

Jaguar JN-100 – Uhhh . . . Accessory? – 2001

OK, here's a really odd one. The Jaguar JN-100 was a sewing machine that came with a Game Boy link cable. A GBC cartridge called *Mario Family* was released that contained thirty-two little patterns for you to copy. Or the machine could copy them for you. I don't know, the only evidence I can find about this machine is, unsurprisingly, all in Japanese, and to be honest this might all be a mad 3 a.m. writing session fever dream.

Game Boy Advance – Handheld – 2001

The GBA passed me right by when it first came out. The GBC was still fairly new, 2D pixel art looked dated compared to the 3D world of consoles and nothing the GBA had to offer really stood out to me as a wee nipper. Only in recent years have I discovered the pleasures of *Metroid: Zero Mission*, *The Legend of Zelda: The Minish Cap* and the one-more-turn-then-I'll-go-to-sleep-oh-God-it's-5-a.m.-I-have-to-be-up-for-work-in-two-hours joy of *Advance Wars*.

The most impressive game on the system is *Robot Wars: Extreme Destruction*, a game that is not only one of the few fully 3D games on the GBA but also features a proper functioning physics engine. You can build a robot, name it Jeffory and then weep as Chaos 2 flips it realistically across the arena into the jaws of a very blocky-looking Sir Killalot. It's ***glorious***.

Also, shout-out to the Game Boy Advance SP, Nintendo's second iteration of the console, for finally realising that it would be nice if people could actually see the games that they were playing and adding a backlight.[12] Another shout-out to the Game Boy Micro, the third version, for thinking that making a

---

12 Even though the backlight was only on the second version of the SP so buying one pre-owned is a lottery.

console so small that you could accidentally swallow it without noticing was a good idea.

Nintendo GameCube – Console – 2001 (JP & US) / 2002 (EU)

The GameCube was nothing more than a big pile of mistakes. While the industry started to push into more mature titles and complex storytelling, Nintendo decided to release a massive, luminous purple box full of well-worn cartoon characters. DVDs were becoming huge but Nintendo decided to ignore having any DVD playback and made their own teeny-tiny discs instead. Consoles were taking their first tentative steps online too but Nintendo didn't want to be part of any of that nonsense.

Nearer the end of the GameCube's life, Nintendo tried to shift towards more adult titles, like the superbly grim *Resident Evil 4*, but that ended up alienating the small kiddie audience it had amassed. It was like watching Mr Bean run a gaming company. After a half-decade trouncing from the PS2, Nintendo performed an act of kindness and quietly had the GameCube put down. It was for the best.

Nintendo DS – Handheld – 2004 (JP & US) / 2005 (EU)

What does the DS in Nintendo DS stand for? Dual Screen? Well, here's Nintendo's official answer for this question:

*'To our developers, it stands for "Developers' System",
since we believe it gives game creators brand-new
tools which will lead to more innovative games for the
world's players.'*

I know. My brain exploded when I read that too. My whole life has been a lie. Nothing can save me now. Nothing.

'It can also stand for "Dual Screen".'

Oh. That's OK then.

Although, having survived this revelation, I can't help but think that 'Developers' System' is a better title for the DS. It's the bestselling handheld of all time and that's mostly because Nintendo gave developers a whole set of new ideas to play with. First up was the return to dual screens, last used on some Game & Watch consoles. This meant that we could have unique games like *The World Ends with You*, a game where you're fighting battles across two dimensions at once, and *Hotel Dusk: Room 215*, a point-and-click mystery played by holding the DS sideways like a book.

The touchscreen gave life to the completely bonkers rhythm tapper *Elite Beat Agents* and the calm loveliness of Professor Layton's puzzle-based adventures. Finally, the return to limited processing power, much like the Game Boy before it, forced developers to place gameplay over graphics, leaving us with games like Rockstar's *Drug Wars* remake, *Grand Theft Auto: Chinatown Wars*.

That's not all. Nintendo also started to heavily push the console to new markets, especially older and female consumers.[13] Games like *Brain Training*, *Nintendogs* and *Cooking Mama* were deliberately made to attract them. Eventually Nintendo even made XL versions of the consoles, useful for people with worse eyesight than your average Joe or Joanne. The Nintendo DS was a party and everyone was invited.

On top of this massive pile of success, they also remembered the core fans. *New Super Mario Bros.*, *Metroid Prime Hunters* and *Warioware DS* were original, gorgeous and pushed franchises to new heights. *Super Mario 64 DS* brought one of gaming's classics back with aplomb, massive nose and all, and *Animal Crossing: Wild World* stole many days of my life that I'll never get back.

In short, the Nintendo DS is the best handheld console to date. In long, see above.

Wii – Console – 2006

After winning over the casual market with the DS, Nintendo went all-in on appealing to them. Gone were controllers; in their place appeared chunky TV remotes. Button-based controls were abandoned for easy-to-use motion controls and even the UI of the console was as soft and simple as a daytime TV presenter. Nintendo had made a games console for people who had never bought a games console before and, somehow, it became their bestselling console and the third bestselling home console of all time.

---

13   In 1988 Nintendo reported that just 27% of its players were female and that only 20% of players were between the ages of 25 and 44. Now, 30 years later, the Entertainment Software Association says that the average age of a gamer is 34 and that women aged 18 and over make up more of the gamer population than boys under 18. The times they are a changin'.

Sales stats for the Wii are fascinating. *Super Mario Galaxy* and *Super Mario Galaxy 2* are the sixth- and seventh-highest-rated video games of all time according to Metacritic, and yet they were demolished in sales by *Wii Fit*, *Wii Sports Resort* and the genuinely crap *Wii Play*. It's not that they sold badly, it's just that the Wii brand was a behemoth of sales. In fact, Nintendo shifted focus from Mario to Wii as a leading brand. A move that ***totally isn't going to ruin them once the 3DS section is out of the way. Nope***.

Nintendo 3DS – Handheld – 2011

When I was starting up all my online shenanigans, money was tight. I hit a point where I needed to sell some stuff to get through a bad month so I made a list of all of the things I could part with, worked out what I cared for the least, and sold as much as I needed to. The Nintendo 3DS was on that list and to this day is the only games console I've ever sold.

The 3DS had a terrible launch. It was expensive, lacked games and was named after one of the worst 3D effects I've seen this side of anaglyph glasses.[14] The pointless 3D was the cause of headaches, lower frame rates and bad press while being completely impossible to advertise. The machine was looking to be a disaster.

Nintendo didn't give in. They ramped up third-party support, halting the handheld's nosedive, and just about saved it. It's nowhere near the DS in terms of sales, but after that start

---

14 I've never actually seen anyone use the 3D for more than a few seconds before they go, 'Huh, that's neat,' and then turn it off immediately.

they're lucky it wasn't Virtual Boy 2.0.

I bought one again a few years later when I was back in the black. As much as it has quite a solid library, I really only use it to play *Picross*. This isn't important to note. I just really like *Picross*.

Wii U – Console – 2012

The phrase 'spectacular cavalcade of failure' is tossed around a lot these days, but until the Wii U's E3 reveal in 2011, we never really knew what those words meant. Every step of the Wii U's lifespan was nothing less
than a slapstick comedy routine; from cradle to grave the

machine was a disaster. The reveal trailer, and I'm being completely serious here, failed to mention it was a new console. In fact, it failed to *feature* the new console at all, instead focusing on the 'New Controller' and repeating the phrase 'New Controller' so many times that Wii U became synonymous with 'New Controller' and not 'New Console'. To better understand the confusion, here is what CNN had to say about the Wii U:

> *'Will Nintendo's forthcoming Wii U controller breathe new life into its aging Wii console?'*
>
> — CNN, 6 June 2012

Yep, even the media thought that the Wii U was just an accessory for the Wii. Not only that, but this article came out a *year* after the Wii U's reveal. An entire year had passed and the goddamn mainstream press still didn't know what the Wii U was. That confusion spread to the casual market Nintendo had cultivated with the Wii, and before it even came out, the Wii U was dead in the water.

However, in late 2014, a light appeared at the end of Nintendo's tunnel. They were releasing a new *Super Smash Bros.* game for the 3DS and Wii U. This was the golden opportunity, this was the system seller, this was nothing less than the saviour of the Wii U!

Except it wasn't. Why? Because Nintendo decided to release it for the 3DS two months before the Wii U. Everyone just bought that one instead.

Unsurprisingly the Wii U was a flop, making just 13.56 million sales worldwide. That's 8 million less than their previous worst-selling console, the GameCube, and almost 90 million less than the Wii. In fact, Nintendo sold more actual Wiis than it did games for the Wii U.

Summing up the Wii U is tricky but that's mostly because a book won't let me embed a gif of someone belly-flopping into a swimming pool before being choked to death by their own trunks.

Nintendo Switch – Console/Handheld Hybrid – 2017

The Nintendo Switch feels like its entire development was rushed. The console feels cheap, the controllers wobble and the thing has a battery life as long as a mayfly's retirement party. As a handheld, it's heavy and slightly uncomfortable; as a console, it's underpowered. It's a bit of a mess.

But none of that really matters because Nintendo learned

their lesson. First, the console reveal was spot on, with a trailer that repeated the fact it was a console about a thousand times, and second, because they've put so many goddamn games on the thing already. The first-party titles are almost all Game of the Year candidates and third-party support, especially indies, is off the charts. It's my favourite console of this generation, and I don't see that changing any time soon.

Nintendo SWiitch –
Console/Handheld Hybrid – 2023

We all laughed when we saw the name; we all laughed when we saw the new third Mario Brother, Carbonara; but damn it all, we stopped laughing when they showed off the console. A screen suspended in mid-air, fifty centimetres from your face, by a magnetic headband. This meant that you could play full motion-controlled games while commuting, hanging out with friends on a rooftop, or just simply piloting an aircraft. This is set to be Nintendo's biggest game changer yet and the one-in-three fatality rate from the headband is a fine price to pay for some of the best games on the market today. Nintendo are back, baby!

So that's Nintendo's hardware history! In conclusion: they're a billion years old, made some of the most iconic games and hardware of all time, fail a remarkably high number of times and experiment more than the members of a dementia-riddled sorority.

If you're told that there's going to be a birthday party on Friday at 8 p.m., then you'd better be playing then or you're going to miss it and upset a koala

Developer: Nintendo
Publisher: Nintendo
Released: *Animal Crossing* (N64, GameCube – 2001), *Animal Crossing: Wild World* (DS – 2005), *Animal Crossing: City Folk* (Wii – 2008), *Animal Crossing: New Leaf* (3DS – 2012)
What is it? A gentle simulation about life in a village of animals.
What is it *really*? *The Godfather*, with raccoons.

Betrayal exists on a scale.

Level one is a light betrayal; for example, taking a biscuit you know belongs to someone else.

At level two there's light to moderate betrayal; being asked not to take a biscuit, but taking one anyway.

Level three is moderate betrayal; being asked not to take a biscuit, yet taking the *last* biscuit.

Level four is moderate to heavy betrayal; being asked not to take a biscuit, taking the last biscuit anyway, and putting the empty packaging back in the cupboard.

Finally, there's the rare level-five betrayal; being asked not to take a biscuit, taking all the biscuits, putting the box back into the cupboard after filling it with spiders, contacting the company that makes the biscuits and convincing them to stop manufacturing the biscuits before finally ordering the controlled destruction of all remaining biscuits of that type.

Level five is the limit of betrayal. It's believed to be a universal constant, like the speed of light, absolute zero or licking your lips after eating a donut. You cannot possibly go any higher than a level-five betrayal.

Now, that's not to say people haven't tried to go further. Marcus Brutus was a famous early betrayaltician who attempted to break the limit, but failed after he chickened out and brought extra people along. Benedict Arnold, Guy Fawkes and Mir Jafar, while ultimately unsuccessful in the pursuit of the level-six betrayal, have all been credited for their work by the London University School of Betrayal and Bastardness.[1] More recently, a team of scientists experimented with betraying an entire planet at once by downgrading Pluto's status in the solar system from 'planet' to 'pleb'.[2] Sadly, the planet forgave them and spray-painted a big heart emoji on itself to indicate this.

I have experienced a level-six betrayal. It happened once, several years ago, and has stayed with me until this day. When I can't sleep at night and all I can hear is the rain tapping on the windows, I always go back to that moment. It left a scar that runs deep and, like many stories of this type, it's about a girl. Unlike many stories of this type, it's also about an elephant.

First, we need to go back to 2006. *Animal Crossing: Wild World* had just been released and I was in love with it. You play as a human villager, living, fishing and decorating in a village of anthropomorphic animals. The game syncs with real-world time so if you're told that there's going to be a birthday party on Friday at 8 p.m., then you'd better be playing then or you're going to miss it and upset a koala.

---

1   Judas Iscariot has had no such honour. Not many people know this but he wasn't actually a betrayaltician. He was just a bit of a twat.
2   A betrayal so large that the betrayal waves that reflected off the dwarf planet caused over twenty thousand acts of level-three betrayal when they eventually made it back to Earth.

One of the residents of my portable village was an elephant named Margie. Margie and I had an instant connection. I liked fish. She liked fish. I liked chairs. She liked chairs. I liked peanuts. She was an elephant.[3] It was a match made in heaven and we became friends for years. Actual, real years. She was in my top eight Myspace friends. That's how close we were.

Then, one day, she left. No warning, just gone. Off to see the world. I didn't even get a goodbye. It was like that bit when Trapper John leaves *M*A*S*H*. I played the game less and less and eventually stopped. My friend had gone; I had no reason to go back.

In 2013, *Animal Crossing: New Leaf* was released and, once again, I fell in love with it. This time around you were mayor. This meant you could build new community buildings, fund art projects and even set a few rules and ordinances for the town. It was great fun and, for a while at least, I didn't even notice something was missing...

I should have known it was Margie from the outset. A house foundation plonked right next to mine, wiping out my exceptionally rare and fragile blue roses. The next day she moved in. I went over to her, ready to barrage her with years' worth of suppressed, 100% English resentment and... she didn't remember me. She didn't know me. Of course she didn't, this was a new game. It would be weirder if she did remember me.

Slowly, we fell into friendship again. I was cautious at first; I knew she was flighty and didn't want to invest too much into the relationship but I couldn't help myself. She was my best friend. My soulmate, with emphasis on the 'mate'. We played hide and seek together, drank coffee together and went shopping together. She promised she'd stay forever and I believed her.

3   Is that racist?

She left the next day. No warning, just gone. Off to see the world again. I decided to continue playing – my town needed me – but just a day later I was losing interest. I was waiting to see which animal would appear next, and I would judge if I wanted to keep playing based on that. They had to replace Margie in my heart and, well, elephants leave big shoes to fill.

The next day I was talking to my friend Eugene when he mentioned a new elephant had arrived in town. No way, it couldn't be. My heart and feet raced and suddenly I was standing in front of a house I recognised all too well. I went inside.

She didn't recognise me. My heart broke in two. A week later she suddenly moved out again. My heart split into fractals all the way down to the subatomic level.

In a not entirely untidy office in the London University School of Betrayal and Bastardness, an underpaid bald man saw the level monitor flash up to 'six' on his betrayalscope. He assumed it was a malfunction and requested a mechanic to arrive in the morning, before cycling home in the rain.

There were a few aftershocks due to the level six event. A brief Margie appearance in a game of *Super Smash Bros.* distracted me enough that I lost my place in a local tournament. Another time an amiibo card of Margie gave me a papercut. I'm not entirely sure why Margie does this to me. Maybe I'm her Agrajag. Maybe coincidence is just playing silly buggers. Maybe I should stop writing this and go back to smearing 'I THOUGHT ELEPHANTS DIDN'T FORGET' on the walls in blood again.

Yeah. That always helps.

I'll go do that.

The *Black* design document was probably just two
words: 'guns' and 'loud'

Developer: Criterion Games
Publisher: Electronic Arts
Platform: PS2, Xbox
Released: 2006
What is it? A military first-person shooter.
What is it *really*? A love letter to gunpowder.

You know those catapults aircraft carriers have that launch fighter jets from the deck? Well, imagine one of those, but instead of being on an oversized boat, it's in a warehouse.

At the end of it, instead of the open sea, is a very large pile of priceless sculptures and statues.

Now imagine that, instead of a jet, you've attached a skip filled with bowling balls, bricks and marbles.

Now put on your safety goggles, pull the lever and watch as tonnes of heavy objects accelerate to 170 mph before turning the *Venus de Milo* and chums into a mushroom cloud of marble.

Now imagine that noise. The crashes, thuds and bangs that echo round the warehouse as you reduce millions of pounds of antiques into driveway gravel. The noise of devastation. The noise of destruction. The noise of obliteration.

That noise is what the pistol sounds like in *Black*.

In *Call of Duty* the machine gun makes the same noise when firing that a baby does when shaking a packet of Tic Tacs. In *Counter-Strike* the SMG has the same audio punch as Mr Rogers gently laying a bag of Quavers down on a table. In *Battlefield* the sniper rifle has all the intensity and violence of a fart in a church.

In *Black* the shotgun sounds like a train crash. An actual train crash. You click the trigger on the controller and suddenly it sounds like the 19:45 to Bristol Temple Meads has ploughed into a shopping centre.[1] The thing you were pointing at fucks off in the opposite direction with a speed that would make Einstein scratch his head, and enough debris is kicked up that future archaeologists would argue that this was the impact point of the meteorite that killed the dinosaurs.

The *Black* design document was probably just two words: 'guns' and 'loud'. There really isn't much else to the game. The level design is OK, the graphics were pretty good for the time and the plot was added at such a late point in development that I'm pretty sure the first few DVDs out of the factory omit it entirely. The sound design is superb though, with each enemy's weapon being pitch-shifted slightly so you can tell each one apart. That's properly clever design right there.

But the gunplay – God is it ferocious. It's ruined the entire FPS genre for me. Every time I fire a gun in an FPS these days, I just sigh. You pull the trigger, it sounds like someone snapped a pathetic twig, a man falls over, a bit of dust is kicked up. It's just not the same.

I guess what they say is true. Once you go *Black* you really can't go back.

---

1   RIP Rudy.

The mission? Interplanetary rescue

Developer: Squad
Publisher: Squad
Platform: PC, PS4, Xbox One
Released: 2015
What is it? A realistic NASA simulator with a slight cartoon aesthetic.
What is it *really*? Build the last thing a bunch of little green men ever see.

Around a hundred years ago, when I was in my teens, I would volunteer at a children's camp for a week every summer. The idea of living in a tent, doing sports and eating around a fire is, to me, a vision of hell. However, organising events, working long hours and doing near endless washing up for a week? Count me in![1]

The camp, run by the Church,[2] gave a holiday to almost 500 kids who came from less than fortunate circumstances. It was an honour to work there with some genuinely fantastic people, and to this day is probably the only real thing listed on my CV.

Aside from the personal growth, etc., etc., the best part of camp was the basketball court. It was housed in some sort of crater, a relic from a war or massive tractor accident, and was

1   I got my first grey hair on 27 June 2014. I was twenty-five. It suited me.
2   I never asked which church.

set away from the main part of the camp. I can't tell you how good it was as a court – I am morally against all forms of sport – however, what I can tell you is that it was excellent for stargazing. The soft asphalt held the heat from the day into the night and the crater stopped any pesky photons from ruining the view of the heavens. It was perfect.

There's something spiritual about stargazing.[3] The longer you do it, the more you see and the more *terrifying* it becomes. You start by staring at a few pinpricks in the sky and before long you can barely see the darkness through the fireballs. You're looking one way and half of everything else that there is is looking back. The only time I ever feel smaller is while watching porn.

One night at camp coincided with a meteor shower. Just after midnight I wandered over to the court with a few other volunteers and the camp's priest[4] to watch massive chunks of rock explode in the sky for a few hours. You know, the usual Saturday night.

A short while later, just as the existential horror was *really* starting to set in, the padre broke the silence with a line about the majesty of creation. We all agreed that watching space debris crash into our planet's windshield was literally – and I mean this word in its original definition – awesome. I can't quite recall the next bit of that conversation because, at that exact moment, something alive jumped on top of me.

Evolution kicked in. First, my heart used its next beat to scoop up seventeen years of unused adrenaline and fling it wildly into every organ and muscle that it could. I stood up, possibly without even bending my knees, and fumbled around for my torch, eventually flicking it on for a fruitless search of the ground. Seeing nothing, I did the only thing that made sense while riding a natural high that would last about a month. I looked up and checked the sky.

---

3   And I say that as a card-carrying agnostic.
4   Lovely bloke, terrible dress sense.

In hindsight, the creature was a rabbit. We had some food out and rabbits, while adorable, have the survival instincts of a baby wielding a fork next to an electrical socket. In all likelihood it just ran off. If it was unlucky then I may have catapulted it like a buzzer beater across the asphalt as I stood, an adorable missile from a panicked trebuchet. However, as I watched a single bright point of light rocket across the heavens, I wondered – in my defence only briefly – if I'd accidentally just sent Thumper into orbit.

Years later someone made a game based on that moment. I didn't even get a creation credit. Bastards.

In *Kerbal Space Program* your job is to be ACME NASA. You design a rocket, fill it with explosive fuel and cuddly green creatures, then fuck it off into outer space to do science.

When you first start playing, 99% of your designs will explode instantaneously and the tiny green Kerbals inside will burn to crispy cinders. Eventually you'll get something in the air, whereupon it'll flip over, hurtle back towards the ground and explode on impact, leaving three little green smudges amongst the charred rubble. The time after that you'll remember to bring a parachute, but due to what is technically known as a 'cock-up', you'll attach it to the wrong bit, bringing a ladder back down to earth at a comfortable rate, while innocent Kerbals smash into the ocean at Mach 55.

After countless failed launches and more green corpses than the Grinch's family graveyard plot, you'll get something into orbit. The orbit may be egg-shaped and too far out to do anything, and you'll run out of fuel, stranding your Kerbals in space forever, but *you* succeeded and that's what counts.

'I have nothing to offer but blood, toil, tears and sweat.'
— Winston Churchill

Never said it had to be your own blood, did he? Now hand me that spanner, this needs another booster.

It's at this point where, during my time playing the game, a lack of skill and an abundance of overconfidence combined into a foolish plan. I was going to go to the moon and by Jove I was going to land on it. I duct-taped together as many fuel tanks as physically possible, hired a Kerbal to drive the thing,[5] and loaded the resulting contraption onto the launch pad.

You'll never see NASA launch a ship like this, I guarantee you that. The centre was a standard-looking rocket: capsule on the top for Neil, booster and engine under him. This would land on the moon. The rest of the craft looked like a pile-up on a runway that someone had filled with highly explosive fuel. This collection of engines and connectors had to fall off at exactly the right time, in exactly the right order, or we wouldn't make it. As the ship stood there, wobbling slightly in the sunlight, a bit fell off, rolled down a hill and exploded, destroying my hangar and killing around a hundred Kerbals.

It was go time.

Three.

Thirty massive rockets ignited.

Two.

They accelerated, draining an oil rig's worth of fuel a second. All systems nominal.

One.

The solitary green Kerbal on board did whatever his planet's equivalent of the sign of the cross is.

Blast off.

The clamps released, the scaffolding blasted backwards and the USS *Je Ne Regrette Rien* pelted off into space at about three

5   I called him Neil.

metres per hour. Turns out that fuel is pretty heavy, but not to worry, little Kerbal, you'll be on your way when it starts to burn up. Just ignore the warnings that say 'overheating'. I always do.

After about a fortnight, the USS *Je Ne Regrette Rien* was in a steady orbit. Only some of it had exploded or fallen off or both. Things were looking great.

A few controlled blasts later and what was left of the ship was on a path to the moon![6] To save time I'd aimed right for the centre of it instead of all that faffing about with lunar orbits. I'd just flip the ship, boost in a direction that I could now call 'up', and land softly amongst the craters.

Sadly I wasn't heading towards the moon, I was heading towards where the moon *was*. Things move in space, and in all the excitement of survival I'd not calculated for that. This is why I'm dreadful at *Space Invaders*.

Some brisk calculations got me on the right track but this had cost me a huge amount of fuel. Now I was faced with a choice: do I land on the moon, never to return, or do I fling myself round it and head back? I briefly looked over the calculations required for the latter, gave up, and sentenced Neil the Kerbal to glorious, historic death.

Now, landing on a moon is tricky. There's no lovely atmosphere to slow you down, or comparatively soft water to land in. Just rocks, dust and that thing NASA won't talk about for as far as the eye can see. Well, there's the Sea of Tranquillity, but that's dryer than a sand sandwich that you bought at a petrol station.

The upside to everything being rocks is that it didn't matter where I landed, I could expect rocks. I flipped the ship, pointing

---

6   Well, the Mun. *Kerbal Space Program* takes place in a fictional solar system, hence the little green men and decently sized space-agency budget.

it away from all the unsurprising rock and began to slow it down gently. When that didn't work, I fired every engine up to maximum until it did.

500 metres.

I levelled the ship out, ready for the landing.

200 metres.

I could see I was heading towards a bit of a slope; no time to correct that, we'd have to make do.

100 metres.

I increased the speed, leaving the craft almost hovering above the surface of the alien world.

50 metres.

I wondered if I should have installed landing legs on this craft. Never mind, the engine should be flat enough on the bottom.

20 metres.

Coming in a bit too fast. Increasing speed to slow it down more.

43 metres.

OK, too much.

6 metres.

TOO LITTLE! SPEED UP.

105 metres.

Goddammit.

This continued for some time. Eventually I found a speed that left me falling, but only just, and managed to set the ship down gently on this new world. I had done it.

Neil disembarked and, clad in a spacesuit and jetpack, took the first small step for Kerbalkind. He admired the first footprint the planet had ever had on it, planted the Kerbal flag next to it, and turned around just in time to see his ship fall over and explode.

As Neil's retirement home was now just another crater on the planet of the craters, I went back to Kerbal, built another identical rocket, filled it with Kerbals and got my *Thunderbirds* on. The mission? Interplanetary rescue.

The launch was smooth, the orbital positioning was fantastic and soon the rescue mission was hurtling towards the moon's surface. Neil looked up, elated to be saved, and watched as the rescue ship bravely ploughed into the grey terrain, sending shrapnel raining down across the entire planet and a deep feeling of irremovable guilt down Neil's spine.

This happened a few more times. I guess that the lack of fuel in the first flight made the rocket less likely to explode on impact. After much workshopping and many meetings back on Kerbin, we countered this issue by remembering to stick legs on the bottom of the craft. A few days later, the USS *L'appel Du Vide* landed safely, about one Australia away from Neil.[7]

After a trek that fundamentally changed who he was as a person, Neil arrived at the rescue site, delighted to see the one-seater rescue craft – less so to see that the seat was already filled by the rescuer. He had literally no way to get on board. I'd fluffed it royally.

Post-obscenities I had an idea. Not a great idea, but at the time I thought it was genius enough to be getting on with. Neil was going to hang onto the ladder on the side of the rescue ship as it took off, that way both Neil and the pilot could get safely back home. I was pretty sure his spacesuit would keep him alive. Everything would go fine.

Now, I can't pinpoint the exact moment I lost him but I'm pretty sure that the atmosphere of Kerbin shaved him off like a waterslide made of cheese graters. The pilot never noticed as he was too busy trying to not crash into the mountain that he later crashed into.

---

7   You know how it goes. One Kerbal is working in inches, the other is working in miles.

I never attempted a moon landing again after Neil's death. Why would I? I'd done it! Flawless victory! Next stop, the planet Moho! Or maybe a space station! Or maybe I'd see just how Kerbal skin reacts to close proximity of the sun! Science is just so much fun!

[IMAGE REMOVED BY EDITOR]

I put her in one of the skirts from a new collection and it turns out that it's so short I can see her pubic hair from both ends of it. I'm on a list now

Developer: Blitz Games
Publisher: THQ
Platform: PS2, GameCube, Game Boy Advance, PC
Released: 2005
What is it? Uhhh...
What is it *really*? I dread to think.

Oh, Alicia Knightly, what have you done?

Alicia backed the very highest tier of this book during the original crowdfunding and therefore had the privilege of picking any game in the world for me to write a chapter on. Before Alicia stood all of gaming, decade after decade of the greatest entertainment medium of all time, hundreds of thousands of stories, anything Alicia's heart desired. An almost impossible choice, yet when asked the answer came instantly, as if Alicia had been planning this for years.

Alicia picked *Bratz: Rock Angelz*.

... right.

I've not yet played *Bratz: Rock Angelz*; surprisingly I don't even own it. It might be good. Hell, it might be great![1] In fact, Alicia might be using this opportunity to educate me and all

---

1   The double usage of 'Z' instead of 'S' might just be a misdirect.

of you readers about an underrated classic. A hidden gem of a game that you'll all go out and buy the moment you finish reading this.

Tomorrow my copy of it arrives from eBay. Today I shall do research on Wikipedia.

'It is based on the direct-to-video film Bratz: Rock Angelz*'*
— Wikipedia

Oh dear. It's not just a movie tie-in, it's a direct-to-DVD movie tie-in.[2] I can't even think of another one of those. This doesn't bode well.

'Plot: This section is empty. You can help by adding to it.'

Uh-oh.

'The game has sold 1.4 million copies, thus making it one of the bestselling games on both the PlayStation 2 and GameCube.'

Uh-oh... wait, what?

The mixed-bag feel carries onto its Metacritic page, where the reviews are all over the place, ranging from this:

'Combining fun mini-games, hot fashion items and an entertaining story, it doesn't get any better than this game.'
— GameZone (Review Score: 78/100)

---

2   The second of **fifteen** Bratz movies released in a nine-year period.

... to this:

'In a hyphenated word: vomit-inducing. Unpleasant, exploitative drivel aimed at girls who would almost certainly have more fun staring at a blank TV set.'
— Official *PlayStation 2 Magazine* UK (Review Score: 20/100)

That's a hell of a range. I particularly enjoy that a game that 'it doesn't get any better than' only scores 78%. I bet that reviewer is great to buy gifts for.

That's as far as I can go without actually playing the game. I will now sleep, wait for Mr Postman, and experience whatever hell Alicia has planned for me.

Wish me luck.

The game has annoyed me already.

I don't have enough space on any of my memory cards for its whopping 500 KB save file so I've had to dig through them and delete a precious memory. Well, a half-finished save of *Dog's Life* at any rate.

Right, we're at the menu now. Behind the 'Press START Button' demand is footage of some RealDolls that have come to life. The pop-rock background song is a rejection of the societal pressure to 'grow up'. Apparently life is too short to take seriously. This is why people die from curable diseases, you know.

The new game begins. The opening cutscene has faded into a school or a shopping mall, possibly both, I can't tell. One of the four Bratz – I don't know their names – has just found out she's got an internship at *Your Thing* magazine. Everyone is excited because she can go to concerts for free and 'watch supermodel meltdowns'. I've taken a strong dislike to this group already.

Uh-oh, the Tweevils, a pair of evil twins, have turned up. You can tell they're evil because they're skinny, bitchy and heavily made-up, just like our heroes.

Drama! The Tweevils also have an internship at the magazine, which is run by the *Spitting Image* version of *Ab Fab*'s Patsy. Now they've tricked our hero into buying a burger for Patsy. Patsy has fired our hero. She is in pieces. Her life is, like, totally over. I assume she's about thirteen.[3]

The game begins proper! After firing off a text message I'm wandering around the now seemingly abandoned schoolmall, picking money off the ground and running into walls due to the inverted horizontal camera controls. Following an arrow has led me back to my fellow Bratz and a seriously reduced quality cutscene[4] allows our hero, referred to as Jade by friends and co-workers, to explain the anguish in her heart by saying 'my life is over' for the seventy-fifth time this morning.

She wanders off and the remaining Bratz decide to cheer her up with a party. To do this they must all spend their money on clothes and make-up... for themselves. I've come up with a new title for this group: Bastardz.

We're now in control of a new Brat, Yasmin apparently, and *finally* get to go shopping. I put her in one of the skirts from a new collection and it turns out that it's so short I can see her pubic hair from both ends of it. I'm on a list now.

Right, It's Cloe's turn to go shopping. She's into make-up so I use the blush to colour her entire face in green. She looks at me angrily. Or jealously. I can't tell.

The last of the Bratz, Sasha, has turned up. Apparently the skirt/belt outfit and Incontourable Hulk are all the ingredients we need for a great party! People, food, drink, balloons, bubble

3   This cutscene was about five godless minutes long.
4   I'm assuming that the first one was just an edited version of the film's opening.

machine, a mix CD of 80s hits, some sort of banner and literally any actual party necessities are so 1991.

The party is an unsurprising failure. The Bratz sit around drinking orange juice shots until Sasha suggests that they play a 'posing' game. I press a button, the thirteen-year-old child poses, and I get paid. I'm 100% on that list.

Oh Christ, the Bratz have now decided to set up their own magazine in revenge.[5] They all discuss the talents they can bring to the magazine. Nobody mentions publishing, copy editing or distribution. This is what happens when you don't take life seriously. I blame the music kids listen to these days.

Holy shit, they've bought a fucking penthouse studio for this endeavour. It's bloody massive! It looks like Austin Powers decorated it after a *Psychonauts* binge, but still, these girls have some serious capital behind them. I have a nose into the corridor outside and next door are the offices of *Your Thing* magazine. This is like when Subway open a shop next to Jan's Sandwiches, isn't it?

Back in the studio I flick through the plan for the *twelve*-page magazine and realise that I need to write an article on designing your own T-shirts. I go to a shop, create one bearing the slogan 'Bratz ♥ the London Underground',[6] and for some reason get paid by the shop for doing so. I'm not sure if the game really doesn't understand how the economy works or if I just collected some protection-racket money.

Putting aside the fact that we might be building an empire on mob money, it's time to write the feature 'Make-up Makeover'. I take Cloe and put so much make-up on her face that she looks like the Star Gate scene from *2001*. I'm not entirely sure how to

---

5 Nothing says 'party' like filling out small-business application forms.
6 Because I only have about four words to choose from and most of them are illegible.

turn this into a feature so I just slam her face directly onto page three and call it a day.

While Cloe staggers out of the studio, Jade makes an announcement. She's stolen four tickets to a London gig from the magazine next door, flights and fancy hotel included. This is considered a victory moment in a game that, if he were alive today, God would certainly have laid supreme and terrible judgement down upon.[7]

Sasha's off to go get some CDs back from her friends so she can write about what the kids these days call music. After more backtracking than [INSERT CURRENT PROMINENT TORY PARTY MEMBER HERE] we collect all the discs and write about that one that's currently on a loop on every menu, in every building and in my fucking dreams.

Yasmin has decided that the magazine needs photographs of animals, because that's what a twelve-page magazine needs. Filler. I photograph a squirrel, a rabbit and a butterfly. The butterfly doesn't count. I photograph a bird. Doesn't count. I photograph a boy called Dylan. That works. I think it's a political statement.

In a shock moment of retribution, the good people over at *Your Thing* have stolen back their rightful property. Aggravated at the loss of their stolen tickets, the Bratz sidestep any moment of character growth and simply decide to nick them back, picking Yasmin to dress up as a Tweevil and infiltrate ~~Shadow Moses~~ the magazine next door. Also, considering Yasmin is a different skin tone to the Tweevils, I guess I'm going to be committing a hate crime as well.

The stealth operation goes smoothly, albeit with a slight misstep as I took an extra moment to enjoy a rendition of

7   A 4/10.

Mozart's *'Eine kleine Nachtmusik'* that was playfully bounding through the *Your Thing* speakers. Delightful. Pretty soon I was back in the studio and, mercifully before the world of teen pop could engulf me again like an icy plunge pool, the Bratz were off to London.

I've lived and worked in London for the better part of my life and I'm not entirely sure this is a faithful rendition. For one thing, it looks like a small town square in Lancashire. For another, the man with the Union Jack hoodie keeps telling me that he's 'a Londoner, born and raised', when, if he truly was a Londoner, he'd stand there in silence until you went away. Finally, the Underground only goes to one place, and that's back to the travel agent in America, 5,000 miles away. No wonder I've heard that Bratz ❤ the London Underground; for them it's wildly convenient.[8]

We've barely had time to take in the London smog when we're hit with another bout of *drama*. The band we're here to see has split up on the day of the show so it's up to us Bratz to save the day! Are we going to track down the band members and convince them to get back together? Absolutely not! We're going to make our own band! With Blackjack! And Us!

I hate to ask but can any of these girls sing or play any instruments? If they're replacing an internationally advertised band, they'd better get some practice in. With all the deft planning talents of the people from a 'Top 10 Skateboarding Accidents' video, the Bratz decide the most important thing to do isn't to book the venue, organise the setlist or even source instruments. It's to design a poster for the show. Also, to give you an idea of how close this is to the start of the gig, I have just two and a

---

8 The posters back in America are advertising for the gig in London so I assume this isn't just implying they go to Heathrow; the Underground literally goes door to door for them.

half minutes to put all these posters up. This is the advertising equivalent of... well... not advertising.

I frantically head to the gig location and throw together an outfit consisting of more leather and denim than a middle-aged cow. I kick the Bratz onto the stage and wonder what the hell comes next.

Hilarity. Hilarity is what comes next.

They can't sing. They can't dance. They can't play anything. They don't even try. The instruments sit abandoned behind them as they come out and... pose. They just pose. They just fucking pose. It's dead silent and they're posing. An audience that paid to see the hottest band in the world instead watches four teenagers shuffle onstage, point a bit for sixty seconds, and wander off again. If this really was London, that entire building would end up dead behind a skip.

Back in America we discover that the unfinished magazine we wrote four out of the twelve pages of has sold more than *Your Thing*. I give up and eject the game directly into industrial farming equipment.

1.4 million people have played *Bratz: Rock Angelz*. I don't know what they saw in it, to be honest. Maybe they can read the deep satire of how the rules of life don't apply to the rich, or maybe they're people who like stealing from small businesses. Either way I am now one of their number, and for that, Alicia Knightly, I may never, ever forgive you.

Each turn you choose the three things you want to do
from a choice of about seventy and slowly and carefully
turn your company from 1976's Apple into 1980's Apple

Tom Clancy's
ruthless.com

Developer: Red Storm Entertainment
Publisher: Red Storm Entertainment
Platform: PC
Released: 1998
What is it? A turn-based business strategy game.
What is it *really*? A turn-based 'accidents' simulator.

DanCorp has just finished a particularly difficult week. On Monday, we launched a product with such poor build quality that it actually lost us market share to a company that didn't make anything at all. On Tuesday, rival software company Keensoft threatened to take over one of our buildings unless we sent over ideas for products. On Wednesday, we poison-pilled the building Keensoft wanted, making its upkeep huge and halting the takeover permanently. On Thursday, we sold the building because it was too damn expensive to keep due to the increased upkeep.[9] Finally, on Friday, our CEO had an 'accidental' fall down a stairwell and died. Third time this year we'd lost a CEO like that. I'll be honest, if our shares weren't literally worthless, I might have sold them all then and there.

---

9   We sold for far less than we would have got for it the day before, but we did sell it to a slightly less evil megacorporation so it all evens out in the end.

ruthless.com[10] is a game about power, control and pushing people down the stairs. It's played across a large, multi-coloured chessboard where each square represents market share of a software company. You plop buildings down onto this board and fill them with different departments, firewalls and ever-decreasing piles of cash. Each turn you choose the three things you want to do from a choice of about seventy and slowly and carefully turn your company from 1976's Apple into 1980's Apple. Some people can probably do better but, alas, after twenty years of playing *ruthless.com*, I still don't actually know how to play it.

I first came across *ruthless.com* at a market in 1999. I used to pick up six-month-old copies of the US version of *PC Gamer* for 50p a pop[11] and would spend weeks, if not months, afterwards playing with the included demo discs. One of the demos included was, rather obviously, *ruthless.com*. It contained a single scenario but I played it hundreds of times, never really getting anywhere but loving just how different it was from everything else I owned. There was only one problem with the demo disc: the button on the menu marked 'Tutorial' was greyed out. It only worked with the full version. A lack of funds and the fact that nobody but me has ever heard of this game[12] meant that it wasn't until over a decade later that I randomly stumbled across a copy of the full game. It was a cheap rerelease, but I was excited to finally learn how to play a game that I think I loved. I, alongside a decade of

---

10 I had a check and the link is dead. The URL is for sale but sadly GoDaddy have listed it for £52,182.52 so I won't be buying it. Twenty-two other people have checked that price though, so maybe one day soon it'll turn into the fansite the game deserves.

11 I assume they'd fallen off the back of a cargo ship.

12 Seriously, the top three results on Google for this game are the Wikipedia page, the actual, empty website ruthless.com and a video of me talking about it.

anticipation, clicked the tutorial button and was greeted by the following message:

'Please open the ruthless.com manual to the Tutorial section.'

Of course, the rerelease didn't come with the manual.

I think I understand most of it now anyway. You come up with, or bid for, ideas that you then turn into products. You sell those products to get market share or give them away for free to get even more market share. If another company gets too close you threaten them with viruses or stairwell accidents until they go away. If a company is doing too well you can firebomb their buildings or even kidnap their CEO, hold them hostage and *then* push them down the stairs a few turns later. At some point you should probably talk to the people in PR too. They keep threatening to jump.

The thing that really captured my imagination about *ruthless. com* wasn't the corporate strategy or the CEO-shoving, it was the newspapers. At the end of each turn a little 'breaking news'-style jingle would play and you'd get the headlines for the past turn. Brilliantly, this wasn't a recap of the actions all players made that turn, this was the *results* of those actions. I loved poring through the five stories each turn, making notes of who made secret agreements with who, what buildings had switched hands and why my CEO was suddenly dead.

I remember once bribing a company to off a CEO from a different company and pin it on a third company. The tension while waiting to see if that had worked was incredible. The plan actually did work and the entire landscape of the game shifted in that double deniability move. Well, the company that I bribed took the money and then proceeded to spend it on ways to make my life a misery but I was winning until that moment so my point still stands.

Anyway, its brilliance aside, I think the real lesson of *ruthless.com* is a simple one. If you want to get ahead in Silicon Valley, don't make software. Start a stairwell-cleaning service instead.

She's easily one of my favourite characters in
gaming history. It's a shame I'm not like her in any way,
but hey, what can you do?

Developer: Core Design
Publisher: Eidos Interactive
Platform: PC, PS1
Released: 1998
What is it? A 3D action platformer.
What is it *really*? A house-exploring simulator with a 3D action platformer attached.

I love air travel. Getting up early, travelling to a big city, travelling about forty miles back out of the big city, squinting at signs that use a single-digit font size, having a stranger brush your sexual organs, visiting the world's smallest yet somehow most expensive WHSmith, hearing the word 'delay' more times than you would in a *Half-Life 3* production meeting...[1] It's a delightful time.

However, after all of the waiting, the screaming children and the corporately mandated sexual assault, you board an engineering miracle, sit in a chair that someone stole from a dollhouse, and you, and the 400 tonnes of miracle you're sitting in, get catapulted 35,000 feet into the air. Nothing beats the feeling of looking down on Planet Earth and thinking, 'I hope I packed my toothbrush.'

---

1 One day this joke will be out of date. One day...

The downside of flight is flight safety. Before the plane has even left the tarmac, you know where the exits are, where to pull to inflate a life jacket and how exactly the tray table will decapitate you if you don't fold it away before you crash into the ocean. This, combined with the aforementioned miracle catapulting, means that many people are scared of flying. To these people I say... here's a story of the time I thought my plane was going to crash.

A couple of years ago I was pinging myself around the globe quite frequently. This meant that I had got used to all the early starts, trains to London and groping in the name of anti-terrorism that come with flying. I arrived at the airport, bought a violently pricy book that I'd never actually read and, after a spot of queueing, was pretty much the last person to step on board the plane. This is when things started to go wrong.

Firstly, there were some very odd men in the business seats. Three of them to be exact, all in the same tailored suits that were far too perfect than should be allowed at 5.30 a.m. Secondly, they were the only people in the business seats. This flight was normally booked solid. Thirdly, and this was the oddest of all, they were all sitting next to each other. Now, business class on this plane meant that for each row of three business seats, only two were booked. This gives the business passenger an extra three or four millimetres of space between them for their belongings or legs. Having three people sit next to each other was off-putting in a way that only the British reading this will understand. This was the airline seating equivalent of a public toilet without a lock on, calling a teacher 'Mum' or accidentally waving back at a stranger who was waving at someone behind you. Deeply uncomfortable for all concerned.

Oddness aside, the flight started smoothly and before we knew it the giant metal sausage filled with compressed air and people was hurtling between clouds at a speed that, had he been strapped to the wing, would have made Jeremy Clarkson's face fall off. I decided everything was going well and did my usual routine for embracing the miracle of flight. I put my headphones in, fired up Dido[2] and went to sleep.

I am a prolific public transport sleeper. Buses, trains, elevators, you name it, I can fall asleep on it.[3] The advantage of this is that I can basically fast-travel to any destination in the world. The disadvantage of this is that you have to learn to deal with waking up like a twat.

We've all seen it, that sleeping guy on the Tube who suddenly jerks awake and yells, 'Grandma, no!' This happens to me all the time and I find it's best just to laugh along with it. It's funny and I'll only lose around eighteen months of sleep beating myself up about it later. No biggie.

Suddenly, at 32,000 feet, I felt the sensation of falling and jerked awake like a twat. I immediately launched into my clinically rehearsed performance of eye rolls and look-at-muggins-here head wiggles that would see me through any awkwardness. However, today the person next to me didn't reply with the usual small laughs, gently exaggerated impersonations of me and 'tsh' sounds, they just sat there, looking forward, white as a porn star's arsehole.[4] I was confused right up until I felt my stomach perform the finale from Cirque du Soleil. I wasn't dreaming: the plane was falling out of the sky.

As a regular flier I'm OK with turbulence. Sure, this was a seriously bad bout of it, but it wasn't a big deal. I understand the plane's tolerances and the basic engineering holding it in the air. I know that there are many, many safety mechanisms between me and the front page of the next day's papers. The rational part of my brain kept me calm. Everything was going to be OK.

2 If my heart could write songs, they'd sound like these.
3 The trick is to be exhausted all the time.
4 It's 6.23 a.m. as I write this. I haven't been to bed yet. I'm sorry.

Then lightning lit up the cabin. The rational part of my brain got up, packed his bags and went on a six-week holiday to the Bahamas. By boat.

Everyone had just started to give each other the English exclusive look of 'Hahaha, but seriously, we're not going to die, are we?' when suddenly there was a pop. Not a loud pop, but everyone still went quiet and looked in the direction of it. The oxygen masks had deployed.

Now, this was a moment we'd been briefed on. We simply had to take the mask, frisbee it onto our own face, tie it up and breathe normally. This was difficult, however, because the only masks that had deployed were over the three men in suits in business class. They all simultaneously reached up, pulled them onto their faces and calmly carried on reading their papers. The plane fell out of the sky some more.

I became convinced that this was the start of a spy movie where the bad guy does something evil to a bunch of innocent people and, spoiler warning, I wasn't going to be named in the credits. I'd be lucky to make it to the titles with the naked swimming ladies.

This crescendo of red flags gave me one of the mercifully few times in my life where I thought, for a brief moment at least, that I was genuinely going to die. Rationality and imagination had both freaked out simultaneously and now I was going to discover how I'd react to my own impending doom. Here is that thought, exactly as I thought it, on that fateful day:

'Fuck, I'm going to miss Doctor Who *tonight.'*

That was it! In a life-or-death situation my first thought was about the adventures of a fucking fictional alien on BBC One. This is disappointing in three ways. One, I'd clearly just accepted death immediately so probably have lemming blood in my family tree somewhere. Two, I'd totally not be put in Gryffindor,[5] and three, I'd never be Lara Croft. I'm not sure which of these hurts most.

You see, in the original canon, Lara Croft survived a plane crash when she was just twenty-one. After dealing with what Ryanair would call a 'slight diversion' Lara went on to survive, stranded and alone, for two weeks in the Himalayas with nothing but her wits, her finishing-school training and the roasted limbs of passengers less fortunate than her. Not bad for a billionaire.

For most people this intense brush with death would mean therapy for life. For Lara, this was the start of her purpose. No longer would she spend Sunday having afternoon tea with the Earl of Sausage or the Duke of Pitsea. Now she was jetting off to rare and exotic locales, finding long-lost civilisations and shooting more endangered animals in the face than an American dentist visiting Longleat.

While her first two games are classics, I'm going to focus on my personal highlight of the series, and my first ever PC game: *Tomb Raider III*. In fact, I'm going to focus in even closer onto just a single moment from the game. No, it isn't when you get suddenly attacked by a London Underground train. It's not the time when you fight mutants in Antarctica. Hell, it's not even the bit where you find a real alien spaceship in Area 51.[6]

I want to talk about the time Lara visits the South Pacific.

The level starts simply enough. A coastal village, stepping stones in quicksand, an Australian whose leg has been eaten by dinosaurs. So far so nor— wait, dinosaurs?

Yep, in this section velociraptors and tiny little compsognathus will occasionally take a pop at Lara. Nothing too taxing, just got

---

5   Probably for the best. The house that values bravery above all else isn't exactly great CV material.
6   These are all real. Yes, even the aliens. This game is awesome.

to keep an eye out for the bitey buggers. Eventually you'll find a crashed plane with a cannon locked in the back that you can use to destroy a wall to the next level. You know, because video games. You'll need two keys to get to the cannon. One of them is in a dark cave that you slide down a hill into. Doesn't look like an easy way back, but you'll sort that out later. The key is on top of a small crater alongside what looks like the remains of one of the downed aircraft's crew. You pick up the key and then, well, something bad happens. Something very bad.

Firstly, music plays. Now anybody who's played the early *Tomb Raiders* knows that there are only two types of music in the entire game. There's the jingle that lets you know you just found a secret, and then there's everything else, and everything else usually means oncoming death. When music, stings or any noises at all sound in *Tomb Raider III* it's advisable to run away screaming from where you currently are, zigzagging as you go and shooting wildly at anything that vaguely resembles anything.[7]

Secondly, the camera shakes. Usually this means something heavy is coming towards you at a speed it wasn't designed to travel at. Maybe a boulder is about to spring out from a bush like a nudie mag in a high wind. Maybe the cave you are in is collapsing and you'll soon be squashed into pâté. Maybe tigers have formed a secret rugby club, and you just picked up what they consider to be the ball. However, this time it's not a constant shake, it's little occasional shakes. You swear it's accompanied by another sound. Loud, booming... footsteps?

Thirdly, a T-Rex roars out of the darkness and eats you. Usually this means that the scariest part is done; however, this time it means you have to explain to your parents why exactly you shat in the computer chair at three in the afternoon.

---

7   On the PS1 the disc would always loudly speed up before one of these musical cues, giving you a different thing to be terrified about.

I didn't jump at this moment in *Tomb Raider III*. No, I *vaulted*. One second I was sitting down in an office chair, the next I was standing behind it. Either I phased through it or went over it. I swear to this day a backflip was involved.

To regain some form of dignity I vowed to vanquish that T-Rex. I threw attempt after attempt at it, trying to find out where it was safe to hide in that cave and trying to count how many hundreds of pistol bullets it took to put it down. After many, many attempts, it finally fell. I felt like a living god right up until the moment I realised you can just run around, pull some levers and escape without fighting it. Still, the cannon was fun to play with.

To me that's *Tomb Raider*. It's an adventure about discovering the unexpected with bravery, infinite bullets and 34Ds. Lara was a total badass in every 1990s sense of the word and, most importantly, the most honourable character in all of video games history. In the London Underground level she can only progress past ticket barriers with a valid ticket even though she could leap over them faster than you could say 'Oyster card'. She's easily one of my favourite characters in gaming history. It's a shame I'm not like her in any way, but hey, what can you do?

Oh, and in case you care, my plane didn't crash. The oxygen masks dropped by accident and the three men probably just worked together or something equally boring. I landed a few hours later and ended that day by watching a genuinely terrible episode of *Doctor Who*. Still, beats eating the left leg of the stewardess I suppose.

HARDWARE HISTORY: SEGA

I know, I know. After Sony and Nintendo you were expecting a section on Microsoft but, to be honest, Microsoft is a dull company. Even the slightly weird stuff like Kinect and HoloLens have a business feel to them, like they're a tie with cartoon dogs on it worn by a very sensible man in a very sensible boardroom.[1]

Sega, on the other hand, aren't very sensible at all. Much like Spider-Man, Sega fling as much at the wall as possible and hope something sticks. PCs, consoles, handhelds without screens that only work on aircraft – you name it, Sega has cocked it up.

Quick prologue! Sega came into being in 1965 during a merger of Service Games, a company that sold jukeboxes and slot machines to the American military, and Rosen Enterprises, an arcade machine manufacturer. They took the first two letters of 'Service' and 'Games' and made Sega, a way better company name than Sero, Seen, Gase, Garo, Gaen, Rose, Roga, Roen, Ense, Enga or Enro.[2]

With the name in place, a fascinating, odd and gently disastrous history began...

---

1   The tie was bought for the very sensible man by his very proper daughter as a Christmas present. She calls him 'Father'. Sadly, she'll discover alcohol at university and ruin their relationship until a heart-wrenching reunion on his deathbed. He'll have the tie on. Even the nurses will cry. It'll win an Oscar.
2   Actually, I quite like Enga.

Sega-Vision – Television – 1976

Sega's first piece of hardware for the home was a seriously massive for the time fifty-inch TV, designed by Earl 'Madman' Muntz, the used-car salesman turned inventor who is credited with coming up with the word 'TV'. If that's not a great first step in hardware, I don't know what is.

Brilliantly, I found out about this machine while watching a very old episode of *The Price Is Right*. The cost? $1,895 in 1976 money. The contestant trying to guess the price thought it was between $2,000 and $2,100. I therefore conclude that this TV was a bargain in 1976 and now that's a historical fact.

SC-3000 – Computer – 1983

The Sega Computer 3000, aside from being the most 1980s-named product of all time, was Sega's first, and last, home computer. Inside it was a blistering 2 KB of RAM, a phenomenal 16 KB of VRAM and an unfillable 32 KB of ROM. I couldn't find any benchmarks for *Crysis* being played on it, but I assume it did spectacularly.

Wedged under the right-hand side of the SC-3000 was a slot for cartridges that needed to be filled or the machine wouldn't even run. The SC-3000 played both its own and SG-1000 cartridges so it was backwards compatible out the gate. Wait, not backwards compatible; the SG-1000 came out on the same day. Sideways compatible. Yes. Much better.

One of the hardware expansions for the SC-3000 was the gloriously named Super Control Station SF-7000. This VCR-shaped add-on gave the system a RAM and ROM boost but, most importantly, the ability to use 3-inch floppy disks.[3] Yes, that's right. 3-inch. Not 3½-inch. Not 5¼-or 8-inch.[4] 3-inch. I literally didn't know that was even a thing. Floppy drives had a Betamax.[5] Who knew?

SG-1000 – Console – 1983

Sega's first games console, the SG-1000, was released in Japan, Taiwan and, for some reason, New Zealand. It came out the same day as the SC-3000 and, due to

the decisions of someone who was presumably fired, the same day as Nintendo's Famicom. It was mostly filled with ports of arcade games and you played them with a joystick that looked like it had fallen off Kirk's chair from a *Star Trek* porn parody. The best game for it, *Girl's Garden*, by Sonic's future creator Yuji Naka, isn't very good at all.[6]

Normally at this point, paragraph two would turn things around and prove that it's actually worthwhile but, well, it's just not. The SG-1000 was a bit rubbish and it only took Sega a year to replace it with a follow-up. Well, sort of, anyway...

---

3   For the young people reading this, a floppy disk was like a USB drive, except much bigger size-wise, much smaller storage-wise and worked with alarming infrequency.
4   God, do you remember 8-inch floppies? The first PC my family owned had an 8-inch drive and I swear that whenever I put one in and it clunked down into place the entire house shook.
5   For the young people reading this, Betamax was like a Blu-ray, but with much lower quality, durability and popularity. Basically, HD DVDs.
6   Actually, it might be great but that joystick makes everything terrible. I tried it once and the next day my hand fell off.

SG-1000 II – Console – 1984

The SG-1000 II was given a whole new look over the SG-1000. New controllers replaced the terrible joystick and... absolutely nothing else  changed. Internally it was just an SG-1000 again. You could have performed this upgrade at home using nothing but a tin of paint and a marker to add the 'II'. Unsurprisingly, this too was annihilated by the Famicom like a very small bird in a very big jet engine.

Third time's the charm?

Sega Mark III – Console – 1985 (JP); Master System – Console – 1986 (US) / 1987 (EU)

The Sega Mark III, an SG-1000 II with upgraded RAM and GPU, didn't sell that well in Japan. Neither did the Master System, a Mark III  rebranded for the West, when it launched in America a year later. By this point Nintendo owned almost 90% of the entire games market, and Sega's floundering about with the SG-1000 line meant that they didn't have a hope of catching up. Yeah, they were in second place, but first place was nothing more than a very small speck on the horizon of a very large planet.

However, when it came to Europe, Nintendo made a mistake. In the UK, home computers were far, far more popular than home consoles. Nintendo ignored this, opting to sell the NES as a toy in the UK, just like they did in the US market. They hired Mattel to run their distribution so here in Blighty the NES ended up wedged between Stompers Trucks and Strawberry Shortcake dolls. Sega, on the other hand, hired Mastertronic, meaning that the Master System ended up on a shelf with all the other home computers and games. This mistake led to the NES being considered a failure in the UK and the Master System finding a foothold. Sega's success spread across the similar European markets and finally Sega started to become a household name. Hooray!

Best game for the system? Probably *Sonic the Hedgehog*. The Mega Drive version is superior, but it's got some damn fine level design that shouldn't be overlooked. Some even argue that the soundtrack is better. They're wrong – unfathomably so – but that's OK. It takes all sorts to make a world.

Sega AI Computer – Computerish Thing – 1986

And now for something completely different. The Sega AI Computer is something of a mystery, with only sparse details recorded in English. Seemingly it's an educational machine, possibly aimed at

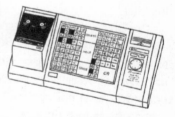

kids, where each game card comes with an overlay mat that you place onto the machine itself, giving each bit of software a unique control setup. It takes its name from the built-in AI that assists learning. No idea if it worked as an educational device or not but considering that nobody with one was literate enough to write an article about it, I'm guessing not.

Mega Drive – Console – 1988 (JP) / 1990 (EU); Genesis – 1989 (US)

The Sega Mega Drive, Sega Genesis or, rather brilliantly, Super Gam*Boy in South Korea, is Sega's bestselling, best-looking and just generally best console. With over 700 games including the *Sonic the Hedgehog* series, *Streets of Rage II*, *Disney's Aladdin*, *Columns*, *ToeJam & Earl* and *Golden Axe*, the Mega Drive was a force to be reckoned with, even against the upcoming SNES.[7]

A fact largely forgotten by history is that the Mega Drive features the greatest console peripheral known to man: the Sega Mega Anser. This was an accessory that let you perform rudimentary online banking using a Mega Drive. You could also get an optional printer to print out statements. How brilliant is that? I told you Sega threw **everything** at the wall.

One thing they maybe shouldn't have thrown at the wall was blood. When *Mortal Kombat* was released in 1993, Nintendo chose to censor the gore. Sega did not. This ended up giving Sega's version higher review scores, but also caused a huge controversy about violence in video games[8] and a senate hearing, and ultimately led to the creation of the ESRB video game rating system we still use today.

It was also my first games console so, as you would expect, I love everything about it.

---

7   Although not in Japan. Never in Japan.
8   Good thing we don't have these any more.

Game Gear – Handheld –
1990 (JP) / 1991 (EU & US)

 The Game Gear, Sega's first attempt at a handheld console, was basically a portable Master System, albeit with slightly improved specs and colours. Sega planned to make the machine's inner workings as close to each other as possible so that Master System games could be ported easily and the Game Gear's library could fill up quickly to compete with Nintendo's Game Boy.

The downside of this was, and you all know this one is coming, the battery life. The Game Boy used four AA batteries up in thirty hours. The Game Gear sucked six of them dry in around three hours. That full-colour, backlit LCD screen and powerful innards took up a lot of juice, and that, combined with a lacklustre set of titles, killed the Game Gear dead.

That said, Rebecca has one and absolutely loves it, so I've been told that if I don't say that it's the best handheld ever, they'll divorce me.

In summary: it's the best handheld ever.

Sega TeraDrive – PC – 1991

OK, so how great does this sound? A PC with a **built-in** Sega Mega Drive. OK, so the PC is an early-90s IBM with an almost decade-old 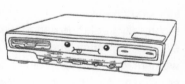 processor from 1982, but that's all just technicalities.

Wonderfully, the PC and console were connected, meaning that the TeraDrive could be used as a Mega Drive dev kit. If you've ever wanted to design games for Sega's best console or just wanted an IBM PC with two Mega Drive controller ports in the front, this is the machine for you...

> *'The system proved unpopular and failed.'*
> — Wikipedia

... and possibly only you!

Sega Mega-CD – Console Add-on – 1991 (JP); Sega CD – 1992 (US) / 1993 (EU)

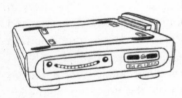

Nestled under your Mega Drive or, later on, glued next to it, the Sega Mega-CD added a nice dollop of increased specs to the Mega Drive while also giving the titular CD support that gave developers more space to play with.

Unfortunately, less than 10% of Mega Drive owners opted to buy one so it fell a bit flat. Why develop a bigger game for the Mega-CD and its much smaller audience when you could develop a little one for the Mega Drive?

It had a few interesting games during its few years of life. *Snatcher* is a pile of Hideo Kojima's weirdness that's technically set in the canon future of *Metal Gear Solid*; *Sonic CD* is... different; and *Night Trap*, a game about spying on women to stop them being attacked in their house, was so violent for the time it featured prominently alongside *Mortal Kombat* in the 90s violent-games controversy. A recent rerelease was rated 'T for Teen'. N'aww, the 90s were so cute.

Sega Action Chair – Accessory – 1992 (UK)

This is a chair controller. You read that correctly. A chair controller. Not a chair with a controller built in; *this was a chair you used to control the game.* Lean the entire chair left and your character goes left. Lean the entire fucking chair right and your character probably goes left because this inevitably wouldn't work. It's a chair. *A fucking chair*.

Sega VR – Accessory – Unreleased

Sega's little foray into VR around this time never saw the light of day, but I just want to mention it because of the great reason they had for axing it. Apparently it was just too damn realistic! They alleged that people would wander around and injure themselves so they scrapped the whole thing. I suddenly feel better about every half-arsed excuse I ever gave for missing homework now.

Activator – Accessory – 1993 (US)

With a VR system failing in the background, Sega decided that now was the time to enter the world of motion controls. Instead of fannying about with a silly glove, they opted for a ring you placed on the floor around you that shot invisible beams of magic[9] into the ceiling. Now all you had to do was break the beams and you'd do the corresponding move. You'd kick, punch and flail in various directions and your on-screen character would do something maybe a bit similar to that! The fighting genre was about to be turned on its head!

Well, no. Fighting games are based on reaction times, and pressing a few buttons is infinitely faster than having to breakdance in seventeen different directions just to do a Hadouken. Additionally, it was terrible at detecting players' movements and frankly didn't work at all if you had something other than a perfectly flat ceiling. It didn't sell well. Shocker.

Sega Pico – Console – 1993 (JP) / 1994 (EU & US)

'How far are we from the first great educational video game console for the home?'

— *Huffington Post*, 2013

Minus at least twenty-five years by my count.

The Sega Pico was a bright and chunky edutainment console aimed at kids and arguably one of Sega's most revolutionary consoles.[10] It was the first educational console to ship worldwide, and one of the first

---

9   Science.
10   Revolutionary in a good way, not revolutionary in a 'let's make a chair into a controller' way.

consoles ever to use a touchscreen as its primary input device. The cartridges were huge because they housed a book inside that was used with the game. It's actually a neat bit of kit!

Unlike almost everything listed in this section, the Pico did remarkably well in Japan! It lasted for ten years and ended up with a library of more than 300 games with titles such as *Ai to Yume no Kuni Sanrio Puroland Chanto Dekirukana Minna to Tanoshii o-Yuugikai, NHK o-Kaasan to Issho Do Re Mi Fa Do~nuts! Oekaki Daaisuki! Omoshiro Oekaki Daishuugou!* and *A Bug's Life*. Guess which of these three made it to the American market?

Aiwa CSD-G1M – CD Player – 1994

When Sega saw the breadth of their domain, they wept... for there were no more random electronics to jam a Mega Drive into. Then an intern pointed at a CD player and they just went with it. It was a Friday, you can't blame them.

Sega Pods – Toy – 1994

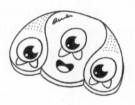

Odd little duck, this. Sega Pods were a set of large, teardrop-shaped devices that could light up, play sounds and detect if your hand was above them. They were mostly used to play variations of Simon Says but the packaging claimed this was 'The Futuristic Game of Lights and Sounds'.

Futuristic game of lights and sounds? Isn't that just... video games?

Sega Channel – Accessory –
1994 (JP & US) / 1996 (EU)

OK, this one is mad, but fucking **brilliant**. Sega Channel was a subscription service for downloading games. You read that right.

After subscribing, you were sent a chunky cartridge that you plugged into your Mega Drive and were given access to a TV channel that broadcast static signals on a loop. Your new hardware could use this static and, through some sort of magic, could translate it into games. These games were stored in the RAM of the Mega Drive and, hey presto, you just downloaded a full Mega Drive game. From your TV. In 1994. Whaaaaaa...[11]

So, am I saying that Sega may have been the pioneer of downloading games? Possibly, but there's more to it than that. Due to the way the Sega Channel was broadcast, any sort of noise or interference would break up the download and cause errors. Sega combated this by working with cable companies directly to clean and improve their cable signal quality, leading to huge improvements in cable infrastructure. Basically, the Sega Channel helped to usher in the era of cable internet that we know and complain about today. Pretty good for a TV channel with more static than a house exclusively fitted with nylon carpets.

---

11   Yes, the games being saved to the RAM meant that they deleted themsleves when the console turned off.

32x – Console Add-on –
1994 (JP & US) / 1995 (EU)

Proving that it learned nothing from the Mega-CD, Sega once again offered up another performance-upgrade peripheral for the Mega Drive that was harder to develop for and had a much smaller audience.

It was meant to bridge the gap between the Mega Drive and the Sega Saturn, but ballsed that up, in Japan at least, by coming out *after* it. The 32x only had forty games and six of those needed the Sega CD add-on too. I don't know what it looks like with both of those plugged in at once, but I assume it looks something like Ron Weasley's house.

Sega Saturn – Console – 1994 (JP) /
1995 (EU & US)

After six years and 2.2 billion unique peripherals, Sega finally replaced the Mega Drive with the 32-bit, CD-ROM-equipped Saturn. Capable of 1.21 gigaflops of polygon bamboozalry,[12] and coming off their hottest console, the Saturn was the surest bet this side of a *Grays Sports Almanac* and a DeLorean.

Of course, it failed.

Why? For a start they buggered up the release something

12   I think that's right…

fierce. It was slated for September 1995 but, at the very first E3 of all places, Sega announced that it had already shipped 30,000 units of the $399 console to certain retailers, available to buy right now. Good hype move, right? Well, no; all the companies that they didn't give stock to started to refuse any and all Sega goods. This meant no Sega presence in tiny places such as Walmart and Best Buy. Uh-oh.

To rub salt laced with itching powder into the wound, at the same E3, Sony Computer Entertainment America president Steve Race announced the PlayStation's price by walking onto the stage, saying 'two-nine-nine' and walking off again. Sadly, unlike Andrew House's version of this in 2013 with the PlayStation 4, nobody chanted Sony's name while whooping. The 90s were a more dignified time.

To hammer one last nail into the coffin, the Saturn never got a proper Sonic game. The one being created for it, *Sonic X-treme*, was cancelled and focus shifted to the Dreamcast. All the Saturn had was a port of *Sonic 3D*; *Sonic Jam*, a collection of Mega Drive games with a neat 3D overworld; and *Sonic R*, a fun racing game with one of the best soundtracks in a game. Ever. Pity it took longer to go to a store and buy it than it did to complete it.

Outside of Sonic, the Saturn has a pretty good library. *Virtua Fighter 2* showed the world just how smooth 60 fps can be, *Panzer Dragoon Saga* is still the best on-rails game of all time, and *Nights into Dreams* is... also here.

The Saturn did well in Japan though, mostly due to its strength in running 2D games and great arcade ports. Actually, thinking about it, I've just realised that Sega's history can basically be covered via one repeatable mad lib:

> In (year) Sega released the (console). It sold quite well in (one country) but terribly elsewhere, resulting in it being regarded as a failure.

Huh.

Sega Mega Jet – Semi-Portable – 1994 (JP)

 This Japanese-only console was a portable Mega Drive. Well, *semi-portable* as it didn't have its own screen. The idea was that you rented it on Japan Airlines flights, plugged it into your seat and could play Mega Drive games on the little screen in front of you. Imagine that: being able to replace the horrific screams of a confused baby with the energetic beats of Green Hill Zone. It worked with your own cartridges too![13]

Eventually Sega even went as far as to sell the Mega Jet in stores. It needed a screen and power to run so was basically just a console with a D-pad, but it was the closest the world had to a portable Mega Drive.

Now wouldn't that be awesome...

Genesis Nomad – Portable – 1995 (US)

I must admit that before I started researching all this Sega malarkey, I had no idea that this

---

13 Back then you could take cartridges through airport security, mostly because there wasn't any airport security. Recently I tried to take a PS3 through security but was informed that I couldn't take it on board unless I could 'open it' first. I missed that flight in the end.

even existed. Now I want one. Your purchase of this book has helped me achieve that goal. Thank you.

The Genesis Nomad is a portable Mega Drive. Well, portable Genesis. Heartbreakingly, it never launched in Europe. With almost the entire Genesis library available to use at launch, except for 32x and Mega-CD games of course, the Nomad was set to be a hit. Sega flung it up for sale and, proving they've still learned nothing about their failures, had another flop on their hands. *GODDAMMIT*, Sega.

It was massive and bulky, far too expensive and somehow, *somehow*, ate batteries faster than the Game Gear. Apparently six entire AA batteries lasted just two hours! To travel my regular journey from Edinburgh to London King's Cross and back again I'd need to bring thirty bloody batteries! Plus, as these were just Genesis games and most didn't have a save function, you'd lose all progress with each battery change too.

Yet I still want one. Nostalgia is one hell of a drug.

Dreamcast – Console – 1998 (JP) / 1999 (EU & US)

This is it. Sega's exit from the console market. The Dreamcast launched just four years after the Saturn and was immediately drowned by the PlayStation 2, a console that wasn't even out yet. The PS2 had it all: DVD playback, massive publisher support and a second analogue stick. What did the Dreamcast have? Online gaming too early to work well, lack of third-party support due to development difficulty and exclusivity arguments[14] and a controller that looked like Voltron's codpiece.

Yet, it wasn't a total loss. The Dreamcast died faster than my will to live in a shoe shop, but in that short time it spawned some incredible games. *Ikaruga* is widely considered to be one of the best shoot 'em ups ever made, *Jet Set Radio* invented the cel-shaded art style that hundreds of games have emulated, *Crazy Taxi* still sells its endless ports to this day, *SoulCalibur* defined the fighting genre for years, *Shenmue* made waiting for the bus in real time almost fun, and *Sonic Adventure* is still the best 3D Sonic game and when I'm king I'll make it illegal to disagree.

Just three years after launch in Japan and less than eighteen months in the UK, the Dreamcast was discontinued. Sega was haemorrhaging money so stepped away to let the modern giants of Sony, Nintendo and Microsoft battle it out. On 31 March 2001, Sega left the console business forever.

... or did they?

Advanced Pico Beena – Console – 2005

Just four years after they faked their own death, Sega launched a streamlined and superior version of their Pico console to the Japanese market. There's not much interesting to write about; however, it has never officially been discontinued,

---

14   EA wanted to be the only company allowed to make sports games for the Dreamcast. Sega rightly told them to shove it and purchased company Visual Concepts, who would eventually turn into 2K Games when they sold them on to Take-Two a few years later. EVERYTHING IS CONNECTED.

meaning that **Sega are still secretly in the console industry**. I don't know why, but this makes me happy.

Sega Vision – Media Player – 2009

No, Sega aren't Benjamin Button-ing back along their own timeline. Not entirely anyway. The Sega Vision, not to be confused with the big TV, the Sega-Vision, is a little media player that plays music, video, ebooks, etc. As far as I can tell it's never been purchasable in stores and can only be won via arcade games in select locations. There's one currently on eBay for £10. I might buy it.

When it was first announced, the Sega Vision was shown playing a few little Flash games. People ran with this and after a while headlines were blaring out that Sega was about to re-enter the game market to fight the DS and PSP. In response, Sega quietly removed the gaming abilities from the machine.

I'm not crying, you're crying.

Sega Dreamcast II – Super Console – 2033

They said it would never happen. They said Sega would never come back but they did, and they did it with aplomb. I don't know what I want to talk about first: the controllers that were individually sculpted for each player's hands, the total lack of terrible peripherals or the incredible line-up of games, all of which featured Sonic and none with a Metacritic score lower than 95. All of this for just £8.99, making it a bargain to boot. Sega was finally ready to rule from on high!

Sadly, however, it was discontinued after three months due to low sales in Japan.

So that's the long, weird and hopefully interesting history of Sega! Giving an interview with the *Guardian* in 2008, Peter Moore, ex-head of Sega of America, said this:

> *'Sega had the option of pouring in more money and going bankrupt and they decided they wanted to live to fight another day. So we licked our wounds, ate some humble pie and went to Sony and Nintendo to ask for dev kits.'*

You know what? That humble pie was the best thing Sega ever ate. They were terrible at hardware. Most of their successes were down to luck and all of their failures were their own fault. They faltered and failed in every way except one. The games.

Each console, each poor DOA console, had a defining library of great games, and with every piece of hardware, Sega got better at making them. Since leaving the console market behind they've given us new series such as the swear-word-inducing *Super Monkey Ball*, the angry-man-punching experience of *Yakuza*, wartime strategy with *Company of Heroes*, the off-kilter hack and slashing of *Bayonetta* and the granddaddy of battle simulation, *Total War*.

Oh, also *Sonic the Hedgehog* (2006).

...

Well, we all make mistakes.

It can stretch out across landscapes, owns a randomly
shaped house and, if it is cut in half, it can eat its
own bum and become whole again

Developer: Namco Bandai
Publisher: Namco Bandai
Platform: PS3
Released: 2009
What is it? I have no idea.
What is it _really_? I have no idea.

In _Noby Noby Boy_ you play as a dog that isn't actually a dog called Boy. It can stretch out across landscapes, owns a randomly shaped house and, if it is cut in half, it can eat its own bum and become whole again.

It has a planet-sized dog-but-not-really friend called Girl. Girl stretches into the cosmos in search of new places to visit and, if she makes it, you can go there too.

There are aliens. You'll meet them. Some of the aliens have cars. You can eat the cars, wheels first.

Occasionally geometric shapes attack you, but I think they're just misunderstood.

I'm not really explaining this well, am I? I think it's time to change literary tactics.

'_What is_ Noby Noby Boy?'

It was late and I was too tired to even turn down the

brightness on the phone. The question stung my retinas.

I scrunched my eyes up and frowned, hoping that this expression would somehow reply to the text message for me. It explained more than words ever could, to be honest.

'*What is* Noby Noby Boy?'

Not only would I have to explain this, I'd have to explain it to my non-gaming mother. I should have expected this when I mentioned playing the game today in my last message. I had set and sprung my own trap.

'*What is* Noby Noby Boy?'

I fell asleep before I could work out how to reply. The next day my phone's battery was flat and Mum was annoyed when I didn't call to say I'd be late home, even though it was technically her fault.

Since that night several years ago I've had time to think and, right here and right now, I shall finally get around to answering that question.

But first, I need to answer an easier one.

'*Is there a God?*'

Yes, I'm aware that a *lot* of books have been written on this subject over all of history and, yes, I'm aware that we still don't exactly know. People far more intelligent than me have all had a proper good swing at this but, alas, the answer eluded them all.

So then, what chance does a silly little book with a naughty word in the title have at uncovering the answer to the most asked question of all time? Well, I have an advantage. You see, I know where to find the answer.

I'm not bullshitting here. I know that there is a single place on this planet, possibly in the universe, where the answer to the question is written down. The full explanation of God's existence. This place is real, easily accessed by you right now, and was invented in 1941 by an Argentinian writer, Jorge Luis Borges.

Jorge wrote a short story called 'The Library of Babel'. It's set in an almost endless library where every possible combination of letters and a few bits of basic punctuation exist, scattered across a massive number of books. This means that almost every book is pure gibberish, just endless random characters, but it also means that literally every book ever written, or that ever will be written, is already in the library. Think infinite monkeys with infinite typewriters and a strong publishing deal.

Still, that's a story. Fiction. What does that have to do with God or *Noby Noby Boy*?

Well, somebody worked out how to build the library and then they put it on the internet. The Library of Babel is now real.[1]

In the library the rooms have long ID codes and the walls surrounding them are numbered. On each wall are sets of numbered shelves and sets of numbered books. In each book are numbered pages and on each page is a unique yet random assortment of characters, periods, commas and spaces. Stored as an algorithm, the library doesn't even take up too much space, even though it houses 10^{4677} books. That's more books than there are stars in the universe. In fact, that's more books than there are *atoms* in the universe. In fact, that's more books than... Well, you get the idea. It's a lot of books.

In the story, the library is inhabited by people who are

1   https://libraryofbabel.info

trapped in there, slowly going mad. In the real world it's very much the same, only here it's filled with senile googlebots trying to index the bloody thing.

Back on the initial topic tangent, in one room, on one wall, on one shelf, on one page of one of ten to the power of four thousand, six hundred and seventy-seven books is the definitive answer to every question we have about the universe, already written down. In fact, this exact paragraph is already there, even though I'm still writing it.[2]

I cannot wrap my head around this place. It's there. All of it. Everything. The meaning of life, how the universe began, how to get red wine out of a white carpet. Your birth, your death, your pin number. Every moment of time logged, filed and stored away permanently, encased in near endless walls of random gibberish. This is the limit of language itself. Every question. Every answer. Every thought anyone will ever think, already written. Original thought is dead. The Library of Babel knows everything.

Brilliantly, the website version has the ability to give you a single book at random. I love hitting that button and poring over the results, trying to find just a single English word in amongst the white noise. Once I found 'tree jam' and nearly fell over with excitement.[3]

Then, half a decade or so ago, I found it. The index book. Four hundred and ten pages of questions, each one followed by the book I could find the answer in.

My heart raced. I had found the answers to all of life's big questions. Now, for the first time in print history, here they are.

---

2   On page 365 of 410 in one of the many books called *ttw,q,hpbb,efo u,obrr*. To be any more accurate I'd need to take up a page and a half with the exact location and I'd rather fill that space with naughty words.

3   A 'tree jam' is when an entire wedge of paper gets caught in your printer at once.

'*Is there a God?*' Big one to start with. Turns out that the answer is yes, but they don't like to boast about it.

'*Is there an afterlife?*' Yes, but it's BYOB.

'*How did the universe begin?*' A faulty microwave and a misguided 4 a.m. snack. Makes sense.

'*Did man land on the moon?*' Yep, just not the moon you're thinking about.

'*Who is the greatest human who has ever lived?*' David Bowie, although he was only half-human.

'*Who is the worst human who has ever lived?*' This one simply led me to a book called *The Big Book of Footballers*.

Now, the big one.

'*What is the meaning of life?*' This answer was one word, but as soon as I read it I was filled with the warmth of understanding, like the jigsaw puzzle of the universe came together in front of me and formed a picture of a nice dog. It simply said, 'Cheese.' I wept.

I turned to the last page of the index book.

'*What is* Noby Noby Boy?'

I sat up, alarmed. The question burned on my screen, silently staring at me.

'*What is* Noby Noby Boy?'

Here it was. Finally. After all these years.

'*What is* Noby Noby Boy?'

I went to find the book. I travelled to the right room. I picked the right wall. I climbed to the right shelf. I selected the right book. I opened it and...

The book was blank. Totally blank.
Outside, the universe began laughing.

In all four games you control Rico Rodriguez,
thing blower-upper and upside-down-plane
abandoner extraordinaire

Developer: Avalanche Studios
Publisher: Eidos Interactive (1 & 2), Square Enix (3 & 4)
Released: *Just Cause* (PC, PS2, Xbox, Xbox 360 – 2006), *Just Cause 2* (PC, PS3, Xbox 360 – 2010), *Just Cause 3* (PC, PS4, Xbox One – 2015), *Just Cause 4* (PC, PS4, Xbox One – 2018)
What is it? An open-world, action-movie homage.
What is it *really*? My not-so-secret crush.

Just Cause is my favourite game series of all time.

In all four games you control Rico Rodriguez, thing blower-upper and upside-down-plane abandoner extraordinaire. Technically he destabilises dictatorships for a living, but in actuality is a sentient half-missile, half-stuntman who is really only ever involved for his own amusement. I therefore understand him on a very deep and personal level.

Each game is set in a supremely massive open world, big enough to fit all the *Grand Theft Auto* maps into in one go with ease, just like your mum, and full to the brim with creative tools to let you unleash your inner ~~terrorist~~ revolutionary. You could drive up to the enemy base, shoot everyone and drive away, but where's the fun in that? What if instead you crashed a 747 into it, strapped explosives to people's faces and flew away on a wingsuit as everyone recreated the only scene that people know from *Scanners*?

That's what *Just Cause* is about. Where some games want you to be creative and others want you to be a psychopath, *Just Cause* wants you to be both. I realise that I'm basically just describing the sort of serial killer who poses the bodies of victims to spell words, but you know, that's not *that* inaccurate...

Just Cause

Released in 2006, the first game in the *Just Cause* series, sensibly titled *Just Cause*, was madness. While the world was still recovering from Justin Timberlake's 'SexyBack', we were introduced to the biggest game world ever,[1] the Caribbean nation of San Esperito, a beautiful set of islands with a ruddy great airport, heavy military presence and a brothel in the crater of a volcano. It's like Torquay if Torquay was the opposite of Torquay.

I never thought we'd see anything even close to *Just Cause*'s world on the humble PS2. The first mission starts you a mile in the air, overlooking the *entire* 1024 km^2 of San Esperito. The biggest world I'd seen before this was in *Grand Theft Auto: San Andreas* and in that you could see about as far as a man in a small box.

While *Just Cause*'s world was a technical achievement, the same couldn't entirely be said about the gameplay. The driving was famously dreadful, with cars skidding wildly about like children on a dance floor at a wedding, the guns felt like fun-size party poppers, and the missions, of which there were about three, were more repetitive than the sound of two clocks ticking.

However, unlike any game before it, *Just Cause* managed to capture the feel of being in an action movie. The ability to climb around and jump between any vehicle, land, sea or air,

---

1   Daggerfall doesn't count because it's shit.

was fantastic and underutilised. The unlimited parachutes that were dispensed like tissues from a box added an entirely new way to get around the vast world, and the grappling hook, while limited compared to later games, gave a thousand new ways to get around and one new way to hit people.

As much as I love the game for what it is, my favourite part of it was a bug. I've got an old PS2 save of the game that, for some reason, and only ever on this save file, turns off the aircraft AI whenever Rico is in an airport. That means that if I go to any airport in the game, it will *rain* aircraft. Planes will crash into runways, helicopters will fall into the sea, and my favourite of them all, massive cargo planes will simply glide sideways back to earth, with all the speed of a pensioner crossing a busy road unaided. I used to play a game where I'd try to grapple onto one of them and take off before it hit the ground. I don't think I ever pulled it off, but I tried for longer than it would take to binge-watch *Prisoner: Cell Block H*.

Just Cause was very much a game whose reach exceeds its grasp. It tried to do so many new things that it could never nail all of them, especially on the creaking PS2 hardware. The PS3 came out just a few months later and, with it, the potential for a fantastic sequel...

Just Cause 2

Once upon a time, I found myself staring at one of those demo stations that you used to see all the time in Electronics Boutique, before the bacteria on the controllers killed everyone who ever used them. Playing on the station was a yet unreleased demo for *Just Cause 2*. I put down my bag, had a quick go, and suddenly it was several hours later. I was in love.

This time, Rico was exploding in the nation of Panau, a gorgeous set of islands featuring tropical beaches, snowy mountains, huge cities, endless deserts and entrenched military installations owned by whoever had a target drawn on their face with an Agency-issued Sharpie this week.

The absolute highlight of the map was the Mile High Club, a fucking great ship held aloft in the sky by two massive balloons. It was supremely impressive, gloriously over the top and full of male strippers. Does it get any more *Just Cause* than that?

Just Cause 2 took all of its predecessor's potential and nailed it like a saviour to a cross. Every weak point of the first was improved upon. The controls were tighter, the shooting was more satisfying and the driving... well, the driving was still shit. But it was *less* shit! That's what counts!

The biggest improvement was to the grappling hook. Now you could attach yourself to any surface, allowing you to scale every building like a chaotic window cleaner. The more dramatic change was that you could now attach any two objects in the world together. This meant you could give someone a gravel facelift by towing them behind your car, create your own wrecking ball out of a helicopter and the heaviest nearby thing your helicopter can lift, or simply force a 747 to noseplant just as it was taking off, likely decapitating everyone on board who ignored the warning to put the tray tables up.

Just Cause 2 was gaming perfection. Almost. The only issue was the Vanderbildt LeisureLiner, a bus that didn't spawn in the game, but was needed for 100% completion. I spent an uncountable number of hours of my finite life searching for that needle in a haystack the size of Dallas, only for it to be a bug that was later patched, meaning that all that hard work never counted for anything.

I missed a funeral for that bus.

Just Cause 3

In 2015 I found myself many storeys above London, in a new suit, looking over the skyline with my father as we both giggled at the stupidity of it all. We were in the offices of Square Enix, a billion-dollar company, because I'd made a video about how much I loved *Just Cause 2* and the developers had seen it. They loved it and, because of that, wanted me to be the first person to show off gameplay from *Just Cause 3*. On that day I learned what imposter syndrome feels like.

Something else I learned that day was how little footage I've seen of big-budget AAA games before they're finished. The *Just Cause 3* I played that day was remarkably smooth and polished for a game almost a year from release, but was full of hilarious bugs that sadly never made it to release.[2]

Occasionally, when Rico would fire his grappling hook, he'd simply fold in half like his spine had suddenly become a deckchair. At one point a bridge exploded and the car on top of it didn't seem to notice at all and, in a very early build of the opening mission, the aircraft Rico flies in on was destroyed, but kept flying anyway. That was particular fun because it apparently hadn't happened before. You're welcome, Square Enix!

Anyway, this time around we find Rico quitting The Agency and going back to his homeland, the Mediterranean-inspired islands of Medici. However, old habits die hard and before long Rico has grabbed a local dictator by the unwhisperables, spun him round and round and flung him into a volcano.[3]

Medici is a collection of farms, caves and wildly dangerous cliff faces, all of which are dotted around the place with the regularity of orange lines on an ordnance survey map. This perilous terrain gives Rico the need for a new traversal method: the wingsuit. Now you can fly further, faster and face-first into flammable fuel

2   'Sadly' is probably not the right word here...
3   The dictator in question, General Sebastiano Di Ravello, is one of my favourite game baddies of all time. The hidden collectables around the island make up an audio diary of his ten-year rise to power and it made smashing his face with an RPG that much sweeter.

factories, flinging fire free from the foe's fortifications and flaring up fruits and flowers in friendly fertile fields.[4]

Alongside the wingsuit, Rico gains the ability to tether together multiple things at once, a pocket that he keeps infinite C4 in and the ability to slap down rocket boosters on *anything*. You'll put them mostly on cows because you're a monster. Also because it's funny to watch a cow spiral off like an unrestrained Catherine wheel.

In short, it's the best game ever.[5]

Just Cause 4

All right, I think they've started making these games exclusively for me. *Just Cause 4* is simply everything I wanted, and more.

In case you needed a reason to distrust clowns any more, in *Just Cause 4* Rico has weaponised the humble balloon. Stick one to an enemy or a few to a car and you can send it skyward, choosing then to burst the balloon and send the victim crashing back to earth, or just keep the USS *Screaming Man* going until it becomes a threat to satellites.

The boosters return, now a part of the grappling hook – and like the balloons and pretty much everything else, they are fully customisable. Speed, power, burn duration, it's all yours to tinker with. You even get to choose what kind of gas goes in your balloons. It's that kind of game.

Weather comes into play in the form of sandstorms, snowstorms, regular storms and a goddamn tornado that after a while becomes your friend and your enemy's nightmare. The featured island this time around, Solis, contains varied terrain, fun secrets and a Ferris wheel that I exploded every time I was vaguely close to it. You can abuse the giant planes taking off from

4   Good luck with the audiobook, prick.
5   I wrote this on a bus once.

the main airport, and in my favourite feature, the vehicle drops now contain the ability to summon a massive aircraft carrier anywhere you want. Sea, land, the top of a skyscraper, wherever. It's a great argument settler. If someone bumps you while driving, you can crush them with 50,000 tonnes of fuck you.

Christ knows where this series goes next. *Just Cause 4* hints that the next game will be against The Agency, Rico's old employers, but after that, who knows? Will Rico take over Earth? Will he burrow into the ground to fight the Worm People or will he be sent to Jupiter to sort out the Jupiterians? I have no idea, but as long as I can crash a large aircraft into someone, I'll be playing.

In *Mario Party* losses are so unfair, unpredictable
and vicious that everyone playing feels cheated,
even if they benefited

Developer: Hudson Soft, NDcube
Publisher: Nintendo
Released: Too many releases to bother to list.
What is it? A digital board game for the whole family!
What is it *really*? The reason my cousin has that scar.

Legend has it that in 1858 confectioner Tom Smith was dozing in his armchair when a loud crackle from his fireplace woke him up with an idea. He was going to add a tiny, surprise explosion to the little packages of sweets, trinkets and mottoes that he sold. The cracker was born.[1] Well, the idea anyway. Tom would initially call them 'Bangs of Expectation'[2] because it was 1858 and that's how people named things back then.

As far as I can tell[3] nobody seems to know exactly when the mottoes in crackers turned into the dreadful jokes we know and hate today. My guess is that in the 150 years since the invention of the cracker we've had two world wars, ten recessions and that

---

1   For you non-Commonwealth lot, a cracker is a colourful cardboard tube with a crap joke, a crap trinket and a crap paper hat inside. You grab one end, someone else grabs the other, you pull, it makes a small bang and your crap falls out. You place the crap hat on your head where it instantly rips and then you have to read the crap joke out loud as everyone groans at how crap it is. This is often the best part of Christmas Day.
2   My favourite Dickens porn parody.
3   And I went as far as the *third* page of Google while researching this.

Mr Blobby single. That's enough to make anyone need a laugh, but the question remains: why aren't cracker jokes any good?

Professor Richard Wiseman, a psychologist at the University of Hertfordshire, believes that cracker jokes are purposely bad to avoid embarrassment. Due to the wide demographic you're likely to have around the dinner table at Christmas, you're never going to find a joke that everyone likes. The kids don't get it, Mum thinks it's offensive, Granddad thinks it's not offensive enough, etc. It's a tough crowd and no joke is going to play well, especially as nobody actually wants to read them out loud. The only way to get around this terminal case of Britishness is to make all the jokes terrible. This way the joke teller isn't to blame, nobody feels left out and everyone gets along and has a lovely Christmas. That is, until the Monopoly board comes out and the evening descends into the traditional candlelit fist fight.

So why did I spend almost 300 words explaining the psychology of Christmas cracker jokes to you?[4] It's because the *Mario Party* series is the video game equivalent of these jokes. Terrible, but terrible on purpose.

But still terrible.

Mario Party is a digital board game for multiple players, currently on its seventeenth game, *Super Mario Party*.[5] It plays like many other board games: you roll dice, collect things and start hating people you once loved. If you land on certain squares you'll need to play minigames against the other players and, here comes the big problem: it literally doesn't matter what you do. If, on the day you play, Lady Luck isn't flashing you her two sixes, you **will** end up in last place. Feeling safe in first place? Doesn't matter. She can, and will, turn her back on you in a heartbeat. Your descent

---

4   Padding.
5   I've had to update this fact **twice** while writing this book. I guarantee this will be wrong three seconds after we go to print.

will not be graceful. No, you will fall with the speed and dignity of a 747 full of elephants, with mercury-filled fuel tanks and a cargo of dynamite, before you crash violently into the ground, exploding into a pile of twisted metal, peanuts and tusks.[6]

Speaking of hilarious disasters, one of the N64 versions of *Mario Party* had several minigames that needed you to spin the controller's abrasive analogue stick so fast that, after a while, your palm would develop blisters. Parents complained, it became a big deal, and Nintendo's solution was to send a pair of gloves to every person who called up and proved they owned the game. I wondered how much these gloves would sell for these days but I can't even find an image of them. As far as I can tell the gloves were just plain white, unbranded and boring. Then again, they're the ones Mario always wears so I don't know why I'm surprised.

Anyway, let's dig straight into the heart of the issue with some exempla. Here are some things that can, and will, actually happen to you in a game of *Mario Party*:

1. The game is over. Stars, the objects you're collecting to win the game, get totalled up. You received the most so are going to win. Then, another player is randomly given bonus stars for something arbitrary like buying more items in the shop or walking more steps. They win. You lose. They cheer. You cry. This happened to me.

2. You play the game with someone who loses interest in it halfway through, leaves, and you finish up without them. You still lose to them even though they weren't even moving in the minigames. This happened to me.[7]

---

6   The reason airlines still give out free packs of peanuts is to commemorate this accident.

7   In fact, this happened yesterday, at the time of writing, on a train. My built-in patriotic duty to remain quiet on public transport was tested somewhat, I can tell you.

3. A player lands on a square that takes everyone's stars away and redistributes them back evenly. The entire game up to this point has been a total waste of time and your lead is a mere fond memory. This happened to me.

4. It's the last turn and you have a very strong lead. You roll and land on a square that takes everything you have and swaps it with another player. They get put in first place and you in last. The game ends. A controller hits the wall. Controller debris and plaster hit the floor. The family tree loses a branch. This happened to me.

In *Mario Party* losses are so unfair, unpredictable and vicious that everyone playing feels cheated, even if they benefited. It's the crap cracker-joke effect: if the game is terrible, then it doesn't matter who wins or who loses, who played well or who played badly. What matters is a bunch of people who wouldn't normally play games at all got together and didn't fight for an hour. That's what *Mario Party* is all about. Bringing people together. They're terrible games, but terrible on purpose.

But still terrible.

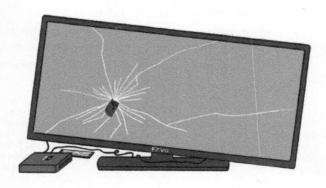

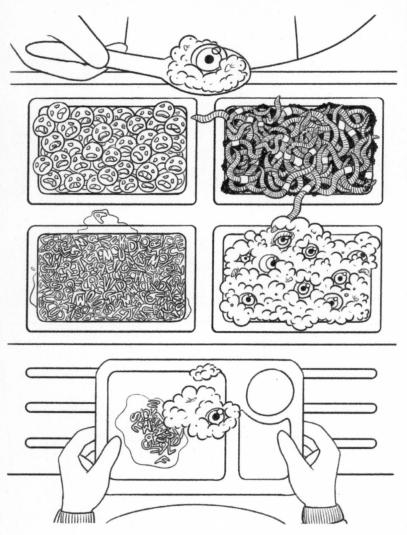

We caught three prisoners having a fight in the cafeteria. Not sure what set it off, but my money is on whatever the cook slopped onto the trays that morning

Developer: Introversion Software
Publisher: Introversion Software
Platform: PC, PS4, Xbox One, Switch
Released: 2015
What is it? A prison construction and management simulation.
What is it *really*? Overtime for the riot squad.

Daily Warden Report – Her Majesty's Prison Slade

Day 1

I arrived at HMP Slade at around nine o'clock this morning, just in time to watch the workmen break ground on this new, glorious cog in the wheel of law and order. It's been a while since I've run a rehabilitation centre such as this, yet I am more than confident that the plans I've laid out will create a safe and fair environment for all who enter.

Mind you, I do hope these workmen get a shift on. Our first eight prisoners are due tomorrow at 8 a.m. and the prison currently consists of nothing but a garbage dump, a door in the middle of the road, and half a reception desk.

Day 2

9 a.m. start again. We've delayed the prisoners by a day due to the unfinished state of the prison. Maybe I overreached when

trying to build an entire prison from the ground up in a day, but no matter. Tomorrow we will house these eight criminals and guide them back onto the right path.

Ah, not eight. Thirty-four now. Right. OK. I might need some more cells.

Day 3

The prisoners arrived at 8 a.m. sharp and I personally welcomed each and every one of them to the prison. An unorthodox approach to my duty as warden, yes, but I needed to kill time so we could get the last of the building materials out of the cafeteria. I do trust these inmates but, off the record, I'd rather they didn't have access to hammers.

Anyway, the first prisoner across the threshold was a young chap named Milo. In for a few bouts of pickpocketing, nothing too serious. I shook his hand – building trust, you see – and told him we would set him straight. He looked back, smiled and said he was looking forward to it! No more than five seconds in and we've already made a connection! Now, admittedly I haven't seen my watch since then, but I probably just misplaced it in my office.

Day 4

Yesterday went swimmingly. Today less so. We caught three prisoners having a fight in the cafeteria. Not sure what set it off, but my money is on whatever the cook slopped onto the trays that morning. I know we have tight budgets, but meat should under no circumstances be a liquid. I let him go and hired a new chef, one with an excellent moustache.

I've set some patrol routes around the prison. Hopefully the presence of my men will be enough to suppress these acts of violence in the future. I've also equipped them with tasers, just in case it isn't.

Update: I've just discovered that the first prisoner we welcomed spells his name 'Mylo'. He seemed very angry when he discovered it spelled the other way on his mail this morning. It's probably a youth thing, like backwards hats, untucked shirts or watching TV shows about genitalia. I'll update it in the records.

Day 5

Nothing really to report. The prisoner population now stands at sixty-four, all of whom are well-fed and happy. Our new chapel opened today, filled with prayer mats and pews. Now I know this might not be PC, but I assigned three guards to it, just to be safe. You really can't trust priests in this day and age now, can you?

Day 6

Another fight in the cafeteria ended with a host of injuries and one death – a guard, unnamed for legal reasons. There will be an inquiry, but seeing as we've got CCTV of a prisoner, legally referred to as Prisoner X, scooping the guard's eyes out with a plastic spoon before spitting down his skull holes, it probably won't be too long an inquiry.

The prisoner in question is currently in solitary confinement for twenty-four hours. We didn't actually have a room for that, so we just stuck him and a chair in a cleaning cupboard for now. In worse news, the psychiatrist has discovered that he has a 'deadly' personality trait, meaning that he's as lethal in hand-to-hand combat as a four-armed Bruce Lee. I've decided to build him his own mini-prison within the perimeter. It's expensive and possibly illegal, but much like James May he'll be best when separated off from the rest of the group.

Day 7

The lawyers here at HMP Slade have done some marvellous work, shredding the i's and removing red tape from the t's. We can now house prisoners in their cells indefinitely, giving legal life to Project Mini-Prison. Prisoner X has been housed and is doing well, despite the fact he'll not see daylight for the next forty years. I've checked his notes and discovered that he used to be a software developer, so there's a chance he won't even notice the lack of vitamin D!

Day 8

Oh dear. Oh dear, oh dear. Today there was an incident in the visitation room. The details are hazy, but apparently a prisoner killed his family, three guards and a workman in the space of five seconds. While we assess the situation we've temporarily placed him in with Prisoner X. I will update as the day progresses.

Update 1: It's Mylo.

Update 2: The situation has been contained, yet the investigation is ongoing. Mylo may have had drug withdrawal issues and snapped when his family didn't smuggle any in for him. I've set up programmes to combat this with the other prisoners, but the damage is done. My mistakes have resulted in seven dead bodies lying in my morgue. Actually, we've only got three slabs so four of them are propped against a wall.

Update 3: We've discovered that Mylo has both the 'extremely deadly' trait as well as the 'extremely volatile' trait. I'm going to build another mini-prison, far away from the main cell blocks to contain him. This man is an explosive monster. I don't know how I didn't notice this before.

Update 4: Prisoner X has been killed by Mylo. OK, that one's on me.

Day 10

'Disciplining yourself to do what you know is right and important, although difficult, is the high road to pride, self-esteem and personal satisfaction.'

I don't know why this Margaret Thatcher quote popped into my head as I bricked Mylo's cell in permanently, leaving him to die. I didn't feel particularly proud of this choice, but it certainly was the right one. Mylo has killed every guard that has entered his mini-prison with food, smashed up every object in it and at one point fought his own reflection for a bit when it made eye contact with him.

Away from Mylo, the rest of the prison is flourishing with reform programmes, educational lessons and workshops, keeping the inmates happy and busy. Happiness is high, the danger level is low. All is finally well.

Day 14

Everyone is dead. It all happened so fast that I couldn't react until it was too late. A guard noticed that Mylo was digging an escape tunnel, so I broke a hole in his cell and sent three armed men in to put him down. He killed all of them and headed towards the prison. I threw the prison into a lockdown but, as I did this during free time, it kicked off a prison-wide riot.

Everything became chaos. I sent in three squads of riot guards with instructions to shoot on sight, but we lost contact with them when they approached Mylo. I hear he kicked one of the guard's heads clean off and it ended up in the school down the road, but the eight-year-old that told me that might have been lying.

Mylo escaped in the end, breaking down the main entrance gate as if it was made of soap bubbles. After he vanished, the last few remaining guards managed to taser order back into what was left of the populace. All three of them were then escorted back to their cells.

I've been given less than a day to correct these mistakes and to get the prison working again. I will redesign, reclaim and rehabilitate. I am the warden and it takes more than relentless loss of human life to stop me. HMP Slade will rise again!

Day 23

My first day in prison, ironically the one I was in charge of less than two weeks ago. I forgot to tell the guards to stop firing at will so a sniper tower took out the entire yard the moment a small scuffle occurred. I was hauled away and placed before a judge to argue that I was both fit to run a prison and not responsible for the hundred or so corpses said running had created.

The trial didn't last long but, in retrospect, my lawyer arguing that placing me back in HMP Slade was akin to a death sentence certainly didn't help my case...

Day 24

The prison is on fire again. I hate this place.

You get captured and escape while entirely naked

TACTICAL ESPIONAGE ACTION

METAL GEAR SOLID 2
SONS OF LIBERTY

Developer: Konami Computer Entertainment Japan
Publisher: Konami
Platform: PS2
Released: 2001
What is it? Tactical Espionage Action.
What is it *really*? Tactical Espiona… Wait, who's this guy?

> *'Mindfuck (noun; taboo, slang)*
> *The deliberate infliction of psychological damage'*
> — Dictionary.com

I'm just going to leave that there. It will become important later and I want us all to be on the same page.

Anyway, Heston Blumenthal's restaurant, The Fat Duck, costs £255 per person for its fifteen-course tasting menu, with an extra cost of £155 per person if you want the recommended wines.[1] You can find it inside a small, sixteenth-century ex-pub in the village of Bray, a community so small that a particularly large yawn on a car ride through it might cause you to miss it entirely.[2]

---

1   I don't understand why wine is so expensive. It's just vinegar mixed with Ribena.
2   Bray, for some reason, contains two out of the five restaurants with three Michelin stars in the UK. Its population is a tad under 10,000 well-fed people.

The Fat Duck isn't a posh restaurant, it's a playground. It's Willy Wonka doing a brand expansion. Every meal is lunacy, from snail porridge to egg-and-bacon ice cream. It's designed as a giant culinary middle finger to everyone who says that you shouldn't play with your food.

It's also been awarded the title of 'The Best Restaurant in the World'.

I couldn't resist. After months of saving[3] and even more months of waiting to get a table, Rebecca and I packed our bags and took a trip to Bray. On the train we tried to come up with the stupidest dishes that we would be served. Bolognese where only the parmesan was visible, a liquid that played your favourite song as you drank it, a smoothie made of spider webs, etc. Our favourite was a single mint, served on the pillow of an entire floating hotel-room bed. If they could pull at least one thing off that was that mad it would be worth the money.

One taxi connection later and we had arrived. Well, we thought we had, anyway. The Fat Duck doesn't actually say it's The Fat Duck, it just has a vague logo dangling off its white front. The windows are blocked off from the inside and the door is solid, wooden and intimidating. From the outside it didn't look like the best restaurant in the world. It looked like your nan's house.

After a small game of 'you go first'[4] we entered into a tiny, entirely mirrored room where a lady stood waiting to welcome us to the restaurant. I caught a glimpse of my own face and hoped I was somehow less terrified than I looked. The lady, one of *eighty* members of staff for this fourteen-table restaurant, took us out of the mirrored room and into a much more normal-looking one. We took our seats in the corner and had a look at our menu that

---

3   AKA not buying any Lego.
4   A game where the winner is the first person to politely force someone into doing something they don't want to do.

was actually a map. The first dishes started to appear and pretty soon I had drunk a flash-frozen cocktail and breathed smoke out of my nose. We weren't in Kansas any more.

It was during the fourth course, a cup of tea that was both hot and cold at the same time, when Rebecca nudged me and pointed to another table. I glanced over, looked back at Rebecca quizzically, looked back again, and my mind fucking exploded.

In the middle of this table, and I swear this is true, was a floating pillow, slowly rotating, with what looked like a little mint on top of it.

I've never felt a feeling quite like that one. It was almost like working out that you're in a nightmare but not quite knowing what to do with that information. The maddest, silliest thing I could come up with was now in the room with me. I tried to vocalise this but any sentence I started fell apart after a syllable or two. I sounded like I was trying to stream my thoughts via dial-up.

The next course was cereal and milk. The milk was eggs and the cereal tasted like breakfast meats. It was presented in the form of a multipack of six small cereal boxes. I opened mine and found that the wooden toy inside had my company logo etched into it. I realised that this wasn't just going to be a mindfuck. It was going to be a tantric mindfuck.

After four and a half hours we eventually escaped The Fat Duck unscathed. Sure, I pooped a colour I'd never seen before for about six weeks afterwards, but it was worth it. I proposed to Rebecca in the Premier Inn that night. Yes, I could have done it in the expensive restaurant and got something free, but I bet that even a bouquet of flowers from that place wouldn't be what it seemed. You'd probably water them and they'd turn into 1990s rock band Deep Blue Something.

When I was planning this book I wrote a list of games I wanted to talk about and fun stories I wanted to tell. Most of them had a natural partner, some got ditched or tied to history lessons about crackers, but this one story didn't have anywhere to go.[5] I needed to attach it to a game that didn't just have one big twist at the end, I needed one that consistently and deliberately messed with you for its entire run. I needed something so bizarre and twisted that people still talk about it to this day. I needed something halfway between genius and padded-walls insane.

In short, I needed a Hideo Kojima game.

If Shigeru Miyamoto is gaming's Walt Disney, Tim Schafer is gaming's Edgar Wright and Peter Molyneux is gaming's George Lucas, then Hideo Kojima is gaming's Stanley Kubrick. No other person involved in gaming has his level of detail, perfectionism and, at points, utter and complete nonsensicalness.

Stealth action game *Metal Gear Solid 2* is, for me, his masterwork. In *MGS2* the lead character, Solid Snake, dies an hour into the game and is replaced by a brand-new character called Raiden.

I remember this happening. I remember sitting there as Raiden took off his mask to reveal his white-blond hair. I remember laughing with a friend and wondering if this was a dream sequence or a VR mission or something. I remember playing the rest of the game dumbstruck that we couldn't play as Snake yet. What the hell was going on?

Every trailer, every goddamn trailer, only showed Snake. Every screenshot, every scrap of information about the game featured Snake. The bastards had even added him into levels he's not in, just for the trailers. Every review danced wildly around the topic of plot to such an extent that it sounded like they were all written by politicians.

5   Plus, if I include this story in the book, then I can classify the meal as a business expense.

It didn't stop there, though. God, no. As the game progresses it just keeps trying to crowbar you away from reality. A Doctor Robotnik cosplayer starts bombing the place, a lady with a rail gun can't be shot and a vampire flies a Harrier for a bit.

It doesn't even stop there! Your dead clone's arm is sentient and now attached to a moustached revolver expert. Snake turns up, but maybe it's just someone who looks like him, and eventually the US president is killed. Don't worry, though, a previous US president is here too! Pity he's the lead villain.

It doesn't even stop *there*! You get captured and escape while entirely naked, limiting your abilities so you can keep a concealing hand on your gentleman's region; the guy giving you your mission starts to break down and might not even be real; and, during that breakdown, your on-screen map turns into a video of a woman and the game pretends that you've had a game over even when you haven't.

It does stop there. Well, after the revelation that there is a shadowy organisation that runs the entire world. Pity that they all died like a century ago. The End.

Metal Gear Solid 2 is a mindfuck. Where most games are happy with a rug-pull right at the end, *MGS2* is a tower of rugs that are ripped out from under you one by one, exactly when you don't expect them to be.

It's also obsessively detailed. There's a cup of ice cubes[6] in an early section that slowly melt if you knock them out. That by itself is already more detailed than 99.9% of games, but did you know that the ice cubes will melt slower if they're near other ice cubes and thus stay colder for longer? That level of detail is normally reserved for space shuttle launches and Wikipedia entries about cartoon horses.

---

6   It's illegal to talk about *MGS2* and not mention these.

Metal Gear Solid 2 is bold, ballsy and batshit insane. It's a combination of the wildest story, terrifying detail and tightest mechanics gaming has ever seen. It also lets you train a parrot at one point because *of course it does.* Go play it if you haven't. Go play it again if you have. It's ready to surprise you all over again.

Now if you'll excuse me, I have to go wash invisible bolognese out of my trousers.

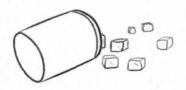

... my trusted housecarl who, without missing a beat,
hoisted her axe, screamed violently and went to war

THE ELDER SCROLLS V: SKYRIM.

Developer: Bethesda Game Studios
Publisher: Bethesda Softworks
Platform: PC, PS3, PS4, Xbox 360, Xbox One, Switch, Every Household Appliance
Released: 2011
What is it? A first-person fantasy RPG.
What is it *really*? A game about trying to steal all the cheese from a country.

It started with a rumour, a hushed whisper on a quiet street. Two citizens spoke of a college of magic, tucked far away in the frozen north-east of Skyrim. A place where mages from all over Tamriel came to study, collaborate and grow more powerful. Yes, the soft words were no more than a rumour, but I was a professional adventurer. Rumours were the reason I got up in the morning. That and the fact that all the mattresses were made from straw.

Being an elf and aspiring mage myself, the prospect of visiting such a place was wickedly tempting. The downside, of course, was that I was only just starting on my journey of dragon slaying and world saving, so the journey to college would be difficult, if not impossible. Then again, the potential benefits could help me in the long run and outweigh the initial risk. It was a difficult choice but eventually I reached a conclusion.

I was going to get my Harry Potter on.

First, I had to pack. This was simple because I didn't actually own anything aside from a fancy dressing gown and a pair of boots made from some adorable animal or another. The perks of being a mage right there: if I wanted a weapon, I could literally magic one out of thin air. I threw a few potions into the bag of my heavily armoured Nord housecarl,[1] Lydia, and commenced the adventure.

The first part of the journey was fine. Everything was bright, green and paved.[2] We had to deal with the odd bandit or assassin but Lydia could cut a bee out of the air with her axe while blindfolded[3] so it was no bother.

As the journey progressed north, the terrain changed. The green forests gave way to ice, snow and more snow. Jagged shards of rock punched through the floor, flat terrain fell into huge ravines without warning and huge, violent creatures stalked from the shadows. Everywhere you looked was white, twisted and full of monsters. It was like reading the *Daily Mail*.

Eventually, we reached the city of Winterhold.[4] At the rear of the city stood a huge bridge, connecting it to the tall towers of Skyrim School of Witchcraft and Wizardry, or whatever it was called.

After gently persuading the guard at the front, I was allowed up into the college and, after a single conversation, was immediately enrolled, given a bed and told where my first lesson would be. They didn't even read my personal statement!

I entered the location of my first lecture, the Hall of the Elements, and jogged over to a few fellow students and a teacher. This was it. I was about to start my journey to become the

---

1 Someone whose job lies just in between a bodyguard and a pack mule.
2 I say 'paved'. It looked more like a very angry person had just wandered about, throwing individual slabs of rock into the ground.
3 She needs a new party trick.
4 It calls itself a city but it has about as many buildings as a cat playing Monopoly.

greatest mage of all time. After brief conversations, I was taught a new spell, a shield, and told to stand on a point. The lecturer would pelt me with fireballs and I'd have to use the shield to protect myself. Simple enough. One small issue was the giant Nord woman in between us. Figuring that I wouldn't need her during my studies, I did the logical thing and dismissed Lydia. She deserved a holiday.

Sadly, before Lydia could even pick up a skiing brochure, all hell broke loose.

Immediately all five mages in the room started firing the *Who's Who* of spells directly at my trusted housecarl, who, without missing a beat, hoisted her axe, screamed violently and went to war.[5] The air crackled and sparked with electricity, ice and fire, while century-old masonry crumbled like your legs when you jump off a trampoline you've been on for far too long. Three seconds before, the scene looked like it had been lifted from *The Lord of the Rings*; now it looked like *The Lord of the Rings* directed by Zack Snyder.

In a snap decision I decided where my priorities were and started kicking the shit out of my classmates. True, this wouldn't look great come parent–teacher conference night, but to hell with it. Lydia scared me more than these Paul Daniels wannabes.

The skirmish ended quickly. We had killed five wizards faster than J K Rowling on deadline day, but it wasn't over yet. The doors flew open and in burst the teachers, mature students and assorted people too scared to leave the comfort of academia. I stood as a distraction in the centre of the room, constantly healing myself and necking mana restore potions, while Lydia

---

5   The college is a protected area in the game so I guess that permission to enter is given to the player and any follower they have, but not to the follower by themselves, so when they separate the follower is treated as an uninvited intruder. Either that or they were all just dicks.

introduced everyone who entered the room to the concept of severe blood loss.

After pulling her axe out of the fifteenth or so mage spine, Lydia fell. A blast of magic sent her body across the room where it hit a wall with the sort of clang a fridge-freezer would make in the same situation. I ran to her side and, one quick looting later, leapt back into the fight, decapitating, disabling and generally ruining the lives of anyone in a three-metre radius with her axe. They would all pay for this. I hate carrying my own stuff.

Villagers in Winterhold would talk about the day that the college burned to the ground. They say that as they stood watching the flames, a single figure slowly made its way down the long bridge to the village, dragging a weighty axe behind it. Burned, bruised and trailing someone else's blood, the elven figure silently walked through the assembled crowd, entered the shop, sold a lot of claret-covered mage robes and left.

Some say the elf was never seen again. Others say the elf was seen again loads and the first people asked weren't paying enough attention. One thing was known for sure: that elf was now, by process of elimination admittedly, the most powerful mage in the world.

I found it much later in the game. A cathedral filled
with a spider the size of the Eden Project

Bloodborne

Developer: FromSoftware
Publisher: Sony Computer Entertainment
Platform: PS4
Released: 2015
What is it? A dark and twisted RPG.
What is it *really*? All my nightmares at once.

Here's another story from that camp I worked at for a while. It was the last full day of the week and everything up to this point had gone particularly well. The birds were singing, the sky was blue and aircraft gently released chemicals into the atmosphere thousands of feet above me. It was glorious. Something was bound to go wrong.

It did. A child suddenly came pelting out of the forest screaming for help. He and a group of friends had 'found something'.

The coaches home were due to arrive in an hour. I sighed and headed towards the forest. I'd picked the wrong day to quit eating candy sticks.

I grabbed another volunteer, partly because this was a bit ominous and partly because, you know, running off with a kid into a forest by yourself isn't a good look in this day and age. Together, we ventured beyond the treeline.

The camp was huge, fifty acres or something,[1] so as we followed the boy it started to get darker and darker. The blue sky was gone, replaced with a weave of gnarled branches and darkened leaves. I half expected to bump into Hagrid in here.

Eventually we heard whispers. Around six or seven other kids were standing around a solitary tree in the middle of a small clearing, giving it a wide berth. I strode up, flung some orders and questions around at no one in particular and stopped the moment I saw... *it*.

Attached to the tree – and now would be the time to remind you that this is very much a true story – was a large and inexplicably writhing black mass. It looked like Venom had jizzed onto it. A lot.

I fell back, joining in the wide berth the group was giving it, desperately trying to process what I was looking at. What was it? A creature? Was it alive? Well, it was certainly moving. Possibly breathing. Possibly watching... I took a step back, placing myself behind the ~~meat shields~~ children.

My train of thought was derailed and replaced with a bus service by a prepubescent voice. It suggested a plan of action that only a prepubescent voice could. The plan was dangerous, foolhardy and just five words long.

'Why don't we poke it?'

A long stick was found and presented to the speaker. The circle spread out, every soul seeking refuge behind a rock, tree or friend. When everyone was settled, the child that I would never see again slowly began his approach. Everything was silent, even the trees held their breath. After what could have been seconds or hours, the stick made contact.

If this was a film this would be the part where, after a luring pause, a sudden burst of music would make you jump while

---

1 Whatever the fuck an acre is.

tentacles would fly out of the black sentient mass, engulfing the child and absorbing him. However, this wasn't a movie. It was highly unlikely that the entire Royal Philharmonic Orchestra was waiting just a few trees over, ready with the sting. This was real life and in real life the black sentient mass instead did something a thousand times scarier.

It *dispersed*.

Bugs. Thousands, if not millions, of bugs suddenly shot in every single direction. It was like someone had used a black paint bucket tool, just on the actual world. Panic set in, everyone ran for their lives. I bolted, making sure to trip up a few of the weaker ones as I made my escape, leaping over tree roots with as much of a plan of looking back as Lot after the salt incident.

I never saw the other volunteer or half of those kids ever again. I assume they died, trampled by quadrillions of tiny legs, suffocated with mouths full of insects or simply eaten by the endless hordes of tiny monsters. Either that or they got on a different bus home from me half an hour later. I'll never know.

It was around this time I inexplicably developed an aversion to insects. I still blame the trauma of that day at camp, but Mum says it was simply from the time when we were in Australia and one of the larger arachnids tried to drag me off into the outback. I'm not so sure. Dad thinks it was from the time that Uncle Fred fell into that pit of stick insects and they ate him alive. I don't think it was that either, although that was a terrible end to my fifth birthday party. I wish he hadn't been dressed as a clown at the time.

This phobia of the creepies and the crawlies extends, bizarrely, to video games. During a playthrough of *Resident Evil* on the DS, a mutant spider dropped down in front of the camera and I jumped so hard my DS flew out of my hands and broke on the floor. Nowadays if I come across a virtual spider, giant or otherwise, I stop, save, quit, mod it out and carry on.

There's a problem, though: consoles, the land that mods forgot. In console games I've got to suck it up, be a man, close my eyes and mash the attack button until it's over. It's not the most effective strategy, but it's all I have. Well, all I had. In 2015 a game called *Bloodborne* came along and my plan became about as useful as tech support run by my mum.

Bloodborne is a game about... well... something. It doesn't directly tell you what, that would be too easy. Instead you have to piece it together from strange conversations, the scrawlings of the mad and architecture that looks like Tim Burton's downstairs bathroom after a fire. Instead of telling you directly what's going on, *Bloodborne* calls your mum up and lets you work it out via her reactions of 'NO!', 'Really?' and 'Well, I never!'

Here are some things that I'm about 80% sure happened. You play as a hunter, wielding a gun, a foldable saw and a rather fetching hat you clearly nicked from a *Pirates of the Caribbean* movie. Something called the Great One is trying to have a baby, the populace of Yharnam[2] have OD'd on the old blood and are now turning slowly into beasts. You go to a different dimension that may or may not be a living nightmare, fight a brain with eyes that drives you mad, meet someone's wet nurse and finally kick seven shades of *salmiakki* out of a monster from the moon. You then... uhhh... turn into a slug. Well, that's only if you've eaten three umbilical cords along the way.[3]

Look, I could dedicate this entire book to unravelling *Bloodborne*, but quite frankly I value my sanity. Just know that things are happening, you're probably involved and there are a thousand monsters between you and the last one. Yes, I know the first one killed you, but that's just the kind of game this is. Anything and everything can and will kill you. It's like living on Canvey Island.

2   A city that's a cross between Victorian London and the apocalypse.
3   Somehow I haven't made any of this up.

Around halfway through the game I got stuck. I was in a big house by a lake and couldn't work out how to progress. It seemed to be a dead end, but FromSoftware games never really have dead ends. Unless they do, which is the case about half of the time. Thinking about it, I think they just hate people who play video games. Understandable, to be honest.

Eventually an old man in the Pope's hat pointed off a ledge[4] and I noticed that the lake had a slight shimmer to it there. I leapt in and ended up on an infinite plane of water, under a massive pale moon. In the distance I saw a mass of life, horrible yet indiscernible. I approached it. The game gave it a name: 'Rom, the Vacuous Spider'. Uh-oh.

Rom, it turns out, is actually quite lovely. Yeah, she looks like the pubic lice of Cthulhu, but at least she doesn't look like a spider. Too many legs, a butt made of dandelion fuzz and the whole 'vacuous' title put me at ease. This was going to be fine.

Then it started to rain spiders.

I shan't describe these ones – I'm feeling faint just thinking about them – but know that they're really quite large and unpleasant. These spindly shits made beating Rom almost impossible. It's hard to judge when to dodge an attack when you're trying desperately hard to not look at the thing attacking you.

It took a long, long time but eventually the power of squinting and sitting far away from the TV won out. Rom was vanquished and the day was saved. Well, I think Rom was somehow holding back all the serious horror and her departure pretty much finished off a broken world, but that's for someone else to worry about. I'm pretty sure that the building-sized eldritch abominations had always been there.

---

4 I've no idea who he was but he dropped a nice item when I carved his spine in two.

Horrors from beyond our understanding aside, I was pumped that I'd conquered my fear and could now keep playing a game I really enjoyed. That was until I heard about the Nightmare of Mensis, a place that apparently made Rom's many-legged buddies look like friendly stuffed animals.

I found it much later in the game. A cathedral filled with a spider the size of the Eden Project. I beat it in one go, laugh-crying the whole way through. I saved at the next lantern and never went back. There may be lots of rare and valuable weapons in that area, but like the dead bodies of a few kids I was hired to look after, the spiders can keep them.

HARDWARE HISTORY: ATARI

Right, I know bugger all about Atari and have had limited access to their stuff in my life, so for this bit I'm handing over to someone who knows what they're on about.

Enter Stuart Ashen, author of *Terrible Old Games You've Probably Never Heard Of* and *Attack of the Flickering Skeletons: More Terrible Old Games You've Probably Never Heard Of*. Ashens (his online alias) is the right man for this job. He's also the *only* man for this job as all the other candidates died in a mysterious bus explosion.

So, take it away, Stuart!

Atari 2600 – Console – 1977

The mighty Atari 2600 is credited with popularising home video games, mostly because it did exactly that. Before it appeared, people were stuck playing the same *Pong* variants over and over until their teeth went grey, but the interchangeable game cartridges allowed for coloured blocks on your TV to pretend to be all sorts of different things.[1]

The primitive graphics forced you to use your imagination more than with modern games. For instance, while playing *The Empire Strikes Back* you had to constantly imagine that you were controlling a snowspeeder attacking AT-ATs to avoid facing the eldritch truth that your TV was showing a leaf attacking those terrifying spindly-limbed elephants from various Salvador Dalí paintings.

It wasn't all Hoth-based self-delusion for 2600 owners – they had to suffer the infamous movie tie-in game for *E.T. the Extra-Terrestrial*. Atari sensibly gave the project to their best programmer, but less sensibly gave him about twenty-five seconds to design and write the game. The result is an awful, boring mess which some people believe is the worst game ever, until they play through the back catalogues of the 80s home computers and realise it doesn't even qualify for the bottom fifty.

Much like every bloody console these days, the Atari 2600 evolved through various versions. The fake wood

---

1   At this point owners of the Fairchild Channel F shouted about how they'd already had cartridges for a year or so but nobody listened to them.

veneer of the early models gave way to black plastic, then later a 'slim' version called the Atari 2600 Jr. was produced for some reason. Plans for a further redesigned model with wireless joysticks were shelved at the eleventh hour after it was discovered that the joysticks transmitted their signal for about 1,000 feet and would thus interfere with consoles in other people's houses. This lack of basic planning continued throughout Atari's existence, and explains why that existence ceased.

Fun fact: Atari 2600 joysticks are the only consumer electronics capable of surviving a nuclear war.

Atari 5200 – Console – 1982

 Essentially a slightly altered Atari 400 home computer, the 5200 was more powerful than the 2600 and was Atari's answer to the Intellivision and ColecoVision.
Unfortunately Atari didn't answer the questions consumers were asking, such as 'Why can't I play my 2600 games on it?', 'Why are most of the games just new versions of ones I've already bought?' and 'Why does the system come bundled with a game that totally fails to show off its power, you twerps?'

The 5200 also had infamously dreadful controllers – weird analogue sticks that didn't self-centre, combined with twelve-button telephone keypads. They also oxidise too easily and will literally break while sitting brand new in an unopened box. Great work, lads.

Atari 2800 – Console – 1983

This was just a redesigned 2600 for the Japanese market. It was released six whole years after the machine came out in America, by which time it was farcically outdated. It went straight up against Nintendo's Famicom and did about as well as you'd expect.

Atari 7800 – Console – 1986

A serious attempt to take on the NES and Master System but not quite as good as either, the 7800 was at least backwards-compatible with 2600 cartridges. Although, as those games were nearly a decade old by that point, people weren't as bothered by that as they were with the 5200.

On the plus side, it didn't suffer from the sprite flickering that was so prevalent with the NES and Master System. On the minus side, it had a really disappointing games line-up and the same awful sound hardware as the ancient Atari 2600.[2]

Ultimately it sold under a tenth as many units as the Master System, and a tiny fraction of the NES. But it did have a great version of *Ballblazer*.

---

2   The idea was that games cartridges would feature their own sound hardware, but very few did.

Atari XEGS – Console – 1987

The XE Gaming System! Atari took their best home computer, the 65XE, and removed the keyboard and tape deck to make a console that just ran off cartridges. Then they sold you back the keyboard and tape deck, or included them in a bundle with a light gun.

Out of the thousands of games available for the Atari 8-bit computers, few were released on cartridge. You really needed the cassette deck attachment… but by then you may as well have bought a second-hand 65XE.

The XEGS is arguably the best attempt at console-ising a computer, mainly due to the ease of turning it into the proper computer it was cut down from in the first place. That pretty much sums up what a bad idea console-isation was in the first place really. If you want to see a real disaster, have a look at the Commodore 64GS or the Amstrad GX4000.

Atari Lynx – Handheld – 1989

To say the Lynx was technically superior to the Game Boy is a terrifying understatement. It didn't just beat it on power – it broke its back, tore it in half and urinated on its still twitching corpse.

It had a clear, bright, full-colour screen. It had custom chips that allowed it to smoothly scale graphics a year before the SNES was released and it did it better too. Unfortunately, it was also too expensive, had a sorely lacking game library, and wasn't anywhere near as portable due to a short battery life and being the size of a small planet. And bundling later releases with the risible *Batman Returns* didn't help. A revised version called the Lynx II went some way towards easing the size and battery problems but the Game Boy had captured the world's imagination while fitting in its pocket.

I absolutely love the Lynx. It's one of my very favourite gaming things, but even I had a Game Boy too.[3]

Atari Jaguar – Console – 1993

A year before the Sega Saturn and the PlayStation were released, Atari attempted to enter the 3D games market with their cartridge-based Jaguar. And as you probably already know, it didn't go well.

By the application of the infamous Atari Logic™ they brought back the giant telephone keypad from the 5200 for the controller, and bundled the console with a half-finished tech demo called *Cybermorph*. And things went downhill from there.

The low point may have been *Club Drive*, an attempt to go up against the fantastic *Ridge Racer* and *Daytona USA*. It was so bad that journalists openly laughed at it when it was unveiled at a big press event. It was not a success.

The Jaguar was a bit of a tragedy, really. Its hardware was never really taken advantage of during the machine's life, and the games library was full of low-quality efforts.

---

3   The Game Gear is still crap though. Worse than the Lynx at everything, and with a screen so blurry you may as well get someone else to describe what's happening to you. A pox on it.

Oddly, the case design of the Jaguar lives on, as the moulds were used to make a piece of dental equipment.

Atari Jaguar CD – Add-on – 1996

It still amazes me this was released in the UK as I have no memory of it at retail at all. It's a little toilet bowl that sits on your Jaguar and allows it to play titles from the Jaguar CD-ROM library! Which consisted of eleven games during the lifetime of the add-on. Only four of those were exclusive to the Jaguar CD, and only two of them are worth playing.

Atari Flashback – Dedicated Consoles – 2004+

A whole slew of plug-straight-into-your-TV-and-play-the-built-in-games things that play 2600 games. Originally a third-party company made ones that were  just a joystick, but then Atari produced ones that looked like little consoles.

There are loads of these. They all have different games, different cases, some can be hacked to add a cartridge port, there are even a couple of handheld models. And if the one I have is anything to go by, some of them just make a 'skrsrksrksrksrk' noise and show a couple of vertical lines when you plug them into a TV.

Ataribox – ? – ?

Some kind of crowdfunded electric box. Probably Android-based. Few people know, and fewer still care.

Atari Cyber Panther – Console – 2026

Famously mocked when announced for being a 3-bit console, everyone changed their tune when the first demos were revealed and the graphics were totally photorealistic. It transpired that the bits were so incredibly powerful that they were sentient, which is why only three were needed.

Unfortunately, no consoles lasted longer than a month before breaking down completely. Atari eventually admitted that in fact the consoles ran on two bits, but the bits had a tendency to argue so a third was installed to keep the peace between them. Over time the third bit would take the side of one of the others, murdering the remaining bit and rendering the console inoperative.

Atari were forced to refund all purchases and burned the faulty consoles in a huge bonfire in a New Mexico desert. Witnesses stated that many of the bits were still alive and 'screamed and screamed and screamed' for the first hour after the bonfire was lit. Atari refused to comment.

I got up, dusted myself off, fell over again
and gave up skiing forever

Developer: EA Canada
Publisher: EA Sports BIG
Platform: PS2, Xbox, GameCube
Released: 2003
What is it? A snowboard racing game set on an entire mountain.
What is it _really_? Cocaine for the eyeballs.

It's snowing outside my window right now. In fact, it's currently snowing outside everyone's window. A snowstorm has rolled in and dusted the whole of the UK with no more than a few inches of snow. Due to this, the entire country has shut down; all that's left on supermarket shelves are jars of pickled owl, and every single mode of public transport has fallen over and caught fire. It's a magical time of year.[1]

I always thought that the UK's inability to deal with more than sixty or so flakes of snow was limited to just work, travel and every basic societal function. I was unaware that it also affected the individual. That's until I went skiing.

Skiing is an odd sport. 'Who can go fast on the slippery thing?' is a game you can play at home with fluffy socks and a recently

---

1   Mid-June.

polished floor.[2] I don't know why you need to go to somewhere in Europe, strap two metre-rulers to your feet, wear a coat in a colour not seen since the 80s, haul yourself up a mountain via a chair on a string before crashing and shattering your femur into so many pieces even the most avid jigsaw-puzzler wouldn't know where to begin.

Alas, a few years back I found myself on a mountain[3] just outside Sofia, the capital of Bulgaria.[4] On my feet were rigid skiing boots, two sizes too small. On my head was a helmet, a rather fetching puce colour. On my body, hardly anything. It was twenty-four fucking degrees centigrade.[5] I've seen more ice on the ground while cleaning out my freezer.

My skiing instructor, a man with an accent thicker than a cement milkshake, informed me that to stop myself from falling down a hill to death, I simply had to twist my feet so that the skis made a triangle shape. I explained to him that my body was about as flexible as the dress code at a funeral, but he decided I was the learn-by-doing type, and pushed me down the mountain.

I fell over about two seconds later, three kilometres from my starting point. As I hit the ground I bent in two, kicked myself in the back of my own head and felt snow shoot up every exposed orifice as well as three concealed ones. The impact gave me an immediate nosebleed, shooting flecks of red blood over the white snow, and made anyone watching from a distance think that I was taken out by a sniper.

---

2   Wood preferable.
3   Mum always wanted a skiing holiday so as a family we traded this for a year of not having to do the washing-up.
4   One of the very few places in Europe I've ever been, yet in a slightly fun coincidence, the exact place my wife grew up as a child. I love it when the universe does that.
5   That's 72° Fahrenheit if you're American, 297° Kelvin if you know your science or 535° Rankine if you're insufferable.

I got up, dusted myself off, fell over again and gave up skiing forever.[6]

As I hung up the boots designed to decapitate me at shin level, I felt a little sad. I've spent so much time playing the SSX[7] series of games, I thought that maybe I would have learned something along the way. With the constant banging on that video game violence begets real violence, why aren't any other skills transferable? If you handed me a gun right now I could apparently clear a museum full of terrorists and yet somehow I don't know how to strap wood to my feet and bomb down a hill? Something's wrong here.

The SSX series focuses on snowboarding rather than skiing, but that's more semantics than anything. The only real difference between snowboarders and skiers is that snowboarders don't have to carry two poles around like an indecisive, ambidextrous javelin thrower. Also the shoes are actually shoes and not bomb-disposal suits just for your feet.

Skiing stories and shoe hatred out of the way, let's get this book about video games back on track. SSX 3, my favourite of the SSX series, was set on a tri-peaked mountain deep in the heart of a country with very lax health and safety rules. You chose from a wide selection of recent escapees from the local psychiatric ward and began your work of 'conquering the mountain'. A quick note on that: you accomplished the 'conquering' with winter sports, not violence. You're going down this mountain on a snowboard, not across it on some war elephants. Any blood spilled will be entirely your own.

There are four main events that you'll compete in to take over

---

6   Happily, though, the balcony of my room overlooked the training slopes and so I spent the next week eating tasty food, getting a tan, and watching people hurt themselves in hilarious ways. It's the best holiday I've ever been on.

7   Short for 'Snowboard Supercross'.

this hunk of rock. First up are races. They start simple enough, more long straights than an exclusively heterosexual basketball team, but before long you're grinding down massive glaciers as they crumble away from under you and leaping over ravines so large that you could easily hide the *Titanic* in them without anyone noticing. This mode culminates in a giant race down the game's *entire* mountain. It takes half an hour. On a vaguely interesting side note, Yuichiro Miura, the man famous for being the first to ski down Mount Everest, went down roughly a quarter of it in two minutes, twenty seconds. This means that the mountain in *SSX 3* is about three times taller than Everest. That's maths.

Next up are Big Air events. These are pretty much just massive ramps in front of cliffs that are as sheer as the emperor's new clothes. You'll gain speed, fly up into the air and then plummet for about seven times as long. Don't mess up the landing, though, or the only score you'll record will be on a seismograph.

Halfpipe events are next. These are great places to practice the biggest, baddest, and rotationiest tricks in your arsenal. Try to combo the entire round into one single, massive trick and snap your controller clean in two when you bugger it up with less than ten seconds left to go.

Finally, it's slopestyle events. Featuring more ramps than an M C Escher painting with wheelchair access, these events combine everything you've learned so far about racing, pulling off huge tricks and punching your opponents the moment the event starts for a special move boost.[8] They're my favourite by far, but that's mostly down to the seemingly infinite fireworks budget these event organisers are working with. Fireworks make everything cooler. Fact.[9]

---

8 This move, like so many others in the era of couch co-op, was something that you only told the other player how to do after you nailed them with it. Usually twice.

9 Fireworks are not toys and can cause serious harm. Please be cool responsibly.

As you start to win races you'll get some cash that you can spend in the many lodges in the game. You can buy new skills, new songs for your custom playlists and, most importantly of all, new clothes. Normally I don't care to play dress-up,[10] but *SSX 3* features the greatest costume item of all time, bar none. You can set your own head on fire. Screw increasing my top speed, I want to ignite my own face!

You know, now I think about it, maybe self-immolation would have helped during actual skiing. No, really! Everyone would get out of my way, the heat would make the snow melt, increasing my speed, and when I inevitably crash into the wilderness I'd be able to cook any deer I hit for dinner! Safety, speed and survivability all in one package. You know, I should patent this...

UPDATE: It's been six months since I wrote this and I'm sad to say that the patent fell through. Turns out it's already been done. Remember that skier on fire during the opening theme of *Malcolm in the Middle*? He's had the patent since the 70s. Bastard. I knew I hated skiing...

10   This applies to real life too. I'm currently in *Star Wars* pyjamas.

During this another team is staring at a wall
until they get a signal, at which point they
flashbang and charge a cupboard

Developer: Red Storm Entertainment, Ubisoft Milan
Publisher: Red Storm Entertainment
Platform: PC, PS1, Dreamcast
Released: 1999
What is it? A first-person shooter with added mission planning.
What is it *really*? Endless proof that I'm not the next Jack Bauer.

Do you ever wonder who sets the waypoints in your video games? You know, those floating, almost omniscient arrows that tell you exactly where to go even in uncharted enemy territory? Down the elevator shaft, into the secret laboratory, past the experiments where the voice in your ear will go, 'My God, what are they doing down here?' and then a left into a room to trigger the cutscene where the colonel betrays you. Who knew all this? Who is controlling you?

In *Rainbow Six: Rogue Spear* the answer is simple. It's you. At the start of each mission you're told the objective – free the hostages, neutralise the terrorists, etc. – and then you're given a big layered map of the whole level and told to plan a mission. You have up to four teams of four and have to plot where they come in, where they go, where they need to wait, what rooms they need to hit, how they have to hit them, who sacrifices themselves for the greater good, where they extract from, who calls Mrs Chavez to tell her about her husband, and whose turn it is to clean out the guttering back at RAINBOW HQ.[1]

Suffice to say, I was never very good at *Rainbow Six: Rogue Spear*. I loved the planning stage but sadly sent many, many counterterrorist officers to their deaths while fiddling with it. I flung so much human life into the unknown that Doctor Mordrid wrote an official letter of complaint. On one glorious occasion I sent three whole teams into a single room from different entrances at the same time. They all died. To this day I have no idea what killed them. Probably crossfire.

For any of you concerned about my nerd credentials, fear not: this next sentence is a doozy. I used to print out screenshots of my plans so I could check and annotate them mid-mission. Am I the most boring man in history? Possibly! It gets worse. I found them all in the loft recently. Hundreds of pieces of paper in those plastic bags with the colourful zips. One bag for each mission. I did this as a child. Fear me.

Anyway, here are the highlights!

Pandora Trigger – USA – 04/08/2001

The Museum of Art in New York City is under attack. There are several hostages, including the daughter of the French prime minister. On top of that the walls are adorned with millions of dollars' worth of masterpieces. Precision is crucial.

Crucial, but apparently not essential. Basically it looks like I ran everyone into the hostage room and ran out again. Not my finest hour, especially as I'm sure there was a whole bunch of trial and error beforehand to find that room. Well, it can only get better from here on out.

Right?

---

1 Remembering to designate someone to set the VCR to record *The Simpsons* at the right time was always the hardest part.

Arctic Flare – Japan – 09/09/2001

An oil tanker has been attacked. Hostages are on board and the terrorists are threatening to blow up the entire ship. The leader is on the bridge by a very large window. He has the remote that controls all the explosives. I start the opposite end of the boat to him with fifteen sniper-rifle-wielding friends. The glass breaking makes every other terrorist go and see what made the noise. Doesn't take long, this one.

Sand Hammer – Oman – 04/10/2001

A water treatment plant is under siege. Terrorists are threatening to put deadly neurotoxin in the water. I think they stole this plot from an episode of *Lassie*.

Goddamn, my plan for this one is impossible to follow. The paths I've laid out look like four sets of headphones that have had a fight in a jogger's pocket. At one point Bravo team goes into a room, leaves, turns around, goes back in and leaves again. During this another team is staring at a wall until they get a signal, at which point they flashbang and charge a cupboard. I guess this one follows the programmer mantra of 'If it works, leave it and back away slowly.'

Lost Thunder – Kosovo – 24/10/2001

This mission is about killing a sniper in a bell tower. There's probably more to it than that but up until a bullet goes through the back of that guy's head, my plan is tight, meticulous and clinical. After that point it goes back to the usual scribblings you'd find on a wall next to any unattended child that owns a crayon.

Perfect Sword – Belgium – 13/11/2001

Usual story. Terrorists, hostages, a grounded plane. Most of the hostages are in the seating area, most of the terrorists are in the cargo area. One terrorist has a human shield at the main door making that a difficult way in. The cargo door is open but, like I said, it's full of terrorists.

Three teams use a moving refuelling truck to sneak under the plane. One team stays on a hill nearby. For some reason only one of the members of that team seems to have a long-range weapon. I assume the rest are picking flowers to give to Sarge when we get back to base.

As the other teams get under the plane one of them lines up under the cargo ramp; the other two wait under the main door. The hill team snipe the terrorist with the hostage; the three teams under the plane move up and in, seize the hostages and escape back to the extraction point. Mission successful.

Well, except for the cargo team. They just run all the way through the hold and die in a hail of gunfire. Their deaths are so certain I didn't even bother to set a waypoint home for them. No hope, no chance, just a one-way ticket to death aboard a 747. On the bright side, their families will probably get a good handful of Air Miles out of that.

Oh, don't look at me like that. Every plan requires a suicidal distraction. Well, every one of mine does, at least. That's probably why they asked me to stop hosting the church fête.

Crystal Ark – Georgia – 19/11/2001

There are eighteen missions in *Rainbow Six: Rogue Spear*. This will be the last one I cover in this book. No, I'm not holding out for the sequel, I just never finished this level. Ever. In eighteen years.

It's simple enough. A stealth mission to plant surveillance bugs in a large house in the country. Detection means failure, and the probable downfall of civilisation as we know it. It took me far too many goes before I realised I shouldn't be sending sixteen men in to do this. I get the feeling that a team of poorly trained geese may have performed better at this than professional counterterrorism team RAINBOW.[2]

I ploughed on, throwing away plan after plan.[3] Sometimes I'd get caught planting the bug, sometimes I'd get caught round a blind corner and, on one wonderful occasion, I just fell right out of a goddamn window. This mission required the stealth and patience of Batman. Shame I brought the Hulk.

I never did finish that level. My dad, who I was taking it in turns with for most of this game, didn't either. He got damn close, though, planting both devices before being scuppered by a guard with a moustache waiting just outside the house. That moment taught me a few new swear words, let me tell you.

For this book I actually went back and played that level again. I did it with ease, watching and waiting for guards to come and go, planting both devices and legging it out of the front door. Moustache Face nearly spotted me, but I took cover in a nearby bramble. A few minutes later and the mission was done. My white whale of a level, conquered disappointingly easily. I assumed I'd fail and this bit would end with hilarious japes. Instead it ends on this rather dull note. Sorry about that.

You were right, Thomas Wolfe. You can't go home again.

---

2   Super terrifying name there, by the way.
3   One of the printouts for this mission has a large splatter of blood in the dead centre of it. I'm not sure where this came from, possibly a concentration-based nosebleed. It does, however, explain the sheer number of bats we have in the loft.

God, I miss LAN parties

Developer: Ironclad Games
Publisher: Stardock
Platform: PC
Released: 2008
What is it? A space-based real-time strategy game.
What is it *really*? The reason I never got my degree.

Did you know that in 2007–08 there was a UK-exclusive energy drink tie-in to the TV series *24*? '24 CTU: The Energy Drink', to give it its full name, was a can full of all the sugars and chemicals you need to finally eradicate the concept of sleep from your life forever. I tracked down the press release for this 92p can of heart palpitations and found this beautiful line:

> *'As a point of difference from other energy drinks, 24 CTU has been developed with a unique citrus taste.'*

I note this simply because my only memory of the drink was that it was the foulest thing I've ever tasted. It sat somewhere between concentrated lemon and what I imagine the inside of a battery tastes like. Somehow they managed to create the flavour equivalent of stepping on Lego.

However, for two glorious days in what is now generally

considered to be a wasted time at the University of Leicester,[1] it was all I drank. No water, no coffee, just something that tasted like it was bottled in Fukushima.

The counter to this influx of caffeine and B vitamins was a tower of around twenty Domino's Meateor pizzas. A pizza of such heavily condensed meat and cheese that any attempts by the 24 drink to speed my heart up would be ruthlessly countered by the sheer amount of fatty build-up the pizzas would cause me to develop.

God, I miss LAN parties…

Two dorm rooms in the university[2] had been overrun by four beefy, LED-filled PCs that were doing their best to bring about localised global warming. A single LAN cable ran out the window of my first-floor room, down the building, and into the enemy territory of Team Downstairs. At 8 p.m. sharp, the game began.

Then, at 9.12 p.m., we finished troubleshooting why one of the PCs couldn't find the game[3] and we began, again.

Sins of a Solar Empire is a whopping great space strategy game. Your objective is to conquer your way across one or more solar systems, taking over planets, blowing up people with different flags to you, and generally dealing with all the red tape that comes with running a galactic government. Last person to have their planets turned into molten slag wins.

We fine men and women of Team Upstairs started quickly, agreeing to focus on expansion first and worry about defence later. Our scout ships found a set of four planets in a line around two-thirds of the way across the solar system that we

---

1   A lovely university, mostly for the fact that the main building looks exactly like Optimus Prime's head. Look up the Charles Wilson Building if you don't believe me. It's uncanny.

2   Well, I say 'in the university'. My dorm was actually a fifty-two-minute walk away from the university itself. My attendance that year was 26%. I wonder why…

3   Goddamn IP forwarding.

started in. The map was across two systems, but the only way to travel to the other was via the sun in the centre. If we raced across and stole the planets then we could cut Team Downstairs off from the rest of the map and the other system. We quickly assembled our colony fleets and sent them out into the black, hoping that Team Downstairs wouldn't have the same idea. They didn't. A short while later the planets were ours. This was a huge advantage and we'd achieved it with no resistance. No resistance whatsoever...

It was quiet. Too quiet. Even for space, which is pretty bloody quiet.

I was just unpacking my last few planetary moving boxes when they turned up. An enemy fleet that darkened the sky. Admittedly it may not have been the enemy fleet that did that – space is sort of dark by default and it was night at the time – but it was still a lot of ships. They opened fire.

My planet fell almost immediately. The rest of Team Upstairs scrambled a defence and attacked back. Team Downstairs seemed surprised at this. I'm assuming they didn't know we had other planets in the area, and retreated. I managed to recover the planet but it was clear that the wheels were looking to come off our plan. If they attacked again, we were finished.

They didn't attack. In fact it was four hours later when we next even saw them. We'd spent the time taking over the two-thirds of the solar system we'd cordoned off and had built a rather huge armada to defend it all. We sent a few scouts through to their side to see what was happening but they got shot down instantly like the geeky lead at the start of a coming-of-age film. Maybe they were lying in wait, ready to spring a huge trap on us. Maybe they'd all died of heart attacks or energy-drink poisoning. One thing was sure: we needed more information. We just didn't know how we'd get it.

Cheating is a word with far too many negative connotations.

Hacking and things like that take the fun away, but there's that fun, inventive level of cheating that in my opinion gets a bad rap. Creative cheating is an art and, as I lowered the desktop microphone out of the window to listen in on Team Downstairs' conversations, I couldn't help but wonder which famous artist would appreciate this level of cheating most. Probably Caravaggio. He was a bit of a lad.

For the next few hours I monitored every word from that room like a sci-fi Radar O'Reilly. Strangely, nothing they were saying made any sense. They were talking about planets that weren't on the map, resources in abundances that made no sense and fleet movements they weren't making. I thought they might have made it to the second solar system but they couldn't have without getting past us. Then again, the little tracker on the bottom of the screen placed their team in the lead in economy and military strength. What the hell was going on?

The sun started to rise. I was about to pull the microphone back in when I heard a word. One word that had the potential to be our complete downfall.

'Wormhole.'

They *were* in the other system. We'd not bothered to research the technology needed to take us there so never checked. We thought we'd been clever and taken two-thirds of the map when, in actual fact, we'd locked ourselves into just a third of it. We pushed forward hard, obliterating the defences they had abandoned there, and found the wormhole. A few scouts were sacrificed to discover the massive armada on the other side. Our defensive lines moved, covering the wormhole and the sun. We'd both dug in and waited for the other to make a move.

Suddenly, words that would make even an Australian blush filled my ears. It was morning and I hadn't brought the microphone back up. They'd seen it.

This meant war.

For the next twenty-four hours straight we engaged in trench warfare. Sleep was caught in between skirmishes, toilet breaks were rapid and the pizzas had formed a thin layer of grease over every surface in the room. Thousands of ships were designed, dispatched and decimated. Nerves started to fray, mistakes were being made and arguments sprang up like pyramid schemes from your Facebook friends.

Finally, the pressure pushed Team Downstairs too far. Late on Sunday, the door to my room opened, a hand appeared, and a cockroach was thrown in.

I'll never understand why people cheat. I think it's morally wrong to try and use outside forces in a friendly game like this, especially when you know everyone in a room is terrified of bugs. Anyway, this wasn't a time for ethics, there was a huge creature in the room that needed addressing. After around ten minutes of freaking out, my citrus-flavour-addled brain came up with the incredible idea of smashing it with a bin, the result of which was a dented bin and an unharmed cockroach. It flew out of the window shortly after that, presumably to go and leave a bad review of my room on the cockroach internet.[4]

Emergency over, we went back to our PCs just in time to see our defensive line fall and the beginning of the end of our empire. It held on bravely but finally collapsed in the early hours. We met up with Team Downstairs, had some laughs over breakfast and then all slept for a few days straight.

I like this story because it shows how good video games are at bringing people together. This wasn't just an excuse to skip lectures; this was the forming of an unbreakable bond that would last forever. Thanks to caffeine and fat we all lost a few years off our lives, but isn't that a fine price to pay for something as

---

4   I checked but it still looks like it's in beta. Loads of bugs.

wonderful as friendship?

To put a slight dampener on that lovely point, I've never spoken to any of these people since I left university and can't even remember their names. I think there was an incident involving a Twilight Imperium playing piece and someone's neck but my memory of that time is hazy at best. Apparently intense amounts of sugar can rot your brain right out of your skull. Who knew? Not me. Unless I did. I can't remember.

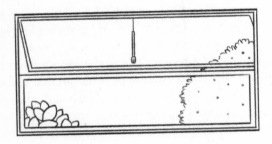

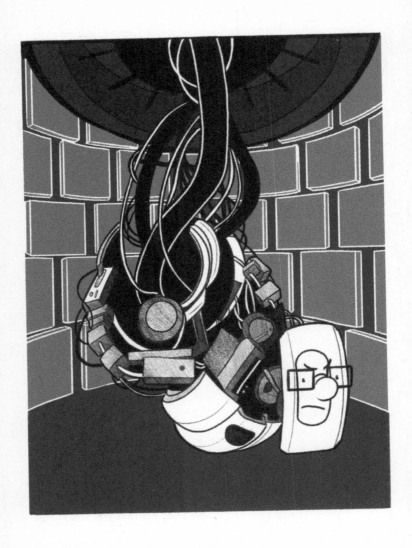

GLaDOS, like Master Control Program, HAL and
Carol Vorderman before her, is a totally evil
computer hell-bent on just two things: making you
feel stupid and killing everyone

36 PORTAL

APERTURE
LABORATORIES

Developer: Valve Corporation
Publisher: Valve Corporation
Platform: PC, Xbox 360, PS3
Released: 2007
What is it? A reality-bending first-person puzzle game.
What is it *really*? Delicious and moist.

I'm surprised that the English language doesn't fold up into itself and vanish when people use the expression 'nothing's perfect'. If that were true then the phrase itself would be perfect, and therefore would be wrong. If it's not true, well, what was the point in saying it?

Contrary to popular yet incorrect sayings, some things *are* perfect. The look of wonder in a child's eyes as they slowly understand a little bit more of the world they've found themselves in. Watching the sun softly set at the beach while eating an ice cream. Tits. All these things are perfect.

Portal is perfect. Designed by Kim Swift and based on her award-winning student game, *Narbacular Drop*, *Portal* was really only supposed to be filler, released as a little extra in *The Orange Box*,[1] and yet it managed to surpass everything else

---

1 A compendium of Valve's games featuring *Half-Life 2, Half-Life 2: Episode One* and *Two* and *Team Fortress 2* from back when Valve actually made video games.

inside. It was like buying a box of cereal and finding out that the free gift at the bottom of the bag was better cereal.

In *Portal* you place portals. Two of them. They can only be on flat surfaces that are stationary or in constant motion. Anything, including you, that enters one of the portals comes out the other one. Momentum is conserved during this transfer. The laws of thermodynamics, however, can go take a running leap into a perpetual motion machine. You could spend hours debating the physics of these portals, but don't. Leave that to me. That'll be my next book.

The superb puzzles in the game come from the fact that you can tell the space–time continuum to swivel on it and connect any wall, floor or ceiling in the world to any other wall, floor or ceiling. This lets you fling yourself across gaps, sneak up behind adorable murder turrets or simply use bridges made of condensed light to travel large distances over what may or may not be raw sewage.

The star of *Portal* isn't the mute, unnamed player character,[2] but rather the evil AI berating you throughout the length of the game. GLaDOS, like Master Control Program, HAL and Carol Vorderman before her, is a totally evil computer hell-bent on just two things: making you feel stupid and killing everyone. Occasionally both at the same time.

The rising tension that GLaDOS brings to this collection of clinically white test chambers is almost full-on horror by the end. She knows what you're doing and is definitely going to kill you when you're done testing. Well, she says that there will be a party but you know what she's talking about. Murder, and not of the 'on the dance floor' variety.

Then, after you smash her into pieces, she berates you one final time. In song, of course.

---

2 The only mention of her name, Chell, is in the credits. 'Thanks for the use of their face' is credited to 'Alésia Glidewell – Chell.'

In short, *Portal* is a masterpiece of design, pacing and tension. In long, it's the same sentiment, only with fancier words. Like equanimity. Or Machiavellian.

A must-play.

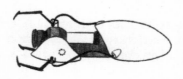

You know the drill: lots of inflatable things, a ball pit that you could theoretically hide a blue whale in and the overwhelming smell of feet

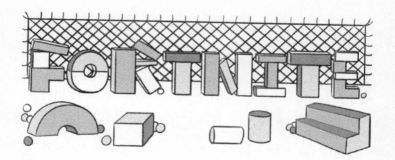

Developer: Epic Games
Publisher: Epic Games
Platform: PC, PS4, Xbox One, Switch
Released: 2017
What is it? An online, battle royale-style shooter.
What is it *really*? An excuse to kill children.

During my time at primary school[1] there were certain items that made you instantly cool. Shiny Charizard cards, Game Boys, Pogs; have any of these on you and you'd basically get a playground promotion. Once I saw a kid with a Pog sticker on his Game Boy that had the Pokémon Card Game on it and the next day he was teaching us numerals.

Above all of these things, however, there was the holiest grail of cool. Get this baby and you'd be cool *for life*. It was rare, impossible for some, but if you were very, very lucky, you could have a birthday party... at Kids Kingdom.

Kids Kingdom is *the* soft play centre for kids.[2] You know the drill: lots of inflatable things, a ball pit that you could theoretically hide a blue whale in and the overwhelming smell of feet. For adults it's a chance to get a half-hour break from

---

1 Six years, but I was out after five for good behaviour.
2 And by 'the' I mean 'the local'.

hyperactivity. For kids, it's nirvana.

For years Kids Kingdom eluded me. Parties happened, but outside my social circles.[3] Reports from these visits were tortuous, yet addictive. Apparently there was a death slide, ball pits as far as the eye could see and, slap bang in the centre of it all, Jelly Mountain. An inflatable so large that you need oxygen canisters to climb it.

I progressed through school, constantly keeping up with the cafeteria grapevine, trying to find out who was next to go to the promised land. I'd make friends with anyone, even if they were years below me. I just had to go. I had to see its beauty with my own eyes.

As I approached double figures, I started to worry. Pretty soon my knees and back would give out from old age, I'd not have the energy for the full thirty minutes and I'd have pubes that would snag on the rope swings, whatever pubes were. I was in crisis, and in a moment of madness I took a final, desperate shot at happiness. I decided to make friends with girls.

Now I know what you're all thinking, and yes, I had my cooties jabs before this. I'm not an idiot.

It worked, though. A female friend of mine, who shall remain nameless,[4] had a birthday at Kids Kingdom and, fanfare please, invited me! For three weeks I didn't sleep, I just lay there, fantasising about Jelly Mountain. The day couldn't come quickly enough.

It never came. My friend fell ill and cancelled her birthday party. A few weeks later she came back to school, but Kids Kingdom was never mentioned again. I was hurt. I couldn't believe she had done this to me, even after I wrote all those nice

---

3　My circles included Paint Eaters Anonymous and Friends of the Attendance Register.

4　Mostly because I've forgotten who it was.

things about her on the inside of my science textbook. Yeah, she had to have an organ removed, but what's life without Jelly Mountain? Worthless, that's what.

Days, weeks, months passed. Exams came and went. I could barely go on. Cartoons bored me, video games were too expensive, Pogs... well, honestly, Pogs were shit from the get-go, I just didn't want to say anything. My education was in a downward spiral and my voice was the highest it would ever be. Life was dreadful.

That's when I got the invite. Not a paper one, someone couldn't make it, but an invite all the same. Kids Kingdom. Next Saturday. Bring a present.

It was happening.

I remember stepping into Kids Kingdom, eyes wide, hands unencumbered by presents because I was a secondary invite and you don't get shit for that. It was breathtaking. Rope bridges dangled from every surface, slides tied knots around each other and the balls in the ball pit lapped gently at the shore. A hundred kids ran around it, filling the air with the sounds of pure glee. In the middle of it all, the height of many men, was Jelly Mountain.

Words cannot do Jelly Mountain justice, but I shall try my best. The mountain itself was a multicoloured inflatable pyramid with a flat top, gleaming in the fluorescent lighting. It was on a base, also inflatable, also multicoloured. Around the base was a ball pit moat, about three miles deep. I wept openly, tears of joy stinging my cheeks. It was everything I'd ever hoped for.

I didn't approach Jelly Mountain to start with. It was too intimidating. I worked my way around the mazes of slides and climbing walls, watching children fail to climb to its peak whenever I got a clear view. One boy got close, but a loose sock caused him to tumble back down. Some girls laughed. I made a note.

'Five minutes left, guys!'

I was on the top of the death slide when the call went out. What? No! Impossible! I shot down the vertical slide and was on my feet before the momentum was quite on my side. I had to get to the mountain, and fast. I must conquer it. It was my destiny.

Alas! It seemed that every other kid in the world had had the same idea. By the time I got to the mountain it was nothing more than a huge pile of bodies. Undeterred, I leapt majestically from the entranceway to the base of the mountain. The impact caused three children near me to fall into the ball pit, never to be seen again.

By this point I'd seen a few children make it, but they didn't last long at the top. I watched as someone tried to pull his friend up, only to be betrayed and cast into the ball pit below. Things were getting dirty, and I don't mean in the fun mud-pie sort of way.

I flung myself at the mountain, trying to climb its ice-smooth surface. It was no good; nothing to grip onto and zero friction from socks made it impossible. I needed a better opening gambit and, as the fat kid next to me fell, I realised that God herself wanted me up this mountain.

I leapt, propelled by the air displacement of Porky Roebuck's landing. My arms extended, fingers outstretched. Boom. I'd managed to grab onto the very edge of the mountain's peak. Sadly, I didn't have the arm strength to go any further. If only I'd spent more time on the monkey bars. God damn you, jungle gym. GOD DAMN YOU!

Distraught, but still holding on, I looked around. It was carnage. Bodies everywhere, limbs pointing every which way, huge tidal waves of balls flying around from the impacts. Then I saw *her*.

Everything stood still and got very, very quiet.

A strange feeling threw itself against my chest.

I'd never felt this way before.

I caught her eye, she caught mine.

We smiled.

I placed my foot on her stupid, appendixless face and pushed hard.

She fell into the balls.

I pulled myself up.

The view from the top of Jelly Mountain was exquisite, made even more so by the failure of my peers surrounding it. I stood, raised my arms to my side, and basked in the warm glow of victory. I had won. I had finally won.

They say you never hear the bullet. I didn't. One minute I was on top of the world, the next I was falling, catching the hollow plastic ball that just bounced off my skull out of the corner of my eye. I landed on the base but the height of the fall made me ricochet into the ball pit. I lay where I landed, slowly sinking beneath the wash. In the distance I heard a member of staff blow a whistle and tell my assailant off for the throw. It didn't matter. The damage was done. I'd had my Icarus moment. I'd flown too close to the sun; now was my time to burn.

I slowly sank beneath the balls.

So, yeah, *Fortnite Battle Royale* is basically that but with guns.

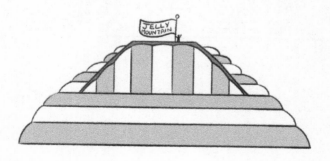

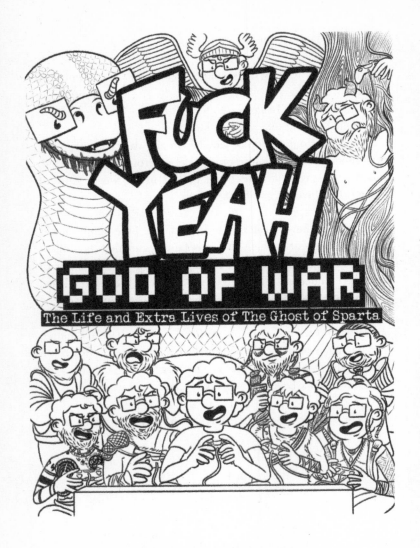

Fuck Yeah, God of War

Developer: SIE Santa Monica Studio
Publisher: Sony Interactive Entertainment
Platform: PS4
Released: 2018
What is it? A hack-and-slash set in Norse mythology.
What is it *really*? A funeral procession.

I don't like children.

The reason for this is simple: I keep getting asked to make one.

> *'So, have you thought about having kids?'*

Yes. I've thought about having them. I've also thought about what would happen if my house were to suddenly fall into a volcano. To be honest, I'm not sure which is worse. You can probably get insurance for the latter.

Kids by themselves are fine. I look upon their struggle to learn about our complicated world with a certain fondness, much as I would a dog with a blanket over its head. My personal issues with them come from the social siege they inflicted upon my life the moment I was married. Between 'I do' and the first sliver of confetti slamming into the ground we'd been asked about them no fewer than 126 times.

At my age[1], every fucker[2] I know[3] is shitting out a kid.[4] Interesting, fabulous people are now all endlessly posting the same pictures of unaware, gormless flesh lumps alongside captions such as, 'Look, Madge is asleep.' Of course Madge is asleep. She's a baby. It's what they do. If she busts out the speech from Act V of *Love's Labour's Lost* in between levels of shitting that would rival someone with lactose intolerance drowning in milk, feel free to let me know.

Let me put it another way: kids are like Harrier Jump Jets. The Harrier is fun and important, but I wouldn't want to own one myself. They're loud, take up loads of space and are wildly expensive. They can also levitate using only strong bursts of air but I fear that to further expand on that point would lower the tone of this book to the point of crassness.

Violently segueing this back onto topic, video games are slowly starting to include more parents as lead characters and, therefore, more kids. A decade or two ago, developers went out of their way to avoid having children in games. *Half-Life 2* features an energy field that suppresses procreation,[5] *The Elder Scrolls Online* seems to have perfected birth control, yet not invented the mattress, and for a city built and named after sin, Vice City's citizens seem to see about as much action as the Apostolic Palace.

However, times are changing. During E3 2016, Sony revealed that one of their classic characters was now a dad. It was *God of War* star Kratos, a man who we'd last seen punching his father's face so many times that what was left looked like a watermelon that had been thrown off the London Eye.

---

1   29 Part II.
2   Friend.
3   Follow on Twitter.
4   Experiencing the miracle of childbirth.
5   The closer you get to the point of climax, the more the field makes you think about every English teacher you've ever had.

This wasn't going to work.

Making Kratos a father is like hiring a blender full of knives as a babysitter. Kratos isn't a man, he's solidified anger. In his first three adventures on PS2, anyone who stood up to him ended up as pâté. The series starts with him killing his wife and daughter, somehow without even noticing, and ends after he's destroyed the whole world by accident. He's about as ready to look after a kid as a top-heavy cabinet that isn't attached to the wall.

But there he was, bearded and now living in Norse mythology – probably because there wasn't any Greek mythology left alive to live in – and hunting with his son, Atreus. Gone was the zoomed-out camera, replaced by an over-the-shoulder number. Gone was his iconic weapon of choice, the Blades of Chaos. Gone was pretty much every identifier that this was the same game, series and even bloke.

This really wasn't going to work.

Eventually 2018 rolled around[6] and *God of War* was released. It was reviewed exceptionally well so, having a schedule about as packed as the inside of a blimp, I picked up a copy to play over the weekend.

Fifty hours later I watched the credits roll on my favourite game of this generation so far.

Somehow, *somehow*, director Cory Barlog took a character whose main hobby is making people headless, and humanised him. It's all still there, the eviscerating, the butchering and the deicide, but that all becomes the B-plot to what is, quite frankly, one of the most enthralling relationships in gaming history.

You see, video games have never been great at love. Romantic relationships peak with a twenty-second cutscene of some squelching and 95% of that looks like it was shot by a

---

6   I'm sure 2016 lasted about a decade.

cameraman who only has interest in a nearby wall or lampshade. That's probably for the best, though; when two characters kiss during a cutscene, more often than not it looks like mannequins that have accidentally fallen onto each other in the front window of a Debenhams.

Parental love is somehow even worse. If your character has a parent, then they're either the secret baddie, are dead to add some angst, or have a mysterious past. Usually all three. If your character has an offspring, then... well, aside from a bit of cow herding in *Red Dead Redemption*, I actually can't think of another game where you simply get to parent a child. *Crusader Kings II* is the only game to spring to mind and in that I'm normally trying to off the little shits if they're born anything other than genetically perfect.

Finally, horse love is well represented and tastefully presented most of the time, but I'll stop talking about *Crusader Kings II* now.[7]

God of War doesn't let you get your equine lust on, but it does understand how raw and cutting love can be. Kratos and Atreus have just lost the most important person in their lives, a wife and a mother, and are taking her ashes to be scattered on the highest point of the nine realms as her last request. On the way they grieve, fight and eventually open up to one another. Every step feels honest, natural and loving. Every emotion deserved and real. This isn't a story about saving the world or murdering gods, it's a funeral procession. The gods just get in the way a bit, much to the dismay of their own necks.

Right, enough blabbing on about mushy stuff like love, emotions and anything that isn't shouting. Let's talk about weapons.

Atreus' go-to is a bow and arrow, with his mum's dagger on

---

7   You can sleep with a horse, promote it to a bishop, breed it with your family and eventually let horses run the world. Note: this only applies to *Crusader Kings II*. This is not a comment on the Royal Family.

the side. He's basically an unkillable distraction, like a fly in a meth lab, but watching him stab a nether demon in the nethers always brings a proud tear to my eye. I taught him that. Literally. The game has RPG elements.

Kratos has a magic axe that he throws away more times than you do those plastic bags local charities post through your letterbox. Then, when the time is right, he recalls it, causing it to detach from whatever entrails it happens to be nested in and fly back to his waiting hand. This is up there with *Spiderman 2*'s web-swinging for most satisfying game mechanic of all time. The feel of weight this axe has when returning is simply delightful. I spent many hours throwing it into trees and bringing it back, while my son sat there, wondering why I'd play catch with a bush and not him.[8]

Enemies are a nicely varied bunch. There's bastards, big bastards, double bastards with wings, sneaky bastards and magic bastards. There's a boss fight with a right bastard very early on in the game that I'd argue is the greatest superhero battle ever captured in any medium, and the secret Valkyrie bastards are some of the most bastardly bastards to ever bastard.

I can't write a chapter on this game without talking about the camerawork. From start to finish, the entire game features one single shot. No cuts. You're with Kratos from the opening menu to the closing credits. Some of the moments, like the arrival of the whoppingly massive world serpent, Jörmungandr, took my breath away for minutes at a time. I don't think we'll see a game pass this level of visual flourish and care until the next console generation. Maybe not even then.

Did I mention that I *really* like this game?

You should play *God of War*. Buy or rent a PS4 if you have

---

8   It's because you can't throw it at the kid. Oh, fuck off, like you didn't try it too.

to, just go and play it. Life is good and the fact that *God of War* exists is proof. *Battlestar Galactica* composer Bear McCreary outdoes himself with the soundtrack, *Stargate SG-1*'s Christopher Judge[9] scores a second career-defining performance as Kratos, and I've just thought of about forty more things I want to mention so I'm stopping now before the book title has to be changed to *Fuck Yeah, God of War*.

To conclude, I've found out something interesting. In 2015 the *Daily Telegraph*, a paper for the sort of people who think recycling would make them too liberal, said that the average cost of raising a child in the UK was £230,000. In 2011 a Harrier sold on eBay for £70,000. In 2014 one sold at auction for £105,800. With that £54,200 left over you could rent a hangar at about £850 a year[10] and fuel them for a couple of grand.[11]

OK, so I was wrong. Kids aren't like Harrier Jump Jets. They're far, far more expensive.

---

9   I met Christopher Judge once. He's as lovely as he is massive and he's seriously fucking massive.

10 I called my local airport for this piece of information.

11 The guy at the airport knew so much! Also, I might be on a government list right now!

The sun was starting to set as I drove down
that long desert road

AFTERWORD

About a decade ago I was roaming around America. This was my gap year and, somehow, I found myself heading towards Tucson, Arizona. Long story short, I'd had to flee a film set due to a funding mishap and a little bit of a visa issue. I think by this point I'd headbutted at least one TSA agent, maybe more.

The sun was starting to set as I drove down that long desert road. My vehicle was a stolen blue Ford Mustang Boss 302, already stolen when I stole it, and I had Christian rock on the radio. If the radio's dial hadn't been shot off, I'm sure I would have been listening to something else.

I'd just finished yet another solo game of I spy when I noticed a man at the side of the road. He waved me down and, as I pulled up, I noticed that his parked car was more than a little bit on fire. He asked if he could borrow a phone. I explained that a large scorpion had run off with mine some twenty or so miles back, but I'd be more than happy to give him a lift somewhere. He thanked me endlessly, grabbed a few things out of his burning husk of an automobile, and took the seat next to me.

As we drove along the dust bowl that makes up half of America, I realised something. I'd seen this man before somewhere, I just couldn't place him. I mentioned this and, to my surprise, the man said the same thing back to me! We'd met before, but he couldn't remember where either!

For the next half hour we sat there, trading places, names and events, trying to find the connection. Brother's wedding?

No. The traditional Christmas piss-up after work last year? Nada. That time someone gently bumped into me on the London Underground on 12 August 2003 at around 3.10 in the afternoon? Nope. This went on for some time and eventually we slipped into a thoughtful, awkward silence. Where the hell did I know this guy from?

Wait, that was it! I worked it out! Stacie Monroe's birthday in 1994! I'd had a bit too much Ribena and was deciding if I wanted to cut the hair of her favourite doll! He convinced six-year-old me to do it! I knew I recognised him! It was the devil!

Satan laughed and slapped his rotting knee. How could he have forgotten that! She cried for hours! The rest of the journey was full of laughter as we caught each other up on the past few years of our busy lives. My dodgy A-levels and new flat, his perpetual fight with the Eternal Lord and Creator of All. It was like we'd never missed a beat!

By the time we'd pulled up in Tucson night had fallen. The stars shone over us as we said our goodbyes. Lucifer thanked me from the bottom of his lack of heart and said if there was anything he could do for me, I shouldn't even hesitate to ask.

Anyway, long story short, that's how I became a successful and famous YouTuber.[1][2][3] This book was just an inevitable part of that.

Next up for my career, *Strictly Come Dancing*.

...

Fuck.

---

1 Some of the details are fuzzy but I'm sure that's it...
2 Also, if you're reading this after the year 2020, YouTube was a website that hosted the videos of egomaniacs.
3 'Successful' and 'famous' compared to, say, a Victorian juggler.

FUCK YEAH

VIDEOGAMES

THE LIFE & EXTRA LIVES OF A PROFESSIONAL NERD

Daniel Hardcastle
Foreword by Tim Schafer
Illustrated by Rebecca Maughan

This is why I've spent the last year and a half writing
a book about video games. They're fucking amazing

After afterword

Hang on a second. I'm not quite done with you yet.

You can find out who someone really is through how they play a game. Any game. Video games, board games, a sandpit with a bright red bucket on top – play is the ultimate expression of creativity and personality. Let me prove it to you.

My mum is the loveliest person I know. She's kind, brilliant and is definitely getting me a massive Christmas present after this sentence. I gave my mum the controls to *Grand Theft Auto V* once and she played tennis, dressed the characters up in fancy suits and complimented every person she walked past on the street. Basically, a loveliness overload.

However, at one point an NPC tried to steal a car right in front of her. In response, she shot at him to make him back off, stole the car herself and chased him down in the car while he was still on foot for *over half an hour*. It was like a horror movie. Yet, for some reason, hearing this guy plead for his very life was also strangely familiar. Then it clicked. The guy was feeling exactly how I used to when I hadn't done the chores I'd promised to do as a kid. Dread it. Run from it. Mum finds you hiding under the duvet all the same.

Let's take some more examples from the rest of my family when they play games. My soulmate Rebecca panics during every single battle, yet wins them all anyway through steely determination and handwritten notes. My sister can kick the shit out of me at anything, even if she's never tried it before, and my dad... well my dad just does his own thing.

This is why I've spent the last year and a half writing a book about video games. They're fucking amazing. Not only do they bring us together, giving us great memories and lasting friendships, but they help us understand each other a little better. Games are about connecting people, whether it's the people on your couch, friends you've made online, or even the people who make them to share the stories in their heads. This world of ours is better when we work together, when we understand each other, and games are brilliant at helping us do just that.

One final example, then I'll get out of your hair until the next self-indulgent book of mine comes along.[1]

The best thing about playing video games for a living, aside from the look of sheer jealousy when I tell that to children, is the ~~money poontang~~ people. Pretty much every single person I've met has been polite, delightful and further reinforced my own belief that this world is a brilliant place that we're lucky to be a part of.

One of these people was a kid called Jay. We met Jay through the Starlight Children's Foundation, a 'Make-A-Wish' type charity for ill children. Jay had beaten cancer and simply wanted to play some games with me. During the process of setting this up, Jay had a relapse, beat cancer for a second time and, years after the initial email, was finally ready to play.

I've never met anyone like Jay. While I react to a single paper cut as if a shark has just bitten me in half, Jay beat off cancer twice like it was a bit of a headache. The only evidence of cancer ever being in his life was the fact he had a wicked dark sense of humour about it. He was an absolute blast to play with and we ended up becoming friends.

Sadly, Jay's cancer returned for a third time, this time for

---

1   Writing a memoir at twenty-nine: what the fuck is wrong with you?

keeps. I visited him in hospital, not entirely knowing what to expect but fearing the worst.[2] I entered Jay's room and was taken aback by just how much the cancer had destroyed his body. He didn't look like my friend any more.

Then *Mario Kart* was put on the TV, the cheating prick gave me motion controls instead of actually usable ones, and I spent the next few hours in the company of the exact same mate I'd always known. We ended up having a really fun day, and kept playing games online together until he died a few months later, outliving every life-expectancy goal he was ever given just because he could. I'm really going to miss that kid.

I've said it before but I'll say it again as I'm wrapping up. Video games connect people. While writing this book I lost two good friends from my life. Jay, and fellow creator and critic John 'Totalbiscuit' Bain. Both of them taught me so much, both of them showed incredible strength and both of them came into my life because of video games. Those silly little programs that go blip have connected me with so many fantastic people, all around the world. People I'll love forever. People I'll never forget.

Plus, in some of them, you can attach rockets onto cows and fuck them off to the moon!

Fuck yeah, video games! Forever may they reign!

2 As my friend Wot pointed out, 'A cancer ward for terminal children' is basically the ultimate Cards Against Humanity card.

The Top 101 Games of All Time

If I was to include every single game that I wanted to, this book would have been thick enough to beat a mountain to death with. To make up for all the ones I missed, here is a list of the games that I genuinely think are the very best.[1]

Your homework is to play them all. Enjoy.

101. Evil Genius
Play as an angry bald man, a seductive lady or a racial stereotype and try to take over the world from the insurance nightmare that is a volcano base.

100. World of Goo
A puzzle game where you smush blobs of goo together and pray that the bridge they make holds while knowing in your heart of hearts that it won't.

99. Pokémon Red, Blue and, sure, why not, Yellow, too
Force animals to fight each other unconscious in a world where doing that is not only socially acceptable but actively encouraged.

98. Armadillo Run
Help a balled-up armadillo get home by building elaborate Rube Goldberg machines in places where a simple bridge would do.

---

1   It's mid-2018 when I put this together so if the greatest game of all time has since come out, just pencil it in yourself.

97. Burnout Paradise
Race in a city where cars don't have drivers, corners must be driven around sideways and Axl Rose is somehow still relevant.

96. Star Trek: Voyager – Elite Force
An FPS where you help Captain Janeway defend *Voyager* from the Borg, Klingons and giant blue moths that communicate by shooting you in the face.

95. PixelJunk Shooter Ultimate
Fly your ship around levels filled with different types of fluids. Get a gun that fires lava. Accidentally kill yourself and anyone you're playing co-op with over and over again.

94. Thomas Was Alone
A lovely story about a rectangle and his friends, filled with more wit and warmth than a hug from Stephen Fry.

93. Resident Evil 4
Spanish Gap Year Simulator 2005.

92. Gunpoint
Experience the life of a spy with spring-loaded trousers, a rewiring kit and a penchant for throwing himself through double-glazing.

91. Far Cry 3
Visit the beautiful Rook Islands! Soak in the sun on the glorious beaches, meet the local murderous cult, kill all wildlife you encounter and make a rucksack from skin. Call now!

90. Just Cause 2
Bring peace to a nation by systematically setting all of it on fire from a parachute.

89. Broforce

America's greatest action heroes gear up and band together to kill Satan, terrorists and anyone in the way.

88. Spelunky

Delve into randomly generated caves and collect as much treasure as you can before you fall and impale yourself on the naturally occurring polished metal spikes.

87. Euro Truck Simulator 2

Load up your truck and spend several hours driving across Europe before reaching your destination, turning around and doing it all over again.

86. Sid Meier's Alpha Centauri

Humans settle in the light of a new star while bombing, backstabbing and being bastards to each other. Also, Mind Worms!

85. Beyond Good & Evil

A female reporter and her pig of an uncle (literally) fight an alien invasion using a kendo stick and investigative journalism.

84. Batman: Arkham Asylum

Enter a prison for the insane and beat up all the inmates while playing as everybody's favourite fridge with a cape attached.

83. Star Wars: Battlefront II

The year 2005 gave us 'My Humps', that terrible *War of the Worlds* reboot and Camilla. However, it also gave us the best *Star Wars* game ever so I'll forgive it. For now.

82. Tomb Raider III
Lara Croft returns with a globetrotting adventure that sees her fighting Tigers, T-Rexes and Ticket Barriers.

81. N++
A clean, crisp and pure hardcore platformer that currently has over 4,000 levels. Rumour has it they used actual ninjas to beta test it.

80. Re-Volt
Race remote-controlled cars around cul-de-sacs, supermarkets and toy shops before weeping into the tax forms you now have to put up with as an adult.

79. Driver
Undercover cop Tanner must travel across four cities solving crimes, running away from the police and making cool, edited videos of it all.

78. Far Cry 2
Visit Africa! Burn to a crisp in some desert! Dig a bullet out of your arm with a knife! Or simply keel over because you forgot to take your malaria pills! Call now!

77. SoulCalibur 2
Large men, larger weapons and even larger breasts do battle in this tale of swords and souls. Ignore the bendy bondage guy. He doesn't like eye contact.

76. Grow Home
Explore the complicated relationship between a boy and his mother when the boy is actually a robot and the mother is his spaceship. Also, gardening.

75. Scott Pilgrim vs. the World: The Game

Edgar Wright's cult hit is turned into a side-scrolling beat 'em up in one of the rarest types of games in the world: the good movie tie-in.

74. Age of Empires II

Build a town, an army and a very large wall and watch it all collapse because an enemy priest has invented the most potent form of religion ever recorded.

73. Plants vs. Zombies

Horror meets horticulture as you defend yourself from zombies via the teachings of Alan Titchmarsh.

72. Terraria

Uncover the riches of the earth as you delve deep underground in search of fortune, power and the one particular type of enemy you need to kill to finish a chair.

71. Stacking

Explore a society made up entirely of matryoshka dolls by going inside people, possessing them and using their abilities. It's somehow not as dark as it sounds.

70. Dragon Ball Z: Budokai 3

Start a fair fight and, across the space of thirty seconds, power up so much that even Thor would struggle to beat you. Then blow up the entire Earth. Fun!

69. Hitman: Blood Money

Stealthily infiltrate the darkest corners of the globe to find and put down your targets before they even know you're in the country. That or kick the doors in while wielding two AKs. Up to you really.

68. WWE 2K16

Oil up and throw down with the most extensive character creator this side of actually being God.

67. Animal Crossing: New Leaf

Buy a house you can't afford, make friends who will never love you back and then go to bed, boot up your 3DS and play *Animal Crossing: New Leaf* to numb the pain.

66. Dishonored

A man with the same powers as a VIVE controller must stab or not stab his way across a list of targets set against a backdrop of Victorian depression and rats.

65. Tom Clancy's Rainbow Six: Rogue Spear

A terrorism-stopping tactical shooter that strikes the careful balance between failing to prepare and preparing to fail.

64. Ratchet & Clank 3

A cat-thing with a wrench and a robot celebrity have to save the galaxy from a different, evil robot with a green fish tank for a hat. Standard PS2 plot there.

63. Rocket League

Rocket-powered cars playing football set in the future. Sequel to the terribly named *Supersonic Acrobatic Rocket-Powered Battle-Cars*. Seriously.

62. Wario Land 3

The heavier yin to Mario's yang falls into a magical music box, fights monsters and saves the day. Guess Mario is the evil twin after all.

61. Left 4 Dead 2

Recreate the feeling of being a security guard during Black Friday with this FPS about four survivors, some pills and a billion fast zombies.

60. Black

Fire a gun and watch as the enemy flies away, a nearby building collapses and everyone in a one-mile radius is immediately deafened. That was just the pistol.

59. Spore

Construct wild and wonderful creatures and send them off on adventures like it was the New Year's Eve party at the local genetics facility.

58. Liero

Two worms made of pixels and gallons of blood go to war underground. Turn off reload times and watch the unmatched cartoon carnage.

57. Tearaway

A little envelope man has a sweet adventure across the land made of paper where the only rule is to have fun. Oh, and no naked flames.

56. Metroid: Zero Mission

Head to planet Zebes, the only planet in the world to invent the elevator before the staircase, and shoot a big brain in the... face?

55. Castlevania: Symphony of the Night

Beat the game, boast about that a decade later and find out that there's a secret second map that doubles the size of the game. Also, angry books!

54. Prince of Persia: Warrior Within

Parkour your way across crumbling ruins, fall into a spike pit, die, rewind time until you just stumbled and die again. Occasionally stab demons too!

53. Psychonauts

Run away from the circus to a summer camp for psychics and get into the heads of everyone around you. Literally.

52. The World Ends with You

You've died. Now you have to work out who killed you. Battle multidimensional beings and keep up with all the latest fashion trends in the heart of Tokyo.

51. Spec Ops: The Line

This is just a normal war shooter. Nothing special about it. Nope. Just a normal shooter. You should play it. It's totally normal. Yep. Normal.

50. Cities: Skylines

A fighting game. Yes, I know it's a game about building a city, but considering you'll be fighting traffic issues for most of it I stand by my initial classification.

49. Antichamber

You look into a room. You see a floating, abstract shape. You turn around and then back. You are now in a new room. Welcome to the Antichamber. Solve it.

48. Theme Hospital

Bloaty head? Invisibility? Third-degree sideburns? My hospital is exactly where you want to be. Don't forget your wallet!

47. Metal Gear Solid 3: Snake Eater

Crawl through the mud, strangle a man and eat a raw snake for sustenance. It's just like being back at Butlin's!

46. Devil May Cry

Imagine *Die Hard* but John McClane is an angsty half-demon, half-angel and Nakatomi Plaza is a big gothic castle. Then add swords.

45. Tony Hawk's Pro Skater 3

Flip, trick, revert, fall on your face and destroy a million-point combo in what is considered by many to be the peak of this skateboarding franchise.

44. Just Cause 3

Ever wanted to strap small rockets to a cow and watch it fly off and explode a train as you wingsuit down a mountain? Well, this game is an alarming coincidence.

43. The Stanley Parable

This is the story of a man named Stanley. Stanley realised that he couldn't quite convey the point of his game in a few lines, so he gave up. Stanley then ate a small sandwich he brought from home.

42. TimeSplitters: Future Perfect

Single player: a brilliant, time-twisting, genre-blending romp. Multiplayer: I HATE MONKEYS. DEATH TO MONKEYS.

41. Crush

Move around 3D levels by crushing them into 2D ones. Play as a man called Dan who cannot sleep. I connect with this game on a very spiritual level.

40. Elite Beat Agents
Tap your DS screen to make a group of people dance to save the day. Never ever hear the song 'Jumpin' Jack Flash' again without tapping your fingers.

39. Job Simulator
Enter the peaceful world of menial jobs reimagined a little bit wrong by robots from the future. Imagine *Office Space* meets *The Matrix*.

38. Watch Dogs 2
An intelligent, bright and fun playground set in the scary technological future we're all catastrophically hurtling towards.

37. Worms Armageddon
What do an old lady, a banana and a sheep with a cape glued on have in common? Nothing, but throw them at the opposing team anyway.

36. LittleBigPlanet 2
Take one cuddly mascot, one ridiculously packed level editor and the ability to share those levels, and what are you left with? That's right! No free time.

35. Kerbal Space Program
Learn about aerodynamics, orbital mechanics and interplanetary travel by sending small green men to hilarious, fiery deaths.

34. Minecraft
Punch a tree. Get some wood. Build a pickaxe. Get some minerals. Continue on like this until you've recreated New York City on a 1:1 scale.

33. Sonic Mania

Take a high-speed trip to the glory days of Sonic with tight gameplay, redesigned classic levels and one of the best soundtracks of all time.

32. The Legend of Zelda: Link's Awakening

My personal favourite of Link's adventures. Explore an island filled with secrets, danger and adventure. Just leave the chickens be. They don't like to be bothered.

31. Red Faction: Guerrilla

Tear entire Martian buildings to the ground with a hammer in this open world with an unrivalled destruction engine. Also, you *might* be a terrorist.

30. Fable III

Enter a world where magic is real, you can become king and, for some reason, 90% of the voice cast are acclaimed British comedians.

29. Yu-Gi-Oh! Tag Force 5

One of my most played games of all time. Collecting almost 5,000 cards spread out across 60 different packs takes a long while.

28. Burnout 3: Takedown

The game that taught me that the difference between a car going 200 mph and a hunk of scrap metal by the side of the road is a well-timed nudge to the back wheel.

27. Sins of a Solar Empire

Expand out into the dark reaches of space to conquer the galaxy. It'll all be over by Space Christmas. Space Christmas AD 3776, that is.

26. Spider-Man 2
Play with proper web-swinging in the best superhero game ever made. Also, pop the balloons of crying children because they're annoying. With great power... etc., etc.

25. Prison Architect
Build a prison. Run a prison. Watch prisoners escape the prison. Crack down on the prison. Accidentally kick off a riot in the prison. Get put in your own prison.

24. Mirror's Edge
A pure white city dashed with vibrant colour has a dark underside. You are a runner. That means you are paid to try to not fall off things. You won't be paid much.

23. Red Dead Redemption
The US and Mexico of 1911 come to life in this game about cowboys, horses and a good man who occasionally ties people up and leaves them on train tracks for fun.

22. Bloodborne
It's the night of the hunt and that pesky old blood is acting up again. Explore the darkness of man, the darkness of nightmares and various other assorted darknesses.

21. Papers, Please
Play as an immigration officer for a fictional dystopian country without first having to read the complete works of Clarkson.

20. Metal Gear Solid 2: Sons of Liberty
When the protagonist is killed off and replaced an hour into the game, you know you're in for a wild ride. With *MGS2*, you have no idea how wild that ride will be.

19. Bastion

A narrator with a voice like melted sex and a stunning soundtrack draw you into a beautiful and breathtaking world. Pity it ended yesterday.

18. Saints Row 2

A perfect mix of silly and serious, *Saints Row 2* is the only game I know where you can spray exhibitionists with liquid sewage. Why isn't that in more games?

17. Heat Signature

Get egotistical whiplash when your heist attempt backfires and you're launched into space for the seventeenth time that day.

16. The Witcher 3: Wild Hunt

A country ruined by war, beasts straight out of your nightmares and a lead character as attractive and gruff as a buttered Jeff Goldblum with a cold.

15. Grand Theft Auto: San Andreas

Somehow Rockstar managed to crush an entire state onto a PS2 alongside all-American pastimes such as monster trucks, corrupt cops and weight gain.

14. The Binding of Isaac: Rebirth

Religion meets violence for the first time in recorded history as a young boy hides from his mother and her new BFF, God.

13. Fallout 4

I hear that this RPG features a story but I didn't realise. I was too busy building, decorating and defending my adorable, if a little draughty, post-apocalyptic towns.

12. FTL: Faster Than Light
The captain is dead and three seconds after you unpause a missile will destroy your ship. Hope Dwayne can run to engineering and get the shields back on time. Shame he's literally a slug.

11. The Sims
Look after tiny people and help them to love, laugh and put out near endless fires in the kitchen. READ A GODDAMN COOKERY BOOK, SUSAN. CHRIST.

10. Dungeon Keeper
Nothing beats slapping around an imp that won't do your bidding. Well, one thing. Possessing that imp directly and slowly walking him towards an enemy dragon.

9. Super Mario Odyssey
If you flung two copies of *Super Mario Odyssey* round the Large Hadron Collider the resulting collision would leave nothing but particles of pure fun. That's science.

8. RollerCoaster Tycoon 2
Build rides, overcharge for toilets and clean up vomit in a game that's about designing rollercoasters that occasionally don't even kill people.

7. SSX 3
A pumping soundtrack, breathtaking visuals and a cast of probably insane stunt junkies combine to make this epic, deep and satisfying snowboard 'em up.

6. Grand Theft Auto: Vice City
Vice City is a smoothie made from neon colours, glam metal and shoulder pads. Also, cocaine. Lots and lots of cocaine.

5. Planet Coaster

The team behind *RollerCoaster Tycoon 3* took that template and updated, improved and revolutionised every single bit of it. It's like having a second, far better baby.

4. God of War (2018)

An angry man and his boy lead a funeral procession up a mountain, across several realms and through piles of recently created dead bodies.

3. Portal

A mute test subject and an evil computer do battle via the usual mediums of comedy, puzzles and a gun that bends the properties of space to its will.

2. Shadow of the Colossus

A mysterious boy travels to a mysterious land to save a mysterious girl by defeating mysterious giants for a mysterious guide. Mysteriously.

1. Bully

Relive your school days except this time you're popular, you'll get into fights, you'll kiss girls, you'll kiss boys and you'll pass all your classes.

Glossary

A

AAA – Games made by thousands of people, millions of dollars and eventually get a 7/10 on Metacritic.

Achievement – So you've just killed 550 enemies with a hammer made from jam? Here's a picture of a trophy and a half-second sound effect for your trouble.

Action-adventure – The Hufflepuff of game genres. If people don't know where to put you, you'll go here.

AI – Artificial intelligence. Thousands of lines of code that control exactly how your digital opponents will run into a wall.

Alpha – An unfinished game that's about five years away from being abandoned.

Ambient occlusion – No idea.

Anti-aliasing – Makes your games look like you're squinting at them.

Arcade – Where video games used to live before they got a real job.

Avatar – A self-created yet better-looking digital version of you.

B

Battle Royale – What they call a Big Mac in Japan.

Beat 'em up – Just you, an opponent, and their knowledge of 100x combos.

Beta – A game that's finished enough that people can look at it, but not finished enough that that people can look at it for too long.

Bethesda – A company that releases games that are more open, more luscious and more buggy than a safari park that specialises in insects.

BIOS – An operating system's dad.

Bit – Video game atoms.

Bonus stage – A secret area filled with lives, money and fun. Basically every party you've never been invited to.

Boob physics – The scientific pursuit of accurate breast tissue. Unfortunately all we have so far looks like water balloons under custard.

Boss – That big guy at the end of a level who just wiped you out in three hits even though you had the Sword of Megasmush.

Braking – A mechanic in racing games where you can slow the vehicle down. Utterly pointless.

Bullet hell – Where NRA members go when their child inevitably shoots them.

C

Camera – The dark magic portal that allows us to see into the realm of video games.

Camping – The art of not enjoying a video game so that you can win a video game.

Capture the Flag – A well-named multiplayer game mode where you capture a flag. What you do after that is, to this day, a mystery.

Cartridge – A prison for bits.

Casual game – A game you play on your phone while half listening to a DVD boxset of *Cheers*.

Cheats – Because sometimes having a character with a big head is fun.

Co-op – Play a video game with friends because you ran out of things to talk about years ago.

Console – That shiny black box under the TV that makes the magic happen.

Controller – The middleman between your fingers and a spinning plastic disc. Alarmingly aerodynamic.

Cover system – Press a button to make a character attach to a wall and never work out which button unattaches them.

CPU – Central processing unit. Does... stuff.

Cutscene – That bit when a game writer decides that his job is more important than your fun.

D

Dance pad – A way of playing video games and not looking cool at the same time.

Dating Sim – Talk to anime girls about their high-school troubles until you get to see cartoon boobies.

Deathmatch – Black Friday but there's only one 4K TV that's 50% off, everyone is armed and reincarnation is real.

Demo – The tiny slice of cake you have before you say, 'Oh, go on then,' and end up dying of diabetes.

Developers – First of all, keep them out of the light, they hate bright light; especially sunlight, it'll kill them. Second, don't give them any water, only energy drinks. But the most important rule, the rule you can never forget: no matter how much they cry, no matter how much they beg, never feed them unless they get an 85 or more on Metacritic.

Devkit – A software development kit. Basically a specially built PC that matches no more than 30% of a console's inner workings for a stress-free development process. Did I say free? I meant inducing.

Digital – Physical, but the opposite.

DLC – Downloadable content. A bit of the game that fell off during production.

DNS – No idea, go and read a library book.

Draw distance – A slider in the options menu that allows your character to repel any and all fog to a certain distance.

DRM – Digital rights management. Stops pirates accessing video games by stopping everyone else accessing the game too.

Dual wielding – Using two guns at the same time. As cool and inaccurate as a shark with an eyepatch.

Dungeon – A place in fantasy games where everyone in the area stores their money, weapons, clothing, magical items and lit candles.

E

E3 – The Electronic Entertainment Expo. A yearly gathering in America where massive companies get together and show off pre-rendered trailers for video games that won't be out for half a decade.

E-Sports – Regular sports, but the games are somehow even more confusing.

EA – What would happen if Satan fucked a credit card.

Early access – The game isn't finished? This seems like a perfect time to buy!

Easter egg – Hollow chocolate egg, usually covered in silver foil.

Edutainment – Education and entertainment mixed together with the same results as oil and water.

Emulator – A naughty way to play old games. Also, pretty much the only way to play old games.

Escort mission – You know what this gameplay section needs? Someone who wanders off, gets in your line of fire, shrieks a lot and makes you fail the entire game when you rightly put two shells in the back of their head.

ESRB – Entertainment Software Rating Board. Spoiling if games have boobies in them since 1994.

Expansion – Back in my day... grumble grumble... something... incoherent grunts... VHS... grumble...

Experience points – That thing on the bottom of a job listing that crushes your chances of getting it.

F

Fanboy – Someone who will defend a game with a 3/10 Metacritic score to the death.

Fast travel – A fleet of artists took years crafting the very ground that you walk upon. Fuck 'em, I've got shit to sell.

Field of view – A number in the settings that will be complained about if it's under ninety.

First-person shooter – See through the eyes of a merciless killer as you snuff out more people than live in Sweden. Wheeeeeeeeee!!!

Fog of War – The area outside your base where all your enemies gather to make up rude names for you.

Force feedback – The reason your mum caught you with a DualShock down your pants.

Frames per second – In economics, the measure of how many picture frames Amazon can sell in a second.

Free to play – Not even once.

FMV – Before graphics could render the lint in Link's belly button, actors were paid very, very small amounts of money to film little cutscenes in a resolution that could display comfortably on a regular calculator. Cheesier than the moon after being dipped in fondue.

G

Game engine – The core of all video games, built by the darkest of creatures. To know of their secrets is to know madness itself.

Game over – The bit where the game is over.

Gameplay – The stuff you do in a video game. Running, jumping, baking a pie, flying a plane, sending a lemming off a cliff for fun – all that and more.

Games as a service – You know how most long-running TV shows get terrible as they go on? Well that, but for video games.

Games industry – A place where creative people and people in suits go to fight.

Glossary – A place in a book for when the word count is just a little bit short.

GPU – The bit inside your PC that makes the games shiny. Often screaming.

Griefer – Digital sandcastle kickers.

Grinding – The act of replaying a section of a game over and over and over and over and over and over again until you unlock the one Level IV Red Platypus Muff you need to craft armour that you'll throw away in an hour or so.

H

Hack and slash – Original name for Guns N' Roses.

Hacker – A dark and mysterious individual that knows how to use Google and double-click on a file they downloaded. Man, they're so cool. I bet they wear sunglasses indoors.

Handheld console – Play video games while you shit because the future is now and it's fantastic.

Hardcore gamer – Someone who has spent more on their PC than they did their house.

Hardware – Your PC.

Hardware requirements – Something much more powerful than your PC.

Hats – An artist spent months perfecting that character design but you're right, it needs a sombrero.

Health – A bar that indicates how close you are to death. Replenish it with food you stole from a bin, swigs of magic potion or just by sitting still for like three seconds.

Hitbox – The area around a character that can be hit by enemies. Will periodically shift when nobody but you is in the room.

Homebrew – What Hawkeye and B.J. were making in that still.

HUD – That one guy with the camera in *Cloverfield*.

Hype – Excitement that ends up costing you money.

I

IGN – A website that attaches a randomly generated number to the end of their game reviews to cause arguments on the internet.

Indie game – A game made by one person in a garage because they believe in it. Will win a BAFTA if the ending is ambiguous.

Inverted controls – Making it so that when you press up on an analogue stick or mouse, the view goes down. *AKA THE RIGHT WAY TO PLAY.*

Invisible wall – Because something has to be coded at 4 p.m. on a Friday.

IRC chat – Internet relay chat chat. Sure, the 'chat' isn't necessary, but it sounds so weird without it.

Isometric – 3D that doesn't try very hard.

J

Jaggies – The name for fans of Mick Jagger.

JRPG – Japanese role-playing game. People with spiky hair leave their idyllic village after a disaster and go and kill God. Also, cleavage as far as the eye can see.

K

Kotaku – The sort of gaming website that would bring a guitar to a party.

Kickstarter – A website where you can pay for a game that nobody ever actually intends to make.

Killstreak – The act of killing someone in a game while nude.

L

Lag – The real reason you lost that last round of *Counter Strike*.

LAN – Convenient local play for PCs once you've dragged yours up the seven flights of stairs to my flat.

LCD – Liquid crystal display. A type of screen made from melted diamonds that explains why old handhelds were so expensive.

Leaderboard – A place for the very best to write the word 'ASS'.

Let's Play – Videos made by talentless fucks on the internet.

Loot – A reward for playing a video game. Damn millennials.

Ludonarrative dissonance – Mention this at a party and watch as people roll their eyes so hard that they end up in their throats.

M

Mana – A banana, for men.

Manual – My favourite *Fawlty Towers* character.

Matchmaking – A type of practical joke where you take low-level players and throw them into the meat grinder of the elite.

Metacritic – A website that takes all the made-up numbers that video games get and produces another made-up number for it. The reason is unclear at the time of printing.

Metroidvania – A description of games that nine times out of ten aren't metroidvanias.

Microtransactions – The ironically named reason why your three-year-old racked up a £3,000 phone bill this month.

Minigame – A game, but smaller.

MMORPG – Massively multiplayer online role-playing game. Basically, where nerds hang out now they've shut down all the libraries.

Mobile games – A type of game that peaked with *Snake* and has been flushing itself down the toilet ever since.

Mods – Little changes to games that fans make; 95% of them either add Iron Man or remove clothing.

Motion blur – That option you turn off before you even hit 'New Game'.

Multiplayer – A way of playing video games for people who think they're too good for AI.

Multiple endings – Videos that you watch on YouTube after playing about a fifth of the game so you can decide which one you're aiming for.

N

Noclip – The ability to move through walls and floors like a ghost, or the noise from the builders next door.

Noobs – The first time you see a new pair of boobs.

NPC – Non-player characters. The sort of people who don't care if you break into their house, steal from their chests and smash up all their pottery.

O

Online – The opposite of offline. Duh.

Open world – Level design is hard; let's just copy-paste New York again.

Operating system – Windows for babies, macOS for 'artists' and Linux for people who desperately want attention.

OST – Official soundtrack; 90% of the time you'll only listen to the YouTube rip of the audio even though you agreed that one time that you wouldn't steal a car.

P

Party Game – It's not a party until Grandma drops an f-bomb over a virtual bowling ball.

Patch – An update for your game that makes it crash more for you and literally nobody else.

PC – A type of games console where you spend more time making a game run properly than actually playing it. Also, spreadsheets.

Permadeath – Die, lose everything and go back and try again. Nothing says fun downtime like mortality!

Pixel – The little squares that make up screens and monitors; 100% sentient, they fear death.

Player – You, presumably.

Pre-Alpha – An idea on a whiteboard.

Procedural generation – Are you a level designer who hates designing levels? Well, have I got the math for you!

Point-and-click adventure – A type of video game where you must get very, very drunk to understand what to do with the rubber chicken and pulley you just picked up.

Polygon – Long story short, it's a 3D pixel.

PvP – Player vs player. When two pimps fight.

PvE – Player vs Elmo. When shit goes down on *Sesame Street*.

Q

Quest – Your mighty and heroic goals in virtual life. Ranges from defeating dragons and saving the world, to getting 120 bottles of milk for Ms Bittermann's cat.

QTE – Quick time event. A button prompt on a time limit that interrupts a cutscene, causing you to fail a part of the game you weren't even playing.

R

Rage-quit – A word for tantrum that the internet invented to sound cooler.

RAM – Random-access memory. The reason that Madonna's 'Material Girl' suddenly pops into your head for no reason and stays there.

RTS – Really terrible socks.

Reboot – A 1994 kids' TV series with nightmare-inducing early CGI.

Respawn – Popping back into the world after you died like Phil Connors having a bad day.

Retro – Anything from more than three years ago.

RNG – Random nun generator. Generates a random nun.

Rockstar Games – Just run over a sex worker with a taxi? You're probably playing one of Rockstar's games. That or you're a horrible person.

Romance – Three conversation options plus a cutscene of heavy petting and, congratulations, you just did a relationship.

Rougelike – An off-red.

RPG – Role-playing game. Create Tim Tabernacle and help him save the world from monsters/men/cling film/two out of the five Spice Girls, etc., etc.

S

Season pass – Buying dessert before you've even touched the main course.

Sidequest – The quest you don't tell your main quest about.

Silent protagonist – Only acceptable if you're making a Penn & Teller video game.

Simulator – Because I was arrested the last time I tried to drive a train in the real world.

Shovelware – The Wii's library.

SLI – Scalable link interface. Making two £2,500 GPUs work together to increase frame rates by a whopping 0.4%.

Speedrun – You've not seen *Mario 64* until you've seen someone complete it in about six minutes.

Spoiler – Snape killed Bruce Willis all along.

Sprite – A lemon-and-lime-flavoured drink.

Square Enix – Company I accidentally took over for a short while.

Stealth – Crouching in a spare bush.

Survival horror – Ammo and weapons are scarce. Your health is low. It's dark. It's raining. Then a monster eats you on the genitals.

T

Tank controls – Walk out the nearest door. Did you walk in straight lines, pausing to turn? No? Then WHY ARE THESE CONTROLS STILL A THING?!

Text adventure – A book you can interact with that's trying its damnedest to kill you.

Teabagging – The cup is your opponent's face. The teabag is... more of a sack really...

Third-party – When you overbook yourself one evening.

Tower defence – When royalty take potshots at the plebs from the Tower of London.

Turn-based strategy – Think chess, but with more exploding worms.

Turtling – Hiding behind seventeen miles of anti-air turrets is legitimate strategy, OK?

U

Ubisoft – Makers of a Mario game with crazed mutant rabbits and turn-based shooting. They can now do no wrong in my eyes.

Unreal Engine – A game engine for developers who want all their characters to look like they're smeared in Vaseline.

Unlockable – Want to play as your favourite character in multiplayer? Collect all 6 billion onion slivers! Hooray!

V

Video game – If you don't know what this is, I bet the past few hundred pages have been mighty confusing.

VR – Virtual reality. Put on a headset and enter video game worlds! Then take it off again because they're almost all scary.

W

WASD – The keys of power. Also, walking.

X

XP – One of the precursors to emojis.

Y

YouTube – A website that turns this interactive medium into an un-interactive one.

Z

Zone – A different word for levels. Yeah, OK, I couldn't think of a good Z word. For a while I had Z-buffering but it's not exactly a high point to end on now, is it? Stupid alphabet. What's it ever done for us, huh?!

Acknowledgements

Daniel would like to thank
Rebecca, for everything.

Mum, Dad and Hannah for 30 years of love and support.

The team at Unbound, especially DeAndra for putting up with my inability to hit deadlines or reply to emails.

Matt, for making sure that the tax man doesn't murder me to death.

Stuart Ashen, for giving me the first sweet hit of book writing.

Tim Schafer, because he's every bit as brilliant as I hoped he'd be.

My brilliant supporters on Patreon, YouTube and Twitch. Thank you so much.

Rebecca would like to thank
Regan, Matilda, Peanut and Eli. <3

All the dogs in the whole world.

Seriously, pat your dog for me.

About the Author and Illustrator

Daniel Hardcastle, Author

Hello! My name is Daniel and I've said approximately 15,000,000 words across over 4,000 internet videos in the past nine years. It's probably time I wrote some of them down.

My love for video games started in 1991 when I discovered that I could magically control the small blue hedgehog on my TV with a special remote control. My passion for writing came about when a boy wizard stabbed a snake man in the face. My interest in dinosaurs came from a visit to the Natural History Museum, but that isn't important right now.

I live in *REDACTED* with Rebecca, the illustrator of this book, and our many, many pets. When I grow up, I'd like to be a bit less fat.

Rebecca Maughan, Illustrator

Interview between Daniel and Rebecca, recorded 29 May 2018 at 19.21.

TRANSCRIPT BEGINS

```
DH:   OK, time to do your one now.
RM:   Hello, I'm Rebecca and [long pause]
      I don't know what to say.
DH:   You have to sell yourself, it's
      like writing a personal statement
```

or something more important like a
Twitter bio.

RM: I hate writing those.

DH: Everyone does.

RM: Why do I have to do this again?

DH: Because people want to know about
you to see if your work is worth
spending money on.

RM: I like dogs.

DH: Great start! Add to it!

RM: I like dogs more than people.

DH: Not quite what I had in mind.

RM: I'd kill all the people...

DH: So... how about those qualifications?

RM: ... to save a dog.

DH: It says here that you have a degree
in software engineering for computer
games!

RM: Just one dog.

DH: And that you've been drawing for
longer than you've been walking.

RM: My dream...

DH: Uh huh...

RM: ... is to find a dog so big...

DH: Yes?

RM: ... that it can eat people.

DH: I'll make something up.

TRANSCRIPT ENDS

Unbound is the world's first crowdfunding publisher, established in 2011.

We believe that wonderful things can happen when you clear a path for people who share a passion. That's why we've built a platform that brings together readers and authors to crowdfund books they believe in – and give fresh ideas that don't fit the traditional mould the chance they deserve.

This book is in your hands because readers made it possible. Everyone who pledged their support is listed below. Join them by visiting unbound.com and supporting a book today.

Jaime A. (Reboot-101), Andreas Aagaard, David Aakvaag, Joshua Aarons, Bilal Abali, Ash Abbink, Billy Abbott, Ethan Abbott, Simon Abbott, Nicholas Abbs, Jacob Abernathy, Liam Abney, Courtney 'Grrenix' Abraham, Michael Abraham, James Abrahams, Alex Acaster, Ravenna Accalia, Arturo Acevedo Bravo, Tim ramspaz Ackley, Callum Ackroyd, Jonathan Ackroyd, Jack Acres, ActFast231, NotMy ActualName, Matthew Adair, Cameron Adam, Adam, Robert Adami, Jack Adamou, Andrew Adams, Benjamin Adams, Caleb Adams, Elizabeth Adams, Jack Adams, Joseph Adams, Josh Adams, Kayleb Adams, Liam Adams, Owen Adams, Paul Adams, Thomas Adams, Timothy Adams, Trevor Adams, Karin Adar, Dan Addams, ADESONOM, Aric Adiego, Robert Adler, Steven Adsitt, Carl-Johan Agebratt, @AgentOink, Axel Ågren, Elijah Ah-Sha, AHanses, Liam Aharon, Keanan Ahern, Aysha Ahmed, Junaid Ahmed, AhmedFullMD, Eric Ahnell, Marko Ahonen, Christopher Aikens, Ben Ainsworth, Jackson Aird, Zion Aitken, Patrick Akbar, Ben Akerman, Vilhelm Åkerström, Shie Ako, Adam Akorita-Burkin, Joseph Al-khaldi, Faisal M. Al-Subaiei, AlanHart.co.uk, Joseph AlanNapeir, Samppa Alatalo, Robert Alavoine, JD Albero, Devin Albertson, Steffen Albrecht, Stian Albrigtsen, Nathan Albury, Luis Alcantara, Matthew Alden-Farrow, Audry Aldridge, Ryan Aldridge, Tony Alegria, Bart Alewijnse, Darren Alexander, Helen Alexander, Jodie Alexander, Kate Alexander, Katie Alexander, Kevin Alexander, Natasha Alexander, Niall Alexander, Filip Alf, Aqua Alford, Peter Alfred and dammit I'm getting my money's wor,

Andreas Lie Algrøy, Omar AlHashmi, Leevi Alho, Tariq Alhussein, Haydar Ali, Humza Ali, Aliasmuse, Richard Alison, Naseer Alkhouri, Kyle Allan, Giacomo Allen, Jordan Jamie Allen, Josiah Allen, Matt Allen, Oliver Allen, Paul Allen, Randy Allen, Rebecca Allen, Silkie Allen, Tom Allen, Rowan Allender, Chaz Allington-Lodge, Drew Allison, Bryanna Allman, Dan Allsobrook, Jack Allwood, Stefan Alm, Joseph Almahmid, Gonçalo Almeida, Liam Almond, Alec Almoosa, almostzen, Peter Laust Almvig, Wyatt Alpers, Blake Alps, AltExt, Noah Althouse, Kevin Alvarez, Isak Alvebro, Ben Alvis, Alexander Aman, BeAkale Amanuel, Arthur Amason, Sindre Vatnamot Amble, Jacopo Ameli, Emma Amfelt, Matt Amies, Beth Amphlett, Dalton Amundson, Andre Anastacio, Albert Anderberg, Kaden Andersen, Rune Andersen, Yrsa Andersen, Charlie Anderson, Craig Anderson, Craig 'CooroSnowFox' Anderson, Denen Anderson, Derek Anderson, Dylan Bryant Anderson, Jake G. Anderson, Jordan Anderson, Justin Anderson, Kyle ShirtLifting Anderson, Lee Anderson, Logan Anderson, Matthew Anderson, Mitchell Anderson, Ryan Anderson, Thomas Anderson, James Anderson Brown, George Anderson-bush, Cody Anderson-Salo, Connor Andersson, David Andersson, Oscar Andersson, Valter Andersson, ANDO, Bruno Aveleira Andrade (bavandrade), Norbert 'ICE Trance' András, Zoe Andraska, Agnar B. Andreassen, Landon Andreatta, My guy Andrew, Alex Andrews, Cayden Andrews, Daniel Andrews, Jack Andrews, Katelyn Andrews, Luke Andrews, Sawyer Andrews, Andyface, George Angel, Marissa Angell, Tommy Angus, Henry Anning, Jason Annunziata, Domenic Anselmi, Zachary Anstee, Phoebe Anstis, Mack Anthis, H. Anthony, AntiSocial-Gamer, Jean-Paul Antoine, Luca-Dorin Anton, Theo Antonov, Omari Antony, Brian Christopher Antosh, Matt Antosik, Craig Apfelbeck, Apollo101Z, Dominic Applebee, Xander Appleby, James Apps, Oskar Apps, Sam Arber, Arcane Flame, Mark Arce, Alex John McChungus Archambault, Aeolus Archangel, Logan Archer, Simone Archer, Jenn Archibald, Louis Ard, Eyal Arditi, Jesse Arends, Anthony Arias, Fabian Santiago Arias, Sebastian Arias Araquistain, Lauren Armandi, James Armitage [Armo], Adam Armstrong, Callum Armstrong, Stuart Armstrong, William Armstrong, Sean Armstrong-Brodie, Ryan Arnold, Zachary Arnold, Zachary Arnould, Henrik Arnøy, Tony Arredondo, Nicolas Arreola, Hiss '1000' Arrettrez, Taylor Arsenault, Alex (blitz) Arseneau, Dawson Arseneault, David Arthurs, Andrew Artioli, Love Arvidsson, Erin Asadourian, Asajz, Sophie Asbery, Emily Ash, Jason Ash, Joe Ash, Lucas Ash, Haydon Ashby, Sam Ashby, Stuart Ashen, Lucas Ashenbrenner, Jacob Ashman, Adrian Ashton, Callum Ashton, Matt Ashwell, DJ Ashworth, Reece Ashworth, Sophia Ley Ashworth, Tharglet Asimis, Sam Askew, Tobias Aspman, Ravi (Fuck) Asrani, Will Assenheimer, Chris Astabie, Summer Astleford, John Aston, Luke Aten, Murat Ates, Connor Atherton, Declan Atkin, Thomas Atkins, Troy Atkins, Ben Atkinson, Hayley Atkinson, Levi Atkinson,

Supporters

Nathan Atkinson, Luke M Atkiss, Matthew Atta, Rocco Attala, Zoe Attenborough, AtticSalt, Callum (Sayiman) Attwell, Darren Attwood, James Atwell, Robin Au, William Aubrey, Brian Aubuchon, Nick Aucamp, Liam (please stop bullying Matt) Audley, John Ault, Sven O. Austad, Nicholas Austill, Andy Austin, Chad Austin, Lewis Austin, Will Austin, Im Australian, Daniel Auty, Peter Avey, Tyler Axenderrie, Axius27, Jonas Ayers, Joel Ayliffe, Cameron Ayre, David Azzarello, Aron B, Mike 'Clownrock95' B., Sam B., Sophie B., Alex B. - Feduje, BA_Crag, Ilya Babansky, Michelle Babb, Jason Babcock, Liam Babington, Kevin Bacak, Fran Bačić, Emil Backhausen, Jake Backman, Joey Backus, Sebastiaan Backus, Ashton Bacon, Justin Bacon, Kaleb 'Arjirr' Bacon, Kelly Bacon, Martin Bacon, Thomas Baddeley, Phillip Badenhorst, Joseph D Badham, Oliver Baer-Benson, Ben Bagley, Joe Baguley, Ciar Baharie, Callum Baigent, Robin Bailes, Aaron Bailey, Christian Bailey, Harry Bailey, Lisa Bailey, Richard Bailey, Ryan Bailey, Sarah Bailey, Timothy Bailey, Daniel Bainbridge, Madalyn Bair, Oliver Baird, Bairees, Richard Bairwell, Ovidiu Baisan, Richard Baister, Adam Baker, Jack Baker, Joey Baker, Jonathan Baker, Josh Baker, Michael Baker, Nicolas Baker, Rhys Baker, Ross Baker, Lincoln Bakker, Mikołaj Balcerzak, Justin Baldock, Alex Baldry, Brendan Bale, Adam Ball, Liam Ball, Aaron Ball (Raj_Gaming), Jon Ball (Tidmouth), Jackson Ballard, Eamon Ballenger, Jeffrey Baltazar, Standerino Bambino, Titusz Ban, Christopher Bandmann, Mikkel Bank Henriksen, Jeremiah Banks, Julian Banks, Logan Banks, Alex Bannerman, Jack Bantock, Daniel Baranowski, Alex Barber, Che Barber, James Barber, Jamie Barber, Max Barber, Richard Barber, Robin Barber, Samuel Barber, Stuart Barber, Christy Barcellona, Anthony Barclay, Jake Barclay, Kit Barker, Liam Barker, Damon Barley, Eric Barley, Danny Barlow, Noah Barlow, Tanner Barlow, Sam Barnard, Alexander Barnas, Mathas Barnby, Avery Barnes, Brandon Barnes, Calum Barnes, Liam Barnes, Matthew Barnes, McKennan Barnes, Jonah Barnet, Dylan Barnett, Logan Barnette, Ross Barnie, Chris Barr, Harry Barr, Jake Barr, Shanna Barr, Graham Barrass, Dean & Mandy Barrett, George Barrett, Isobel Barrett, Joe Barrett, Mark Barrett, Peter Barrett, Travis Barrett, Dan Barriskell, Andrew Barron, Josh Barron, Tyler Barron, Ty Barrot, Jack Barrow, Joe Barry, Meriadoc Barry, Oliver Bart, Toby Bartholomew, Tom Bartle, Callum Bartlett, Nicholas Bartolomei, Tamara Barton, Elliot Bartram, Jacob Bartynski, Matthew Barus, Daniel Bascombe, Michael H D Bashner (TI100), Ashley Bass, Gareth Bass, Brody Bassett, Peter Bassom, Alex Basta, James Bastone, Cruze Batcheldor, Jacob Batchelor, Lydia Batek, Andrea Bateman, John Bateman, Richard Bateman, Rob Bateman, Zoe Bateman, Alice Bater, Charlotte Bates, Chloe Bates, Elliot 'Rogue' Bates, Noah Bates, Sean Bates, Tom Bates, Yaleni Prisca Bates, Marcin Bator, Scott Battensby, Matthew Battersby, Jake Batting, Harry Battle, Nate BattleFly, K.C. Bauer, Niklas Bauer, Dillon Baulch, Zach Bauleke,

Stephan Baum, Eric Baumann, Lucas Baumgartner, Jonas Baur, Diego Bauza, Nicolai Bavnbek, Gus Baxter, Alex Bayfield, Stephen Bayliss, Alice Bayly, Lauren Bayly, Stepan Baziuk, Ewan Bazley, Karen Beach, Callum Beale, James Beale, Wade Beale, Eden Beales-Harper, Hunter Beaman, Josh Bean, Nathan Beard, Thomas Beard, BeardedDuckWitch, Euan Beardmore, Joe Beardmore, Brandon 'Demolisher BPB' Beardsall, Connor Beaton, Michael Beattie, Jason Jackie Beaven, Steven Beavis, Sarah Bebbington, Jaison Bechar, Jeb Beck, Matthew Beck, Simon Beck, Steven Beck, Daniel Becker, Frederik Becker, Josef Becker, Koen Beckers & Fabienne Daalhuisen, Hayden Beckett, James Beckett, Richard Beckett, Nathanial Beddall, Robin 'UniRob' Beddow, Nathan Beddow (Mr_chestnut), Grayden Bedford, Reilly Bednar, Hill Bednarski, Andy Bee, Hannah Beebe, Oliver Beeby-Rigby, Sarah Beecham, Spencer Beem, David Beentjes, Tristan Beer, Tobias Beesley, Sam Beeston, Will Begley, Andrew Behrend, Keir Beigel, Nicholas Beith, Morgan Belanger, Adrian Belcher, Sam Belcher, Adam Bell, Cameron Bell, Luke Bell, Matthew Bell, Michael Bell, Peter Bell, Quentin Bell, Jack Bellaby, Gideon Bellamy, Stewart Bellamy, Josh Bellas, Declan Bellchambers, Thomas Bellekens, Alan Bellio, Will Bellman, Vicky Belousova, Gabe Belton, Ryan Beman, Ben, Jon Benard, Rachael Benfield, Taylor Benge, Kieran Benham, Benji, Cameron Bennett, Connor Bennett, Dan Bennett, Daniel Bennett, Daniel 'minorman' Bennett, Edd Bennett, James Bennett, Joshua Bennett, Kian Bennett, Lucy Bennett, Michael 'Spud' Bennett, Owen Bennett, Ross Bennett, Thomas Bennett, Marty Benoit, Max Benoiton, Charlie Bensley, Cooper Benson, Rollins Benson, Mason Bentley, Tom Bentley, William Bentley, Gabriel Benton, Matthew Bentvelzen, Beny, BeowulfWLOG, Hayley (AlyxisSix) Bepple, Nick Berenbroick, Johan Berg, Signe Berg, Bernhard Berg Arup Seip, Stian Bergersen, Oskar Bergkvist, Jakob Berglund, Tijmen Bergman, Jake Bergstresser, Ethan Berk, Jonathan Berkolds, Nikolas Berlinghoff, Brittany Berna, Myles Bernard, Alexander Bernhardt, Thomas Berrisford-Williams, Mirko Bertermann, Emil Bertilsson, Nate Bertrand, James Best, Jordan Best, Dylan Beswick, Bethe, Liam Betteridge, Luke Betteridge, Joseph Bettinger, Lucy Bettison, Lars Betts, Florian Betzler, Christoffer Beurling, Philipp Beutler, Robby Bevacqua, Hayden Bevan, Jack Bevan, Paul Beveridge, Carl Bevis, Domantas Jonas Bezaras, Joshua Bhe, Greg Ivan Bicknell, Harry Biddulph, Alex Bidwell, Joshua Bierwiler, TJ Bifano, Luke Bigg, Emma Biggins, Patrick Biggs, Phill Biggs, Noah Bigner, Jord Bijker, Sjoerd Bijl, Harry Billings, Declan Billington, Corbin Bilund, Jazz Binding, Jamie Bindon, Joe Bingham, Ryan Bingham, Dominic Birch, Robert Bird, Samuel Bird, BirdPlane, Danny Birdsall, Byron Birkby, Aleksander B. Birkeland, Anthony Birkett, Harry Birks, Dominic Birn-Pratt, Adam Bishop, Alec Bishop, Kelly Bishop, Scott Bishop, Sebastian Bishop, Tyler Bishop, Luke Bisset, Lucas Bissey, Aubrey Bisson, Kasper Bistrup, Ranjeev Biswas, Rhys Bithell, Bitraver, Bizomm, Alexander Már

Supporters

Bjarnason, Isabelle Wennerbeck Björkbacke, Lukas 'Ben Dover' Björklund, Kim Roger Bjørnø, Aidan Black, Gabriel Black, Riley Hayley Black, Joe Blackburn, Joseph 'tronjitrot' Blackburn, Nathan Blackburn, Sharon Blackburn-Maughan, Louise Blackman, Daniel Blackney, Alisdair Blackshaw, Ruby Blackstone, Alex Blackwell, Jacob Blackwell, Martin Blair, Alisha Blake, Sam Blake, Stephen Blake, Freddie Blake-Parsons, Jack Blakie, Joshua Blanchard, Adam Blanchflower, Alice Bland, Alex Blandin, Andrew Blane, Mason Blank, Benjamin Blanks, Sean Blanks, Martin Blaskewitz for Julian Naethe (it's a gift), Adam Blatt, Jonathan Blazeby, blaziken1001, Chris Blease, Evert Bleijendaal, Matthew Blenkinship, Ezekiel Blessing, Bryson Blevins, Jonathan Blight, Aidan Bliss, Michael Bliss Jr, Josh Blitz, Blobbem, Vincent Bloemen, Gerwin Bloemhof, Thomas Blomster Jr, Jan Arthur Blomvik, Emma Bloodworth, Mitchell Bloom, Karl Blow, Lucas Blucher, Alec Blue, Rhane Blue, Its BlueRio, Josh Blundred, Karl Blythe, Konrad Boberg, Boberto Bobert, Daniel Bobosky, Paul Böck, Brandon Bockovich, Dennis Bode, John Bode, Chris Bode ♥➶, Lucy Bodin, Parker Bodkin, Máté Bodnár, Lars Boere, Jonathon Boerema, Luuk Boersma, George Boff, Stijn Bogaerts, Adam Bogg, Christina Bøgh, Jean Baptiste Bogingy, David Bognar, Cody Bogus, Nicholas Bohmer, Eric Bohn, Matthew Boice, Peter Boin, Ryan Boisvert, Ivor Boiten, Benedek Bóka, Emma Mellene Bokaldere, Amit Bokobza, Hayden Boling, Lane Bolinger, Peter Bollhagen, Becky Bolton, Zak Bolton, Eric Bonar, Chloe Bond, Joe Bond, Keith Bond, Michael Bond, Sam Bond, Shea Bond, Wilf Bond, Parker Bone, Lee Boniface, Alex Bonilla, TJ Bonnet, Brody Bonney, James Bonsall, Jason Booher, Aidan Booker, AJ Booker, Haley Booker, Harry Booker, Wilson Boop, Jonathan Boorman, Nick Booth, Zak Booth, Reef Boothby, Elliot Bootle, Ludvig Borch, Julie Borden, David Bordicott, Jaime Borges, Vincent Borja, Christopher Bork, Harry Borland, Jabe Born, R_M_Renfield Borovicka, Nate Borras, Anthony Borrayo, Michael Borrego, Nicholas Borrell, Jamie Borrill, Stan Borst, Nikolay Bortsov, Gerwin Bosch, Sebastian Bosher Williams, Tim Bosman, Jasper Bosschart, Karl Bostock, Peyton Boston, Robert Boston, Klemens Böswirth, Aiden Botfield, Sam Bott, Nic Bottcher, Adam Bottomley, Ya Boi Matthew Bottorff, Rhys Botwright, Harrison Bouche, Ian Bouche, Joel Boucher, Matthew Boudier, Keith G. Boudreaux II, Jack Boughton, Ryan Bourne, Ruben Bouwsma, Emil Aagaard Bovbjerg, Dan Bovey, Casey Bowden, Colin Bowden, John Bowden, Milz Bowden, Zack Bowden, Daniel Bowdery, Archie Bower, Josiah Bower, Alex Bowerman, Mark Bowes, Reece Bowey, Glenn Bowie, James Bowles, Anthony Bowman, Grayling Bowman, Sam Bowman, Joshua Bown, Will Bowring, Scott Bowsher, Michael Bowyer, Max Box, Charlotte Boxall, Song Boxi, Maria Boyce, Cameron Boyd, Brandon Boyer, Andrew Boylan, Glen Boyle, Niels Braam, Tyler Bracey, Forest Brach, BradCubed, Andrew Bradford, Ben Bradley, Douglas Bradley, Richard

Bradley, Sean Bradley, Edward 'Invaraid' Bradshaw, Nathan Bradshaw, Todd Bradshaw, Chris Brady, Danny Brady, Joseph Brady, Sam Brady, Tom Braide, Alec Bramham, Samantha Bramley, Torin Bramley, Jack Branca, Eli Brand, Mark Brand, Ross Brand, Eric Brandel, Sean Brandenburg, Bram Brandhoff, Tigh Brannagaanagon, Mackenzie Brannan, Brody Brannon, Wesley Branton, Heather Brasher, Matthew K. Bratrsovsky, Josh Bray, Adam Braybrook, Sebastian Brazel, Aaron Brazier, Christopher Brazier, Sophie Brazier, Jessica Brearley, Liam Breen, Nathaniel Brelsford, Andreas Cornelius Bach Bremer, Braedon Brenna, Michael Brennen, Sam Brenninkmeijer, Ally Brett, Jess Brett, Meghan Brett, Alexander Brevik Slavov, Alex Brew, Tom Brewe, Jackson Brewer, Nicholas Brewer, Simon Brewin, Álvaro Brey, Benjamin Brian, Billy Bricker, Stephen Bride, Jacob Brideau, Scott Bridewell, Sean Bridge, Matt Bridger, Adrian Briggs, Bee Briggs, Jason Briggs, Amanda Bright, Charlie Bright, Theoden Brill, Ethan J Brimage, Jack Brimble, Max Brindley, BringForthTheCheese, Jakob Brink, Luke Briscoe, Duncan Bristow, Joseph Britcliffe, Aaron Britton, Gabriel Britton, Louis Britton, Ray Britton, Matt Broadway, Anthony Broccoli, Dominic Brock, Matt Brock, Ryan Brock-Matthews, Peter Brocklehurst, Adrienne Broderick, Darren Broderick, Bart Broekman, Harm Broeren, Brogan, Calum Bromley, Siana Brooker, Alysse Brooks, Gareth Brooks, Harry Brooks, Katherine Brooks, Ryan Brooks, Sam Brooks, Lily Broomfield, Kathryn Brough, Luke Broughan, Timo Brouwer, Alex Brown, Anthony Brown, Antony Brown, Dan Brown, David Brown, Devin Brown, Finn Brown, Fiona Brown, Hayden Brown, Heath Brown, Huccaby Brown, Iain Brown, Ian 'Ducky' Brown, Jacob Brown, Jake Brown, James Brown, James Stargazer Brown, Jason Brown, Jobeth Brown, Josh Brown, Kevin Brown, Kitty Brown, Kyle Brown, Levi Brown, Liam Brown, Matthew Brown, Michael Brown, Nathan Brown, Nick Brown, Scott Brown, Sean Brown, Tom Brown, Trevor Brown, Trey Brown, William Brown, Zack Brown, Zak 'Floof' Brown, Nathan Brown (Barber100Dr), Anthony Browne, Christian Browne, Conor Browne, Thomas Browne, Ryan Brownewell, Luke Browning, Matthew Browning, James Brownsmith, Mitchell Lee Brownson, Charlie Bruce, Jordan Bruce, Josh Bruce, Sam Bruce, Wallum Bruce, James Bruem, Vivienne Bruen, Manuel Bruß, André Bruynseels, Amy Bryan, Corey Bryan, Zac Bryan, Fabien Bryans, Ben Bryant, Danny Bryant, Dustin Bryant, Jesse Bryant, Karl Bryant, Oliver Bryant, Tristan Bryant, BryceFoxdon, James Bubb, Jonathan Bubley, Adam Buchan-Wyber, Beren Buchanan, Jordan Buchanan, Rory Buchanan, Zackary Buchmann, Sebastian Buck, Luke Buckel, Andrew Buckingham, Henry Buckland, Jesse Buckley, Paul 'Xytrixz' Buckley, Carmelo Bucolo, Thomas Budd, Brooke Buege, William Buerkle, Steven Buffardi, Max Buffkin, Duran Buffonge, Austin Bugert, Sergio Buijs, Jeffrey Buijssen, Daan Buis, Tom Buist, Ben Bulcock, Aiden Bull, Joseph Bull, Paul Bullard, Gage Bullock, Matty Bullock, James Bulman,

Supporters

Raymond Bultynck, Tyler Bunge, Thomas Bunink, Logan Bunning, Addison Bur, Tristan Burch, Andrew Burcham, Johnny Burcham <3, Jesse Burchfield, Scott Burchfield, Alex Burford, Hayden Burger, Adam Burgess, Daniel Burgess, Matthew 'BurmaCuWin' Burgess, Nathan Burgess, Lelan Burgher, Andrew Burke, Dylan Burke, Ray Burke, Drew Burkett, Jacob Burkett, Eric Burkhalter, Collin Burkhart, Jacob Burley, Ben Burling, Daniel Burling, Daniel Burn, Kieren Burne, Rob Burnett, Thomas Burnip, Karl Burniston, Harry Burns, Jacob Burns, Lazlo Burns, OffGridGamer Johnny Burns, Sam Lewis Burns, Andrew Burridge, James Burriss, Alex Burroughes, Alex Burroughs, Joshua Burrow, Cieran Burrows, David Burrows, Sam Burrows, Lee Burt, Amanda Burtchett, Ross Burton, Taylor Burton, Thomas Burton, Yveline Burton, Jack Burton-Self, Jackson Bury, Alef Burzmali, Jonathan (John) Busch, Tomar But, Andrew Butcher, Tom James Butcher 'Typogre', Erika Butland, Amy Butler, Callum Butler, Charlie Butler, Christian Butler, Gary Butler, Jonny Butler, Noah Butler, Stuart Butler, Joseph Butler-Moor, Jonno Butson, Daniel Butt, Matthew Butt, Fergie Buttercup, Sophie Butterworth, Corbin Butts, Robin Butz, Alec Buxton, Joshua Buxton, Dieter Buyse, Jack Byass, Jack Byers, Nathan Byers, Sam Byford, Andy Byrd, Callum Byrne, Christopher Byrne, Hayden Byrne, Patrick Byrne, Paul O Byrne, Reece Byrne, Sean Byrne, Reece Byrnes, Rachelle Byroad, Siobhan C, Daniel Cacioppo, Matthew Cadd, Andrew Caddell, Matt Caddell, Matthew Cadenas, Henry Cadogan, Maggie Caffrey, Taidhg Cahill, Antoine Cahn, Jean-Baptiste Caillaud, Christopher Cain, Ciaphas Cain, Ryan Cain, David Cairney, Emily Cairns, Matt Cairns-Poole, Peter Caldarola, M. Caldeira (Mcportugalem), Harrison Caldwell, Cameron Callaghan, Dylan Callaghan, Sam Callaghan, Stef Callanan, Nicholas Callander, David Callier, Melina Fay Callioni, Matthew Callum, John Calum, Sandy Calvert, Steven Calvert, Craig Cameron, Braden Camilleri, Chris Camm, Joshua Cammock, Ya Boi Cammy, Danny Campbell, David W R Campbell, Erik Campbell, Harry Campbell, Ian Campbell, Jennifer Campbell, Kayden Campbell, Lee Campbell, Levi A. Campbell, Max Campbell, Courtney Canning, Marc Cannon, Thomas Cannoot, Spencer Cantafio, Blake Cantrell, Josh Capewell, Elizabeth Capp, Charlie Capps, Boso Captain, Nicholas Carabine, Genevieve Carbonneau, Kaylee Cardana, Jason Cardno, Beth Carey, Jerome 'Emorejets' Carey, Tasmin Carey, Hugo Caritey, Freddie Carlisle, Jeff Carlisle, Tyler Carlson, Will Carlson, Isaak Carlsson, Aaron Carnahan 'PlumpChimp', Michael Carnall, Gabe Carnes, Alex Carney, Maeve Carney, Ralph Carney, William J Carney, James R Carney Sr Love you Dad Rip, Ryan Caron, Cedric Caron-Lavoie, Steven Carpadakis, Britnie Carpenter, Christopher H Carpenter, Jodie Carpenter, Tristan Carpenter, Zac Carpenter, Alex Carr, Pj Carr, Jacob Carriello, George Carrier, Philip Carringer, Adam Carroll, Andrew Carroll, Hamish Carroll, Josh Carroll, Liam John Carroll, Seán Carroll, Uisca Carroll, Jayden Carslake,

Aaron Carson, Josh Carson, Cole Carsten, Ashley Carter, Ben Carter, Ewan Carter, Harry Carter, Jacob Carter, Jamie Carter, Jessica Carter, Kyle Carter, Nancy Carter, George Cartlidge, Gemma Cartwright, Hayley Cartwright, John Cartwright, Michael Cartwright, Tony Cartwright, Kayla Casabuena, Chad Casale, Alice Casey, James Casey, Michael Casey, Ryan Casey, Mark Casey (PixelPodium), John Cash, Sean Caskey, Casoonn, Jonathan Cassell, Abbie Cassidy, Stephen Cassidy, Caste, Erin and Michael Casteel, James Castle, Liam Castles, Christopher Catalano, Ramsey Cather, Ami Cattrall, Daniel Causton (and Livvy the dog), Sam Cauvin, Restless Cavy, Benjamin Cays, @cdl2002, John Cedergren, Tony Cefalu, Verena Celis, Cem, Matthias 'Bright Spark' Cermak, Cristian Cerroni, Jonathan Chadwick, Thomas Atlas Chadwick, Cullen Chaffin, David Chaira, Michal Chalacinski, Jacob Challender, Marcus Chalmers, Mark Chalmers, Dean Chambers, Jason Chambers, Oliver 'Caldyro' Chambers, Conor Chamiec, Maxime Champagne, Sam Champs, Chris Chan, Wayne Chan, Yanny Chan, Albert Chandra, Tom Chaney, Vincent Channon Keimera, Aaron Chaplin, Craig Chapman, Emma Chapman, Kate Chapman, Kenny Chapman, Matthew Chapman, Matthew Chapman, Will Chappell, Prince Charcoal, Charlotte Chard, Matthew Charles, Ben Charlesworth, Kitty Charlie, Charlie, Luke Charlton, Heidi Charnoski, Kyle Chart, Kiki Chartreuse, Marc Gabriel Chassé, Andrew Chatten, Jose Chavez, Lewis Cheel, David Cheetham, Aimee Chell, Zixin Chen, Oliver Chenery, Jake Cherry, James Chester, ChevronTango, PJ Cheyne-Miller, Tristan Chia, Josh Chica, Alex Chichester, Ben Chilcott, Liam Chilcott, Aston Childs, Lucy Childs, Cedric Chinn, Marley Chinn, Roxana Chiorean, Matthew Chirnside, Phil Chisholm, Miloslav Chlíbek, Chak Man Cho, Jim Choi, Joseph Cholerton, Austin Chomoa, Niyaz Chowdhury, Lene Christensen, Chris Christie, Iain Christie, Jonathan Christie, Joe Christman, Eli Christoff, Christoffer, Johnathon Christopher, Miles Christopher, ChrisWithAKube, Dongwoo T Chung, Nathaniel Churchill, Mikhail Cicala, Avian Ciganko-Ford, Hanno Cilliers, Melina Cirverius, Tim Claessens, Alex Claire, Alex Clare, Jack Clare, Jacob Clare, James Clare, Henry Claridge, Ben Clark, Bethannie Clark, Callum Clark, Christopher Clark, Devin Clark, Ed Clark, Edward 'Squeaky' Clark, Henry Clark, Jack Clark, Jacob Clark, Jonathan Clark, Josh Clark, Kinnon Clark, Liam Clark, Robert Clark, Samuel Clark, Simon Clark, Alex Clarke, Ben Clarke, Charlotte Emma Clarke, Daniel Clarke, Danny Clarke, Fred Clarke, Jake Clarke, Laurie Clarke, Michael Clarke, Tom Clarke, William Clarke, The ClassaNova Team, Sebastian Clatterbuck, Daniel Claussen, Hannah Clay, Alex Clayton, Andrew Clayton, Luke Clayton, Martin Clayton, Thomas Clayton, Danny Clearwater, Cyrus Cleary, Lee Clegg, Nathan Clemann, Hal Clemens, Mitchell Clements, Bartal Clementsen, Lauren D. Clemmet, Eddy Cless, Mac Clevinger, Richard Cliffen, Miles Cline, Steven Clinton, Nicholas

Supporters

Clippinger, Jack Clishem, Harrison Clover, Sam Clowes, Michael Clubb, Filip Čmilňák, CMSeff, Cameron Coakley, Garrett Coakley, Ben Coates, Jared Coates, Alex Coatsworth, Andrew Cobb, Matt Cobb, Stephen A. Cobden, Jared Cochran, Jay Cochran, Harry Cochrane, Philip Cochrane, Matthew Cocker, Marc (The Incredible) Cockerton, Joanna Cocklin, CodeF53, Erick Coe, André Coelho, James Coen, Jurgen Coenegrachts, Christian Coffaro, Erik Coffey, Juan Cofre, Tony Cogan, Kylie Coghill, Daniel (Loves Kay Kay) Cohen, James Cohen, Thea Cohn, Thomas 'teecol' Colbourn, Dexter Cole, Hamish Cole, Jed Cole, Jonathan Cole, Kadence Cole, Matthew Cole, Jade Colebourne, Bryce Coleman, Kerrick Coleman, Charles Coles, Jay Coles, Jackie Coley, James Colgan, Tom Colley, Alistair Colliar, Simon Collier, Tio Colligan, Christopher Collingridge, Aidan Collins, Amy Collins, Benjamin Collins, Chase Collins, Joshua Collins, Michael Collins, Robert Collins, Sean Collins, Simon Collins, Toby Collins-Wren, Henry Collis, Pål Collyer, Aidan Colosimo-Petrasso, Adam Colquitt, Liam Eric Colwell, Tom Combley, Common Denominator-JW, Ricky Compton, Jake Conibeer, Matt Conine, Michelle Conklin, Josh Conlon, Ryan Conneely, Andrew Connell, Rhys Connell, Cian Connellan, Stuart Connelly, Jerrod Conner, Keegan Connolly, Jack 'GiggleSquid' Connors, Dawson Conville, Conall Conway, Sam Conway, Gary Cook, Ian Cook, Jacob Cook, John Cook, Lachlan Cook, Matthew Cook, Ryan Cook, Savannah Cook, Sean Cook, Steve Cook, Harry Cook (Trekkie 135), Joseph Cook-Williams, Jack Cooke, Jake Cooke, Joe Cooke, Jordan Cooke, Lewis Cooke, Neil Cooke, Samuel Cooke, Ryan Cooke-McGuinness, Rhys Cookie, Josh Coombe, Chris Coomber, Sam Coombs, James Cooney, Ben Cooper, Ben Tenshi Cooper, Blake Cooper, Chris Cooper, Courtney Cooper, Daniel Cooper, Hannah Cooper, James Cooper, Joseph Cooper, Josephine Cooper, Keelan Cooper, Luke Cooper, Matthew Cooper, Nick Cooper, Rich Cooper, Sam Michael Cooper, Seth Cooper, Toby Cooper, William Cooper, Zev Cooper-Bennun, Nattie Copeland, Amanda Copier, Aaron Coppedge, Brent Coppens, Joel Copson, Darius Copus, Kyle Corbett, Tyler Corbett-Sourshake, Chris Corby, Colin Corcoran, Jack Corcoran, Chris Cordon, William Cordwell, Zach Cormier, Alex Corn, Josh Cornell, Thomas Cornell, Alex Cornish, Ryan Cornwell, Nathan Corr, Alec Corser, Sean Cosgrave, Lucas Cosolo, Steven Costa, Kelan Costello, Patrick Costello, James Cotham, Michael Cotham, Sophie Cotterill, Michael Cotton, Darragh Coughlan, Chloe Coughlin, Adam Coulson, Alfie Coulson, Christopher Coulson, Matthew Coulson, BM Coulter, Nick Coulter & Toby Hudson, James Coulthard, Aaron Coulton, Harri Cound, Lachlan Couper, Cian Courtney-Long, Jake Cousans, Jimmy Cousino, Grant Cousins, McLaren Cousins, Aaron Coville, Tyler Covington, Brendan Cowan, Frazer Cowan, Sam Cowan, Felicity Cowdrey, Alex Cox, Anthony Cox, Ceceilia Cox, Chris Cox, David Cox, James Cox, Jamie Cox, Joanne Cox, Kaleb Cox, Nicholas

Cox, Oliver 'Kokkusu' Cox, Paul 'Coxy' Cox, Sean Coxhead, Kyle Coxon, Jack Coy, Charlie Coyle, Jennifer Coyle, Rob Coyle, Tom Coyle, Joshua Cozens, Kane Crabtree, Samuel Crabtree, Alexandru Craciunescu, David Cragg, Joshua Craggs-Hill, Ben Craig, Callum Craig, Ewan Craig, James Craig, Samuel Craig, Trevor Craig, Craig & Sam, Angus Cram, Paulwillem Cramer, Conor Crampsie, Steph Crandall, Liam Crane, Matthew 'Mattihase' Crane, Sean Crane, Max Craner, McKenna Craven, Connor Crawford, Khadijah Crawford, Angus Crawley, Elliot Crawshaw, Stephen Crawshaw, Oliver Creasey, Natalie Creed, Jamie Creek, Matthew Cremer, Samuel Creten, Brigid Crevola, Max Crichton, Conor Crickmore, Bram Crielaard, Jack Critten, Magnus Criwall, Benjamin Crocker, Joseph Crocker, Joshua Crocker, Michaela Croe, Alex Croft, Dayton Croft, Jay Croft, Thomas Croft, Timothy Croft, James Crofton, Mark Crolla, Josh Crompton, Cian Cronin, Joseph Cronin, Alex Crook, Oliver Crook, Tonicha Crook, Ethan Crooks, Jack Crooks, Caleb Crory, Mark Crosby, Bradley Cross, Nick Cross, Mitchell Crossland, Matthew Crossman, Andrew Crosswait, Simon Crouch, Stuart Croughan, Alex Crowe, Robert Crowley, Fior Crowstaff, Lachlan Crowther, Matthew Crowther, John Cruickshanks, Sarah Crump, Dan Crutchington, Gonzalo Cruz, Parker Cryderman, Peter Csicsay, Daniel Cso, Alex Cuba, Joseph Cube-Romero, Niche Florett Cudjoe-Jones, Luke Cuellar, Dominic Cuevas, Rhys Cullen, Tom Cullen, Tony Culpin, Fraser Culton, Will Cumberland, Fraser Cumming, Ben Cummings, Quinn Cummings, Jake Cummins, Scott 'Ferby' Cummins, Anthony Cunliffe, Matthew Cunneen, Aaron Cunningham, Lee Cunningham, Oliver Cunningham, Quinn Cunningham, James Cunnington, James Cunnold White, Professor Cupcake, Logan Curnow, Samuel Curnow, Tom Curnow, Kian Curran, Alex Currie, Brandon Currie, Lee Currie, Ross Currie, James Curry, Gemma Curtis, Jason Curtis, Kyle Curtis, Matthew Curtis, Zach Curtis, Miranda Curto, Glenn Curwen, Bradley Cushion, Odhrán Cushley, Zachary Cushman, Will Cuthbertson, Sarah Cuthel, Joshua Cutting, Sarah Louise Cutts, Bryan Czamara, Jacob Czerwan, Harry D-C, Josh D., Joshua D'Angelo, Tommaso D'Argenio, William Dabbs, Andrew Dack, Alex Dadoun, Henry Dadswell, Sam Daffern, Josef Dag, Niall Dagg, Agnar Dahl, Karl Dahle, Sam Dains, Justin Daisy, Fredric Dalqvist, Gerard Daly, Ulf Damkjer, DanDaMan97x, Rajesh Dandekar, Zipffy Dando, Benjamin Daniel, Kevin Daniel, Shane Daniel, Daniel - Tootyfruity, Daniel3032, Angelo Daniele, Toby E.G. Daniell, Nick Daniello, Simon Danielsson, Cameron Dann, Eric Dapp, Jack Darby, Steven Darby, Dark Insanities, Jack Darkens, Nicholas Darling, Jack Darlington, Thomas Darmody, Jonathan Dartnell, Adam Darwin, Vincent Das, Adam Dashper, Väino Daum, Noble Dave, Adam Davenport, Alan Davenport, Auston Davenport, Jack Davenport, Jordan Davey, Reus Davey, Tom Davey, Jacob Davey-Lambert, Clifford LeRoy David, Joël David, Glen

Supporters

Davidson, Jack Davidson, Jamie Davidson, Owen Davidson, Rory Davidson, Sam Davidson, Steven Davidson, Alex Davies, Carlos Davies, Daniel Davies, Dylan Davies, Hayden Davies, Ieuan Davies, Joel Davies, Jon Davies, Luca Davies, Luke Davies, Morgan Davies, Oriana Davies, Paul Davies, Rhys Davies, Vaughan Davies, Nathaniel Davies [StratoV], Adam Davis, Alexander Davis, Ben Davis, Conner Davis, Elias Davis, Haley Davis, Jason Davis, Justin Davis, Kristen Davis, Matty Davis, Rhys Davis, Jerry Davis II, Ben Davis-Lorton, Michael Davison, Roger Davison, Matt Dawe, Aaron Dawes, Neil Dawes, Phill Dawes, Aaron Dawson, Lewis Dawson, Mark Dawson, Michael Dawson, Nathan Dawson, Robert Dawson, Daxwred, Lewis Day, Ruud de Bont, Amber de Bruijn, David de Bruijn, Hans de Bruijn, Henry de Carle, Jessica De Cort, Pierce De Hóra, Douwe de Jong, Merlijn de Jong, Jessica De Maid, Christopher de Mercado, Stephen de Riel, Marvin de Rooij, Vincent de Smet, Elson De Souza Jr., Steven de Vet, Roby de Visser, Stijn De Vleeschauwer, Jur de Vries, Mark De Vries, Rylen de Vries, Charlie de Waal, Boet de Willigen, Alex de Winter, Andrew de-Ste-Croix, Michael De'Placido, John Deakin, Matt Dean, Ricky Dean, Stephen Dean, Tom Dean, Alex Deane, Daniel Dearden, Deathlink10, David Deaton, Matt Debenham-Burghart, Heinrich Dechering, Lisa Decker, Zachary DeConinck, Chris Deeley, Cole DeFallier, Ronan DeFanti, Noah deFer, Joe Defter, Cas Dekker, Floris Dekkers, Matteo Del Gallo, Nick Del Mastro, Jason Del Ponte, Luke Delahoy, Daniel Delaney, Kyle Delaney, Niall Delaney, Ben Delaney-Brownlow, Sven Delanoye, Shane Delany, Hugo Delatorre, Theo Delettre, Cody DelFava, Zachary 'DelirusRex' Delfs, Alex Delk, Harry Dellow, Griffin Delmore, Chris Delones, Grady Delp, Barry Delreu, Alex Demartino, Thomas DeMelo, Clayton Dement, Matthew DeMio, Edward Robert Karol Demkowicz-Duffy, Ciarán Dempsey, Jordan den Heeten, Daniël den Heijer, Saya Denesha, Christopher Denk, Sarah Denman, Steven Denman, Tom Denman, Jacob Dennison, Timo Dennison, Jack Densley, Pablo Dent, Kyler Denton, Matthew Denton, Mike Denton, Alex Denton-Bell, Seb Deragon, Randi Derakhshani, Matthew Derks, Shawn Dermer, Sebastian DeRosa, Fletcher DeRouen, Kieran Derrick, Johnny Deschane, Jackson Desgagne, Nikola Despinic, Jacob Determan, Alex Dethier, Tovly Deutsch, Dylan Devalia, Logan DeVasure, Mark DeVault, Liam Devenney, Christian Dever, Ethan Devlin, Lukas DeVries, Devyn , Jordy Dewerchin, David Dewhirst, Rowan DeWitt, Nick Dewsbury, Dholoken, Marco Di Loreto, Massimo Di Ruscio, Alexander Di Vito, Jacob Dial, Aidan Diamond, Octavio Dias, Daniel Dias Cyrino, Jacob C. Diaz, Conor Dick, Stephen Dickason, Matthew Dicken, Samuel Dicken, Cole Dickinson, Dexter Dickinson, Isaac Dickinson, Evan Dickison, Ryan Dickman, Alexander Dickson, Lucie Dickson, Michael Dickson, Kai Diederichsen, Benedict Dietrich, Don Dietrich, Ashlyn Diggins, Corné Dijk, Eoghan Dillane, Mark Dillard, Brendon Robert Dillon, Fenna Dillon, Oli Dillon, Natalie

Dimasi, Konstantinos Dimopoulos, Fletcher Dinard-Samuel, Arran Dingwall, Garrett DiPalma, Dan Dipllodocus, Tiaan Dippenaar, Patrick Dirks, Robert DiRosa, Phil DiSalvo, disjfa, Sam Disney, Joseph Dispoto, Cody Ditchfield, William Dite, Div the Horse, Caleb Diven, Ashley Divenuto, Ben Dixon, Daniel Dixon, Jack Dixon, Liam Dixon, Matthew Dixon, Samuel Dixon, Mark Dixon-Mersh, Liam Doan, Minh Doan, Joel Dobb, Eleri Dobbs, Jake Dobbs, Alex Dobeck, Izak Dobney, Conor Docherty, Dave Docker, Ewan Dockerty, Colin Dodd, Chloe Dodd (RSkittless), Jason Dodge, Adam Dodman, Antony Doff, Charlotte Doherty, James Doherty, Jennifer Doherty, Joseph Doherty, Rory Doherty, Chris Dohmen, Jack Doig, Joseph James Dollard, Richard Dölz, Jack Domenici, Tyler Domin, Leonardo Domingues, Marvin Dominguez, Rick Dominicus, Jeremy Donald, Harley Donaldson, Stephen Donegan, Matthew Doney, Jerry Dong, Darryl Donnelly, Stanley Donnelly, David Donner, Emma Donohue, Andrew Donovan, Harry Donovan, Fletcher Doolan, Jd Doran, William Doran, Rainer Dorant, Henry Dorman, Steffen 'Dixi' Dörner, Robbert Dorrestein, Carl Dorsett, Corey Dorsey, Colin Doubek, Ethan Doucet, Chris Douglas, Christopher Douglas, Matthew Douglas-Brown, Tom Douglass, Edward Dovey, Jack Dovey, Finn Dowds, Conor Dowler, Josh Downard, James Downey, Jon Downey, Liam Downie, Jack Downing, Jonny Downs, Stephen Dowson, Nic Doye, Anna Doyle, Conor Doyle, Graham Doyle, Philip Doyle, Ryan Doyle, Jean-Raphaël Doyon, Natalie Drabsch, Andy 'Rednic' Dracon, Jan Felix Dräger-Gillessen, DragonNightArt, Nathan Drake, Thomas Drake, Aaron 'Aarwoo' Draper, Jack Draper, Bailey Dremel, Jacob Drew, Jak Drew, Melissa Drewry, Johannes Drews, Chathan Driehuys, Rhys Drinkwater, Nicholas Driscoll, Sam Driver, Mark Drumm, Jack Drummond, Alex Dry, Nathan 'Money well spent' Dryburgh, Harry Dryden, Jack Duarte, Tim Dubbelman, Jacob Dubois, Derek J. Dubuque, DuckTheCow, Luke Duckworth, Tim Ducret, Bethany Dudley, Chris Jan Dudley, Richard Duff, Robert Duffield, Snowy 'Count Frackula' Duffield, Boden Duffy, Ryan Duffy, George Duggins, Zack Duggins, Olaf Duinmaijer, Ella Duke, Nate Dull, Cog Dunbar, Tyler Dunbar, Matt Duncalf, Louise Duncan, Ryan Duncan, Duncan 'NiftyHat', Cameron Dunk, Alexandria Dunlop, Tom Dunmore, Aaron Dunn, Anthony Dunn, Charlie Dunn, James Dunn, Bradan Dunne, Cian Dunne, Daniel Dunsmore, Michael Duntz, Kevin Duong, Cole Dupuis, Ashley Durnall, Aaron Durning, Daniel Durrance, Abigail Duske, JJ Dusting, Jonathan Dutkus, Joss Dutton, Will Dutton, Jeffrey Duvall, Mason Dyas, George J. Dyason, Lindsey Dyches, Matt Dye, Joseph Dyer, Patrick Dyer, Rhys Dyer, Thomas J. Dyer II, Liam Dyke, Jessica Dymphna Rosana Virtua, Joshzua Dysert, Aaron Dyson, Jack Dyson, Josh Dyson, Mr. E, Sarah E, Damion Eaddy, Cameron Eadie, Samuel Ealam (The Second Coming), Lee Chun Ean, Nicole Eannucci, Peter Eardley, Adam Earl, Annmarie Earl, Kieron Earl, Nathan Earle,

Supporters

Ryan Earles, Liam Earnshaw, Matthew Earwaker, Tom Easden, Lewis Eason, Elliot Eaton, Marcel Eaton, Dominic Eatwell, Jonathan Ebsworth, Dylan Eck, Emily Eckman, Moritz Eckrich, Tom Eden, Quentin Edens, Owen Edgar, Rasmus Edling, Kyle Edmond, Timothy Edmonds, Zayne Edmonson, Michael Edmonston, Joshua Edward1s2s4s3, Ben Edwards, Braden Edwards, Conor Edwards, Daniel Edwards, Dion Edwards, Jake Edwards, Jamie Edwards, Joe Edwards, Joseph Edwards, Kayleigh Edwards, Lincoln Edwards, Marc Edwards, Matt Edwards, Matthew Edwards, Nathan Edwards, Rhydian Edwards, Samuel Edwards, Tegan Edwards, Thomas David Edwards, Tobias Edwards, Zoe Edwards-Wainwright, Ethan Edwards-Wells, Harry Efstathiades, H Egan, Matthew Egan, Whitney Egelston, Joshua Ehlers, Matthew Eich, Anthony Eickelman, Henrik Eikrem, Sigve Eilertsen, Daniel Eisen, Stefan Eisenreich, Josh Eitel, Markus Eiterer, Liam 'Eggy1632' Ekeberg, Toms Ekmanis, Kamal El Assal, Ben Elbling, Andrew Elbourn, Natalie-Marie 'Sparky' Elcock, Ahren Elderton, Magid Elgady, Tactician Elgah, Dan Elia, Amy Elizabeth, Katie Elizabeth, Matthew Ellerby, Alexander Lund Ellingsgaard, Sarah Ellingson, Adam Elliott, Amelia Elliott, Brandon Elliott, Darren Austen Elliott, Drew Elliott, James Elliott, Mark Elliott, William Elliott-Bowden, Ayran Ellis, Carlin Ellis, Christopher Ellis, Connor Ellis, Luke Ellis, Peyton Ellis, Samuel Ellis, Euan Ellis-Jones, Amy Ellison, Curtis Ellison, Michael Ellison, Zachary Elliston, Tyler Ellul, Foster Elmendorf, Connor Elmy, Callum Else, Clayton Eltis, Ryan Elwood-Clarke, Digital Ember, Tobias Emberland, Richard Emblem, Emereld master333, Aaron Emerson, Rob Emerson, Chloe Emery, Scott Emery, Alex Emmas, Yoran Engelberts, Jeroen Engels, Lasse Engen, Nilena Engi, Harry England, Jake Englin, Kyle English, Albin Engström, Aurel Eppert, Joshua Epps, Hiussay Equinity, Bill Erhard, Patrick Erhard, Sean Erickson, Simen Eriksen, Oscar Eriksson, May Erise, Zach Ernst, Tiina Eronen, Chris Errett, Daniel Errington, Norbert Érsek, Enrique Escobar, Bryn Escott-Allen, Liah 'The Weejay' Esparza, Gabriel Espinosa, Magnus Espø, Lisa Marleen Esselink, Joel Esson, Daniel Estabrook, Ben Estelle, Justin Estrellado, Ryan Etherington, Derrick Ettinger, Kenji Eva, Adam Evans, Andy Ray Evans, Aron Evans, Benjamin Evans, Cameron Evans, Courtney Evans, Ellis Evans, Geraint Evans, Grace Evans, Harry Evans, Ian Evans, Iwan Evans, Joshua Evans, Kaleb Evans, Luke Evans, Mark Evans, Nathan Evans, Simon Evans, Timothy Evans, Timothy Alfred 'Big slaps Mcgee' Evans, Tom Evans, Zack Evans, Zak Evans, George Evans & Kimberley Gill, Lisette Eve, Nicholas Eve-Kerchey, Sarah Eve-Kerchey, Fjodor Everaerts, Alex Everett-Last, George Everingham, Paul Everitt, Gleb Evteev, Mark Ewasiw, Russell Ewe, Chris Ewing, Dominic Ewing, Thomas Ewing, Daymara Excel, Kiera Exley, Extulen, Alexander Eyers-Taylor, Michael Eyre, Jamie Faben, Jack Fabian, fabnie, Jan Faborsky (Chromerian), Alex Facq, Cristian Daniel Fadón, Simon

Faerge, Edward Fagan, Fredrik Fagerstrøm, Jason Fahy, Alex Faint, Leif Fairbairn, Samuel Faircloth, FalconChipp, Jarrod Falconer, Magnus Faldorf, Ian Faletti, Luke Falgate, Matthew Falle, Lucy Fallows, Mr. Falsey, Cameron Fanelli, Jack Fannon, NoorAldin Farawati, Joel Vatne Fardal, Toni Fargher, Carl Farlow, Conor Farman, Rob Farmer, Adam Farnsworth, Rowan Farquhar, Alex Farr, Drew Farr, Jennifer Farr, Ciaron Farrell, Conor Farrell, Jack Farrell, George Farren, Katelyn Farrugia, Stephen Fasciani, Michael Fase, Devin Fassett Thainzek, FasterThanLlamas, Chris Fasulo, The Fat Vegan Liberator (AKA Anthony Goldsmith), Danny Faulkner, Joseph Faulkner, Archie Faulkner-Lerway, David Fausey, Matthew Favaloro, Fawks the wolf, Cynthia Fay, Derwen Fay, Carol-Ann Fazakarley, Alex Fearn, Jade Fearnley, Declan Feehily, Feelink It, Skylar Fegel, Benjamin Feiler, Simon Feist, Piotr Fejdych, Elijah Feliciano, Luis Félix, Alex Fellas, Paddy Fellows, Markus Fenes, Enicara Cagaerius Fenrir, Jayden Fenton, Jake Fenwick, Matthew Fenwick, Craig Ferels, Andrew Ferguson, Cameron Ferguson, Cooper Ferguson, James Ferguson, Nick Ferguson, Stuart Ferguson, Lachlan Ferguson-Shaw, Jack Fermor-Worrell, Alexander Fernandez, Jonathan Ferns, Samantha Ferns, Ricardo Ferreira, Rui Ferreira, Georgia Ferrol, Lachlan Ferry, Quinton Feser, Henri Fessel, Maria Nektaria Fetta, Tyler Fetty, Jeffrey Fewell, Zack Fewtrell, Edward Feys, Simon Fiander, Steven Fice, Oliver Fiddy, Amit Fidelman, Alex Fido, Daniel Field, Josh Field, Connor Fielder, Ramona Fielding, Max Fifield, Ryan Figler, Sam Figlmiller, Andrew Figueroa, Anna Eve Figueroa, Marlise Fikse, Peter File, Amanda Filipsson, Brandon Fillenworth, Daniel Filler, Braxton Fillerup, James Finch, Liam Finch, Rhiannon Fincham, Aaron Fincher, Max Findlater, Tom Findlay, Daniel Fink, Isaac Finkelstein, Conor Finn, Jack Finn, Jonathan Finn, Rob Finn, Finn, Jack 'The Chin' Finnegan, Quinn Finnegan, Fired_Fly, Max Firestorm, Bishop Firth, Callum Firth, Lina Fischer, Brendan Fisher, Nathan 'TediousTotoro' Fisher, Preston Fisher, Daniel 'puppiesanddogsarebest' Fitch, Simon Fitch, Jacob Fitchard, Kyle Fitness, Morgan Fitt-Boyland, Jacob Fitter, Conor Fitzgerald, Hudson Fitzgerald, Nicholas Fitzgerald, Robert Fitzgerald, Tyler Fitzgerald, Arthur Fitzjohn, Gabriel Fitzko, Austin Fitzpatrick, Luke Fitzpatrick, Angus Fitzsimons, Joseph Fitzsimons, Fizrug, Robin Aasen Fjeldberg, Maximilian Fjellner, Liam Flack, Ryan Flanagan, Shea Flanagan, Mike Flattery, Flavonoidz Explosion, Arran Flay, Robert Fleetham, Jace Fleming, Nathan Fleming, Cameron Flester, Harry Fletcher, Ian Fletcher, Joe Fletcher, Jonathan Fletcher, Anya Fletcher-Jones, Callum Flett, Callum Flinn, Todd Flitton, Alistair Flood, Oskar Florén, Eddie Flores, João Flórido, Johan Florin, Simon Floyd, Julian Flum, Colm Flynn, Sian Flynn, Steven Flynn, Tyler Foehlinger, Moritz Foerster, Paul Fogarty, Scott & Ben Foggin, Kira Foken, Stephen Foley, Phill Folkes, Linus Follert, Michael Fontana, Amy Foote, Ben Ford, Ciaran Ford, Edmund Ford, Glen Ford, Ken Ford, Ross Ford,

Supporters

Cameron Fordyce, Christopher Foreman, Nathan Foreman, Matt Forman, Rhyce Forrester, Jayke Forshaw, Joe Forster, Dylan Fortner, Jose Fortun, Elizabeth Fosbrook, Sydney Foshie, Tom Foss, Ole Steffen Fosseide, Aaron Foster, Alicia Foster, Benjaman Foster, David Foster, George Foster, Kit 'Quick Fastly' Foster, Liam Foster, Megan Foster, Wyatt Foster, Matthew Fothergill, Peter Fowler, Reece Fowler, Joel Fowles, Jess Fox, Joe Fox, Kyle Fox, Tyler Fox, Ronin Foxtail, Aidan Fozard, Roger Fracalossi, Adrian (Cat) Framingham, Rhys France, Christian Franchi, Connor Francis, David Francis, Owen Francis, Michael Francisco, Max Franck, Ethan Francois, Frederik Helmer Frandsen, Diane Frank (nediane), Alex Franke, Kyllian Franken, Emil Frankenberg, Autumn Franklin, Steven Frankowski, Perry Franks, Tyler Frankum, Kyle Fransen, Greg Frasco, Andrew Fraser, Ekaterina Fraser, Jamie Fraser, Jonathan Fraser, Kimberley Fraser, Leanne Fraser, William Fraser, Joaquin Frasu, Kevin Frazier, Nicholas Frederick, Noel Frederick, Anders Frederiksen, David Freeman, Joe Freeman, Johnathon Freeman, Louis Freeman, Benjamin Frege, Brandon French, Gill French, Max French, Frenchy, Bjorn Friberg, Thomas Friedel, Alec Friedman, Jono Friend, Luuk Frijmuth, Eric Fritsche, Joel 'Zyronn' Fritz, Martin Frontz, Cally Frost, Gary Frost, James Frost, Joshua Frost, Philip Frost, Maite Frutos, Alexander Fry, Christian Fry, Elia Fry, Martin Fry, Matt Fry, David Fryer, Edmund Fryxell, Tom Fugate, Victor Fugl, Ethan Fulbright, Ben Fuller, Kieran Fuller, Luke Fuller, Tom Fuller, Travis Fuller, Cameron Fulton, Jane Fung, Joseph Furber, Quintin Furlong, Timothy Furlong, Kyle Furmage, Abbie Furnivall, Tobias Fürstenfelder, Arne Furuseth, Joseph Fustolo, Alexander Futcher, Grant Futcher, Louie G, Matheos G, Nick G, Tom G and Lydia B, Matt G., Ömer G., Anders Gaardbo, Gonçalo Gabriel, Markus Gabrielsen, Adam Gade, Brendan Gadient, Brian Gahagan, Tyler Gainsbrye, Richard Gairing, Zav Galax, Harry Gallagher, Jacob Gallagher, Matthew Kavan Gallagher, Stephen Gallemore, Rachael Galley, Jeffrey Galli, Struan Gallie, Dan J Galliott, Damean Galloway, Kyle Galloway, André Galouchka, Christopher Gamble, Drew Gamble, GamingRack, Chris Gander, Daniel Gannon, Manuel Garat, Aden Garbellini, Savi Garcelon, Brenton Gardiner, Dan Gardiner, Andy Gardner, Brian Gardner, George Gardner, Robbie Gardner, Ryan Gardner, Welf Garkisch, Jonathan Garland, Nathan Garner, Oliver Garner, William Garrard, Ryan Garrett, Weston Garrett, Peyton Garris, Peter Garside, Jeck Garson, Nina Gärtner, Alex Garton-Hill <3, DJ Garwood-DeLong, Stan Gaskell, Seth Gaskins, Zack Gaspar, Austen Gatehouse, Ethan Gates, James (Insane) Gates, Ruby Gatt, Samuel Gatten (Ben is a Bean), Forrest Gauch, James Gauld, Frazer Gault, Nathan Gavin, Rebekah Gawthorpe, George Gawthrop, Chris Gawthrop-Bleet, Ehren Gay, Gary Gay, James Gay, Robert H. Gaydon, Alex Gayford, Joseph Gaynor, Andrew Geary, Leon Gebler, Balázs Géczi, Adam Gee, Brad Gee, Henry Gee, GeekMeetsWorld, Enrico

Geerts, Tom Geerts, Duncan Geissler, Gekoreivax, Patrick Gelvin, Shaun Gendall, Dominic Gentile, Daniel Geoghegan, Niall Geoghegan, Anthony George, CosmicHuwnd George, Klaus George, Sam George, William George, Brenda Georgen, Johan Gerdin, Stefan Gerrish, Will Gerrish, Sander Gerrits, Jeff Getrum, Jort Geurts, Carolyn Geyer, GG-JigglePhysics, Roshan Jade Gharaby, Leonardo Ghelli Luserna di Rorà, Auronyo Ghosh, Luca Giancola, Jordan Giannopoulos, Hugh Gibb, Max Gibb, Wilfred Gibbens, Cameron 'TheGibbonOfLif' Gibbon, Bobby Gibbons, Adam Gibbs, Carla Gibson, Garrett Gibson, Jac Gibson, Jennifer Gibson, Kyle Gibson, Sami Gibson, Jaeden Giesbrecht, Martin Giger, Alexander Gilchrist, Opal Gilchrist, Liam Giles, Nathan Giles, Ted Giles, Mike Gilfillan, Connor Gilhooly, Grue Gilith, Elis Gilkes, Ben Gill, Dr Martine Gill, Elliott Gill, George 'SentryBuster Is Spy' Gill, James Gill, Josh Gill, Polly Gill, Isaac Gillam-Lindo, Rhys Gillanders, Philip Gillberg, Joanna Gillespie, Audrey Gillies, David Gillingham, Maxwell Gilliver, Brody Gillmore, Adam Gilmartin, Adam Gilson, Mike Gilson, GingerYeti95, John Gipp, Liam Girard, Hugh Gisborne, Casper Gislum, Eric Givans, Conor Given, Eric Gladrow, Daniel Gläss, Howard Glaum, James Glavin, David Gleed, Ryan Gleed, Alexander Glegg, Alastair Gleghorn, Stephen Gleitz, Connor Glen, Harry Glen, Jacob Glen, Danny Glover, Will Glynn, Gnegnol, Goaliator, Matt Goble, Max Godber, Mark Goddard, Katie Godfrey, Nathan Godfrey, Bartosz Godlewski, Jack Godley, Craig Goheen, Cameron Gold, Christopher Goldasz, Kevin Goldberg, Ya'akov Goldberg, Tate Golder, Kieran Golding, Sean Golding, Kacper Golonka, Michael Golowka, Elizabeth Gonsalves, Alexis Gonzales, Emily Gonzales, Lucas Gonzales, Michael T Gonzalez, Rachel Gonzalez, Isaac Gooch, Morrie Gooch, Samuel Gooch, James Goodall, Elliot Goodban, Charlie Goodbody, Aiden Goode, Alex Goodfield, Jack Goodlett, Franklin Goodman, Sean Goodman, Hannah Goodwin, Jack Goodwin, Zak Goodwin, Alex Goodwins, Johnny Pigby Goonan, Alyssa Gordon, Harrison Gordon, Jay Gordon, Joe Gordon, Alex Gore, Dylan Gore, Sam Gorlov-Webster, Ben Gosney, Jesko Göttges, Patrick Götz, Bill Gould, Leon Gould, Jake Gould-Reddy, Rob Goulding, Ben Gourlay, Zach Goyette, Oscar Grace, Chris Graden, Max Gradinger, Wil Gradwell, Cooper Graetz, William Grafford, Alexander Grafton, Elliott Gragg, Aaron Graham, Connor Graham, David Graham, Jack (Randsaw) Graham, Karl Graham, Lars Grahmann, Ashley Grainger, Alan Grant, Cameron Grant, Daniel Grant, Gav Grant, Joe Grant, Joseph Grant, Sam Grant, Isaac Grant-Smith, Joe Grantham, Charles Grass, Timothy Grassi, Amy Graves, Michael Graves, William Graves, Alexander Gray, Alister Gray, Allen Gray, Harry Gray, Isabelle Gray, Jack 'Daftlearner' Gray, Jayden Gray, Jennifer Gray, Jess Gray, Jordan Gray, Joshua M Gray, Katy Gray, Tanner Gray, Richard Grayson, Julius Gražėnas, Christopher Greaves, Rares Grecu, Jordan Greelish, Alexander

Supporters

Green, Alicia Green, Brandon Green, Callum Green, Christy Green, Daren Green, Dillon Green, Emily Green, George Green, Jack Green, James Green, Jamie 'Ake' Green, Jed Green, Jessie Green, Joseph Green, Josh Green, Joshua Green, Kristopher Green, Kurtis Green, Maxwell Green, Nathan Green, Nelson Green, Shane Green, Stephen Green, Theo Green, Tyler Green, William Green, William 'Outcast' Green, Zoe Green, George Greenaway, Tom Greenaway, Toni Greenaway, Aidan Greene, Gavin Greene, Luke Greenhill, Rowan Greenhill Timewell, Ollie Greenslade, Owen Greenslade, Corey Greenstein, Henry Greer, Jack Greer, Hans Gregersen, Mikkel Juel Gregersen, Asher Gregg, Ben Gregg, Dan Gregg, Ryan Gregory, Matthew Greig, Oscar Greinke, Simran Grewal, Aaron Greyser, Callum Gribben, Daniel Griffen, Ashley Amelia-Thomas Griffin, DeShawn Griffin, Jared Griffin, Michael Griffin, Carson Griffing, Ruben Griffioen, Gethin Griffith, Oliver Griffith, William Griffith, Aaron Griffiths, Eliot Griffiths, Molly Griffiths, Paige Griffiths, Sam Griffiths, Zea Griffiths, Jack Grigg, Oscar Grigg, Liam Griggs, George Grimley, Nick Grimmer, Ryan Grindley, Kieran Grist, Joshua Grizzell, Kevin Groat, Lars Gröber, Conor Grocock, Reece Grocott, Niek 'Pixle' Groen, The Groener Family, Rory Grogan, Ryan Grondin, Maxine Grooms, Aaron Grosse, Tristan Grossnick, Cameron Grounds, Lisa Groves, Murray Groves, Travis Groves, Daniel Growcott, Benjamin Gruber, Zach Gruber, Andrew Guard, Josh Guarneri, Dani Gud, Cyrus Guderyon, Ellys Gudger, Linus Gudmundsson, William Eugene Guenin Jr., Janis Guerke, Joris Guetens, Flora Guijt, Andrew Guire, Steven Gulberg, Christiaan Guliker, Rohan Gundala, Brandon Gunderson, Chris Gunn, Oscar Gunnell, Adam Gunning, Gunrun Gunrun, Konrad Gunshon, William Gunter, Ankishu Gupta, Dillon Gurney, James Gurney, Hannes Gustafsson, Timmy Gustavsson, Ciaran Guthrie, Helen Guthrie, The right honourable Harry Guthrie, Norbert Guti, Benjamin Scott Guy, Kallim Guy, Maxwell Guy, Damien Gwardys, Scott Gygax, Veturliði Snær Gylfason, Emme H, Kamil H, Martin H, Thor Haag, Matthew Haahr, Jens CS Haarstad, Yannick Haas, Ole Haatveit, Sam Hackett, Cameron Haddock, Matthew Haddow, Abdul Hadi, James Hadley, Stephen Hadley, Frederik Haeusler, Mattias Hagberg, Cameron Hagelauer, Edward Hagreen, Christoph Hahn, Tre Hahn, Alastair 'SheepBeard' Haig, Fawn Hailey, David Hair, Thomas Haire, Leon Halbert, Andreas Halbro, Mathias Hald, Cris Hale, Dion Hale, Jadon Hale, Sam Hale, Trevor Hale, Simon Halewood, Dacoda Haley, Joe Haley, Halferbrain, Coire Halfpenny, halfur, Eivind Halhjem, Alexis Hall, Brandon Hall, Bryan Hall, Cameron Hall, James Hall, Joshua Hall, Kieran Hall, Lewi Hall, Lucas Hall, Matthew Hall, Max Sandwich Hall, Rosalind Hall, Ryan Hall, Taylor Hall, Thomas Hall, Zan Hall, William Hallam, Rob Hallatt, Daníel Snær Halldórsson, Anthony Halloway, Cam Halls, Cullen Halmstad, Håkon Haltbakk, Corey Hamat, Hilman Hambali, Jordan Hamblin, Nicholas Hamill,

Connor Hamilton, Euan Hamilton, Glenn Hamilton, Jack Hamilton, James Hamilton, Jamie Hamilton, Malachy Hamilton, Matthew Hamilton, Paul Hamilton, James Hamling, Russell Hamm, Stian Kjelstad Hammer, Leigh Hammersley, Alan Hammond, Steven Hammontree, Daniel Hampson, Josh Hampton, Karl-Johan Hamrin, Conner Hancock, Kieran Hancock, Liam Hancox, Max Hancox, Szymon Handke, Carl Handley, Joshua Handley, Jacob Handslip, Matt Haney, Ryan Hanley, Austin Hanna, Ben Hanna, William Hannah, Niko Hänninen, Joshua Hansard, Luke Hansard, Adrian R. Hansen, Casper Hansen, Chris Hansen, Gustav Ibsen Hansen, Jonathan Hansen, Joshua Hansen, Louis Hansen, Mads Frederik Hansen, Mark Hansen, Michael Hansen, Nicolaj Paw Hansen, Peter Hansen, Christopher Hanson, Ori Hanson, Rebecca Hanson, Thomas Hanson, Tyler Hanson, Simon Hansson, Manuel Hanzl, John Olav Haraldstad, Remi Harbo, James Harbord, Joshua Harbour, Simon Hardacre, Daniel Hardcastle, Dj Hardin, John Hardin, Jack Harding, Josh Harding, Paul Harding, Will Harding, Zach Harding, Alan Hardman, Tobias Hardt, Thomas Hardwick, François Hardy, Jacob Hardy, Katie Hardy, Keilen Hardy, Lance Hardy, Stephen Hardy, T-jay Harfleet <3, Ross Hargill, Jason Hargrave, Karl Harker, Jake Harman, Dennis Harmel, Stevie-Leigh Harmer, Matt Harmon, Adam Harper, Tobias Harper, Aydan Harr, Joe Harrington, Amy Harris, Ben Harris, Iain Harris, Jacob Harris, Jamie Harris, Nicole Harris, Oliver Harris, Samuel John Harris, Shaun Harris, Simon Harris, Zach Harris, Alex Harrison, Alexander Harrison, Cosmo Harrison, Dylan Harrison, Erik Harrison, James Harrison, Kane Harrison, Kieran Harrison, Leila Harrison, Michael (Conor smells) Harrison, Patrick Harrison, Rob Harrison, Scott Harrison, Seth Harrison, Sierra Harrison, Harvey Harrison-Doyle, Nicholas Harrold, Harrybob, Charlie Harrysson, Daniel Hart, Jack Hart, Luke Hart, Ellis Hartfield, Amy Hartley, Benjamin Hartley, Owen Hartley Jr, Derick Hartman, Harry Hartnell, Paul Hartramph, Ben 'Spoons' Harvey, Benjamin John Harvey, Bryn Harvey, Chris Harvey, David Harvey, James Harvey, Mathew Harvey, Michael Harvey, Thomas Harvey, Tyla Harvey, Franklin Harwood IV, Ethan Harycki, Jack Haseldine, Jordan Hass, Spencer Hassall, Joseph Hassell, Sander Hasselo, Alex Haswell, Moshe Hai Hatan, Tiarnan Hatchell, Jordan Hathaway, William Haub, Anders Bodin Haugen, Kjarton Haugen, Vegar Haugen, Håkon Hauglid, Kevin Hauman, Max Haupt, Alex Hausch, Kieran Havard, Jayson Haven, Eythan Havens, George Haviland, Arthur D Hawkes, Louis Hawkes, Luke Hawkes, Didier Tuscan Hawkey, Adam Hawkins, Charlton Hawkins, Corwyn Hawkins, Jack Hawkins, Jordan Hawkins, Ethan Hawksworth, James Hawthorn, Taylor Hawthorne, Grace Hay, Luke Hayden, Marc Hayden, Thomas Hayden, Garry Haydon, Jamie Hayes, Lachlainn Hayes, Pookage Hayes, Caleb Hayhoe-Castle, Ben Hayman, Nick Haynes, Calvin Hayward and Aurelie Larane, The Haywoods,

Supporters

Matt Hazeldine, Ariez Hazrul, Joseph Head, Luke Headington, J Heal, Joseph Heald, John Healey, James Heaney, Samuel Heaney, Joshua Heape, Jayden Heard, Amber Hearn, Ben Hugh Hearty, Howard Heath, Daksh Saikia Hebbar, Mitchell Hebbard, Michael Hechinger, Thomas Hechl, Max Hecht, Alexander Heckles, Anders Hedberg Magnusson, Benjamin Hedden, Marcel Hedemand, Ryan Hedge-Holmes, Angus Hedger, Benjamin Hedges, Dan Hedley, Hazel Hedrick, Erwin Heemsbergen, Conor Heffernan McGarry, Tim Heffernon, Carlin Hefner, Kinan Hegarty, Oliver Heib, Victor Heide Madsen, Steven Heiden, Malte Heidenblut, Christopher Heighton, Floris van der Heijde, Maurice Heijligers, Glenn-Helge Heimdal, Sara E. Heins, James 'Junkfight' Heis II, Ben Hellis, Hello There, Harry Hellyer, James Helm, Byron Helmrich, Help I'm Trapped In A Book Facto, Help I'm trapped in a book factory, Sam Helstrip, Seth Heltborg, Jeremy Helton, Gustav Hemgren, Ben Hemmings, Gareth Hemmings, Luke Hemmings, Peter Hemmins, James Henaghan, Rene Henckens, Chris Henderson, Egan Henderson, Joseph Henderson, Oliver Hendey, Max Hendrix, Callum Hendry, Darren Hendry, Ewan Hendry, Lukas Hendry, Bryan Hengels, Nicholas Hennell-Foley, Cara Henney, Craig Henney, Ryan Hennings, Brage Henriksen, Cerys Henry, Chace Henry, Daniel Henry, Kacey Henry, Leah Henry, Ryan Henry, Anthony 'NotThatAnt' Henson, Paul Henty, Robert Hepburn, Darragh Heppell, Johan Hepsö, Ashley Hepworth, Bianca Herbert, Andrew Herbison, Kent-André Herland, Ad Herlihy, Derek Hermann, Jared Hermann, Lasse Robsrud Hermansen, Tim Hermansson, Stefán Hermundsson, Brenda Hernandez, Enrique Hernandez, Nick Hernandez, Sebastian Hernandez, Spencer Hernandez, James Heron, Gary Herreman, James Herridge, Charles Herrin, Dave Herrington, James Hersh, Lhiam Herwill, Sarah Hesbrook, Sam Hesler (*poke*), Josh Heslor, John Hesman, Logan Hesseling, Chris Hesselink, Rob Hession, Naomi Heuer, Naomi Heuer @QuartzMoons, Thomas Hewer, Alice Hewett, Kyle 'KaiKat' Hewett, Philippe Hewett, Reilly Hewitson, Alfie Hewitt, Callum Hewitt, Emily J. Hewitt, James Hewitt, Joe Hewitt, Sam Hewitt, Sev Hewitt, Eddie Heyne, Matt Heys, Hi brother. No dinos sorry. From ur fav lil sis., Jake Hibbert, Lachlan Bruce Hibbert-Jones, Alex Hickey, Ethan Hickey, Lillith Hickling, Rebecca Hickman, Robert Hickman, Cole J Hicks, Connor Hicks, Joel Hicks, Justin Hicks, Robert Hicks, Jim Hickson, James Hiett, Alex Higgins, Daniel Higgins, Quinn Higgins, Stu, Katherine and Izzy Higgins, Brooklyn Higginson, Sally Higginson, Nick Higgs, Louis Higham, Jenna Hilario, Alex Hilbert, Tyler Hildebran, Greg Hildebrandt, Jacob Hildreth, Adam Hill, Carly Hill, Carter Hill, Chris Hill, Christopher Hill, Conner Hill, Darythe Hill, David Hill, Eli Hill, Gary Hill, Harvey Hill, Jacob Hill, Jesse Hill, Joe Hill, Kyle Hill, Nathan Hill, Ross Hill, Simon Hill, Steven Hill, Thomas Hill, Tyler Hill, Wilson Hill, Allen Hillaker, Riley Hillard, Bjarke Hillgaard, Daniel Hillman, Dennis

Hillmann, Charley Hills, Ari Fannar Hilmarsson <3, Callum Hilton, Eden Hilton, Jay Hilton, Leroy Hilverdink, Danny Hin, John Hinch, Adam Hindmarch :), Joseph Hine, Adam Hines, Dylan Hinnant, Kyle Hinojosa, Josh Hippe, hippity_hopper, Ethan Hirschowitz, Mark Hirst, Megan Max Hirst, Sam Hiscock, Jane Hiscoke, Sam Hiscox, The Hislop-Croft Family, Jurriaan Hisschemoller, Mantas Hitas, Andy Hitchen, Aaron Hitchens, Adam Luke Hitchin, Victoria Hjelm, Sora Hjort, Jakub Hnát, Steven Hoad, Ethan Hoang, Tai Hoang, Jannik Höb, Bastian Ole Hobbs, Mary Hobbs, Owain Hobbs, Connor Hockey, Lee Hockin, Daniel Hocking, Justin Hodakowski, Clay Hodges, Michael Hodges, Ryan Hodgetts, Tom Hodgins, Kieron Hodgkinson, Peter 'Strike' Hodgkinson, Douglas Hodgson, Martin Hodgson, [Bradin Hodgson]^3, Sam Hoejenbos, Sam Hoenes, Jonathan Hoffman, Jeroen Hofland, Frederik Høfler-Simonsen, Tom Hogan, Patrick Hogg, Ashley Hoggard, Cody Hohnecker, Ambrose Hoilman, Sean Manuel Holcomb, Luke Holdaway, Joshua Holden, Zak Holden, Daniel Holdsworth, Lucy Holdt, Joshua Hole, Eddy Holiday, Bailey Holland, Kai Holland, Luke Holland, Tim Holland, Harry Hollaway, Jesse Holle, Rebecca Hollingsworth, Yannik Hollmann, Chris Holloway, Gareth Holloway, Jack Holloway, Cabot Holm, Anton Holmberg, Isak Holmdahl, Aprille Holmes, Daniel Holmes, Joseph Holmes, Victor Holmgren Ödman, Tommi Holmnäs, Edward Holmwood, Alexander Holster, Jess Holt, Ariën Holthuizen, Henrieke Holtmann, Ashley Holton, Chelsea Holton, Yannik Holzer, Liam Homer, Henning Østertun Homlong, Jonathan Honey, David Honhold, Kieran Hood, Adrian Hook, Lucas Hook, Ben Hoole, Adam Hooper, Joshua Hooper, Maxine Morgan Hooper, Buwy Hope, Christopher Hope, James Hope, John Hope, Luke 'Lukazaide' Hope, Callum Hopkins, Jack Hopkins, Lincoln Hopkins, Matthew Hopkins, Nicholas Hopp, Joshua Horan, Daniel 'Mod' Horgan, Blake Horn, John Horn, Jan Marius Hornberg, Callum Hornby, Joseph Horner, Sam Horner, James Horsman, Austin Horton, Jacob Horton, Jakob Horvath, Ronald Hosang, David J. Hose, Patrick Hoskin, Adam Hoskinson, Justin Hoss, Tom Hostetler, Brandon Hostetter, James Hotchkin, Jacob Hougie, Joe House, James Housego, Kyle Housley, Niklas Hövel, Martin Hovin, Chris Howard, David Howard, Harry Howard, John Howard, Jonathan Howard, Joseph Howard, Joseph D. Howard, Joshua Howard, Liam Howard, Mike Howard, Nathaniel Howard, Nick Howard, Joe Howarth, Justin Chandler Howcroft, Elliot Howden-Roberts, Hannah Howden-Roberts, Jordan Howe, Beth Howell, Edward & William Howell, James Howell, Matt Howell, Rhys Howell, Mark Howells, Michael Howes, Oli Howes, Zach Howes, Sam Howeth, James Howlin, Matthew Howlin, Gavin Howson, Mark Howson, Lasse Höykinpuro, Jordan Hoyland, Jack Hoyle, Casey 'Spreadsheets' Hoyt, Maxim Hrynaszkiewicz, Kevin Hu, Joel Tyler Hubbard, Jack Hubbucks, Ashley Huby, Ross Huchko, Daniel Huda,

Supporters

Isaac Hudd, Sam Huddart, Alex Huddleston, Wesley (Yihuya) Hudgens, Alex Hudson, Charlie Hudson, Jack Hudson, Matthew Hudson, Matthew James Hudson, Olivia Hudson, Tasha Hudson, Fletcher Huelsemann, Hailey Huerta-Nunez, Chase Huettl, Lala Huffman, Aidan Hughes, Charlie Hughes, Charlotte Hughes, Ciaran Hughes, Darcie Hughes, David Hughes, Douglas Hughes, Gareth 'Gonic' Hughes, James Hughes, Keiran Hughes, Luke Hughes, Michael Hughes, Ryan Hughes, Sam Hughes, Sammy Hughes, Tom Hughes, Liam Hughes & Llinos Pritchard, Jack Hulatt, Samuel Hull, Simon Hull, Nick Hulley, Stephen Hulmes, Evano Hulsman, Lukas Hulting, Max Humberstone, Andrew Humbles, Bramwell Humby, George Hume, Christopher Humm, Jack Hummel, Alix Humphrey, Tyler Humphrey, Paul Humphreys, Jo Humphriss, Martyn Humphrys, James Hunt, Joel Hunt, Leah and Rob Hunt, Mexy Hunt, Mike Hunt, Sam Hunt, Sarah Hunt, Cameron Hunter, Connor Hunter, Dan Hunter, Ethan Hunter, Michael Hunter, Sam Hunter, Sean Hunter, Cameron Hunter-Spokes, Quinton Huntington-Silver, Rouven Hurling, Samantha 'Cin' Hurrell, Adam Hurst, Elliott Hurst, Matthew Husband, Robert Huse, Anders Husebø, Zakaria Hussain, Trenton Huston, John Hutchings, Julian 'ChocoFudgelet' Hutchings, Ben Hutchinson, Emily Hutchinson, Jason Hutchinson, Michael Hutchinson, Ian Hutchison, Sebastian Hutter, Savage Hutton, Sam Huynh, Senne Huysmans, Brandon Hynes, Daniel Hyslop, Jorrit Idsardi, Lionel Ieri, Brennig Ifans, Tuomo Ikävalko, Josh Ikin, Ikke776h, Ilari Illamaa, Max Inerfield, infinitehorizon♥, Leon Ingall, Karl Emil Ingebrigtsen, Martin Ingebrigtsen, Dom Ingersole, Mattias Inghe, Eryk Ingram, Mister InSayne, Claire Louise Insole, Bryson Interlandi, Serena Inzani, Claudiu Ionescu, iPat8, Gijs Ipers, Will Ireland, Aitor Iribar, Chris Iriondo, Bradley Iroine, Gavin Ironside, Aaron Irwin, Alex Irwin, Dylan Irwin, Amund Isaksen, Emma Isaksen, Jack Isle, Kimberly Alice Isley, Sam Istvan, Sage ItsAMe, Arty (Drunk Russian) Ivanenko, Sandis Ivanovskis (Expcookie), Harry Iveson, Martin Ivey, Chris Ivison, John Ivison, Daniel Izzard, Harrison Izzard, Joshua Izzett, J W, James Jaap, Ashraf Jabir, Oliver Jack, Tristan Jack (Circus Freak), Guy Jacklin, Ben Jackson, Christopher Jackson, David Jackson, Harry Jackson, Jonny Jackson, Jordan Jackson, Josh Jackson, Karsten Jackson, Patrick Jackson, Stephen Jackson, Toby Jackson, Jackson & Ollie, Conagh Jackson-Cook, Jacob 'Crispy', Alyx Jacobs, Arne Jacobs, Morgan Jacobs, Stephanie Scarlet Jacobs, Victor Jacobsen, Joshua Jacobson, Daniel Jacobsson, Peter Jacques, Jade, Matthias Jaenicke, Joe Jagla, Jaffer Jake, Mads Jakobsen, Richard Jalland, Eric Jälmevik, Aaron James, Alex James, Amaria James, Ben James, Benjamin James, Daniel James, David James, Douglas James, Euan James, Jack James, James James, Keean James, Leon James, Marcus James, Maxwell James, Stephen James, Tom James, James.W.J.Percival, Ben Jammin, Emma Jane, William Jane, Emily Janes, August Janklow, Luka Jankovic, Justin

Jankunas, Alexander Janmo, Matt Jannetta-Wilson, Travis Janney, Cas Janse, Freek Jansen, Joshy Jansen, Matthew Jansen, Robin Jansen, Yoeri Jansen, Lucas Janssen, Ean Janusz, Mitchell Jaques, Hugo Jaramillo, Emil Järf, Tyler Jarman, Paul Jarrow, Billy Jarvis, Callum Jarvis, Connor Jarvis, Euan Jarvis, James Jarvis, Mark Jarvis, Mitchell Jarvis, Nicole Jasaitis, Jacob Jasek, Evan Jasinski, Jasiek Jasinski, Phillip Jay, Andrew Jayamaha, Alexis Jayme, Harrison Jeal, Nick Jean, Matthew Jeans, Jonathan Jebb, Marc Jebelean, Some guy named Jeff, Jeff, Jeff the shark (Adrian Campey), Michael Jeffers, Chris Jeffery, Oliver Jeffery, Harry Jeffree, Stephen Jeffrey, Arne 'S Jegers, Patriks Jegurs, Alexander Jenings, Alec Jenkins, Cameron Jenkins, Honor Jenkins, Katheebs Jenkins, Matthew Jenkins, Odog Jenks, Simon Jenner, Andy Jennings, Ben Jennings, Harry Jennings, John Douglas Jennings, Josh Jennings, Luke Jennings, Robin Jennings, Daniel Jensen, Jonathan 'Yeet' Jensen, Lennart Jensen, Mathew Jensen, Noa Jensen, Niklas Jensen Haunstrup, Oliver Jephson, Tyler Jerman, Jade Jerram, Benjamin Jerrett, Toni Jerrett, Callum Jessamine, Cameron Jessup, Rick Jessup, André Jesus, Michael Jiles, Jimbo!, Jimmy the Eyes aka, acousticfury, Allison JJ, Chris Joberns, Dan Jobling, Benjamin Jodway, Albert Joel, Joel Alcoholic_Aussie, Jakob Joensen, Amy Joestar, Jamie Joggi (trashmonster), Hayden Johal, Philip Charlie Johansen, Tor Edvart Johansen, David Johansson, Kim Johansson, Mattias Johansson, Tobias Johansson, Gareth Aled John, Jacob John, Harrison Johns, Jostein Johnsen, Alexander Johnson, Alice Johnson, Catherine Johnson, Daniel Johnson, Dean Johnson, Gabriel Johnson, Garrett W. Johnson, Ian Johnson, J Johnson, Jacob Johnson, James Johnson, Jamie Johnson, JB Johnson, Jimmothy Johnson, Joey Johnson, Josh Johnson, Kitty Fangtastokitty Johnson, Marc J. Johnson, Matthew Johnson, Nick Johnson, Paul Johnson, Rebecca Johnson, Samuel Johnson, Scott Johnson, Terry Johnson, Wyatt Johnson, Zachary Johnson, James Johnston, Kevin Johnston, Scott Johnston, Logan Johnston (EnigmaticWraith), Christopher Jolley, Aaron Jolly, Liam Joly, Jonah, Aaron Jones, Aidan Jones, Ashley 'Alfor' Jones, Bethan Jones, Daniel Jones, Dave Jones, Elliott Jones, Emily Jones, Evan Jones, Hannah Jones, Harrison Jones, Hayden Jones, Huw Jones, Isaac Jones, Jake Jones, James Jones, Jon Jones, Joseph Jones, Joshua Jones, Joshua O. Jones, Kyle Jones, Liam Jones, Louis Jones, Luca Jones, Luke Jones, Madeleine Jones, Matthew Jones, Michael Jones, Nathan 'Unix' Jones, Nathaniel Jones, Nicholas Jones, Robin Jones, Sam Jones, Siôn Jones, Stacey Jones, Taylor Jones, Theo Jones, Thomas Jones, William Jones, wantadogsobigitcanspoonme (Adam Jones), Jonesy, Remco Jongschaap, Nick Jonker, Ellinor Jönsson, Otto Jönsson, Joost, Daniel Jordaan, Chase Jordan, Daniel Jordan, George 'Azeria' Jordan, Sean Jordan, jordguitar, Samuel Jorgensen, Luca Jorgenson, Joris, Rita Joseph, Ronan Joseph, Joey Josephson, JoshK, Calvin Jubb, Chris Juden, Frederik P. Finnerup Juel, Oli Jukes, Nathan Jung, Callum Juniper, Harry Jupp,

Supporters

Urška Jurečič, Tommy Justus, Harry K, K.L, Anders Wolsing Kaa, László Kabódi, Adam Kadow, Tommie Kaercher, Suphanath Kaewboonruang, Jaakko Kähärä, Nigel Kaitell, Joel Kalich, Mateusz Kalinowski, Tyler Austen Kalmbach, Jakub Kalousek, Jake Kalp, Alex Kalzirdragon, Thomas Kamm, Kammy and Jan, Per Kampman, Nicholas Kanakaris, Kanako The Squirrel, Devin Kanaly, Reidulous Kane, Sam Kane, Jillian Kane-Gallagher, Matias Kangasjärvelä, Russell Kanharn, Koen Kant, Squally Kanto, Divo Kaplan, Josh Kaplan, Ben Karas, Matthew Karasz, Tomasz Karcz, Tanju Kardes, Nathaniel Kargher, Oscar Karlsjö, Marcus Karlsson, Katie Karran-Antrobus, Alexander 'Xan' Kashev, Riley Kass - iamb4u11, Katala & Slider, Søren Katborg-Vestergaard, Marijn Katgert, Rebecca Kath, Brady Katshor, Eden Kaufman, Justin Kaufman, Arjun Kaura, Jack 'Jellex' Kavanagh, Adam Kay, Karl-Georg Kay, Trevor Kay, Jokūbas Kazlauskas, Anders KBB, Aodhán Keady, Josh Keane, Dale Kearney, Jordan Kearney, Josh Kearney, George Kearns, Ben Keast, Matt Keatley, Harrison Keaton, Andrei Keaveney, Jack O Keeffe, Nathaniel Keegan, Danny Keeler-Clark, Robert Keenan, Liam Keft, Mads-Ejnar Kehlet, Markus Keil, Jim Keir, Aidan Keith, Brandon Keller, Chris Kelley, Derrick Kelley, Liam Kelley, Shaun Kelley, Tyler Kelley, Anna Kelly, Charlie Kelly, Daniel Kelly, David Kelly, Dominic Kelly, Euan Kelly, Glen Kelly, Joseph Kelly, Joshua Kelly, Mary Ann Kelly, Michael Kelly, Nathan Kelly, Sean Joseph Kelly, Sophie Kelly, Stu Kelly, Richard Kelsey, Will Kelsey, Bertie Kemp, Ethan Kemp, Ryan-John Kemp, Jacob Kemper, James Kempster, Ed Kendall, Joseph Kendall, Christopher Kennard, Anthony Kennedy, Lawrence Kennedy, Maddy Kennedy, Matthew Kennedy, Dan Kennedy IG:@itskingdan, Hester Kenneison, Kennith Kennithson, Harry Kenny, Michael Kenny, Peadar Kenny, Luke Kenworthy, Evan Keogh, Ryan Kepper, Alexander Kerckhof, Sebastian Kerebs, Tara Kerger, Nicholas Kerins, Nick Kerkhof, Jaxom Kerlin, Andrew Kern, Nick Kern, Nathan Kerns, Keroia, Brendan Kerr, Jack Kerr, Jamie Kerr, Fraser Kerr (OfficialPirateFraser), Louis Kersh, Euan Kershaw, James Kershaw, Mitchell Kershaw, Arttu Keskinen HIMOM, Caleb Kesse-Shepard, Kylie Kestenbaum, Daniel Ketchell, Max Kettenhofen, Richard Key, Kent Keylon, Bashira Khan, David Khoshnood, Michael Kiba, Ashley Kidd, Ben Kidd, Jarryd Kidd, Julia Kiely, Dan Kieran, Justin Kierstead, Jacob Kies, Bennett Kilgore, Joel Kilgour, Ryan Killey, Gabriel Killough-Hill, Aurora Kim, Derek Kim, Thomas Kim, Luke Kimmings, Eliot 'The Butt Puncher' King, Jacob King, Nathan King, Patrick King, Samuel King, Shadow King, Simon D. King, The King Family, Solomon King-Purdy, Holly Kingdon, Robin Kingsley, Kayleigh Kingston, Stefano Kinkade, Ryan Kinloch, Robin Kinnard, Samuel Kinns, Matt Kinsey, Andrew Kinsman, Tash Kinsman, Justin Kintop, Ryan Kipke, Brandon Kirby, Connor Kirby, Nathan Kirby, Jonathan Kirch, Richard Kirk, Will Kirk, Naomi Kirk-Muir, Alfie Kirkham, Andrew Kirkham, Aidan Kirkup, Cody Kirton, Eugene

Kiselyov, Graham Kiser, Adam Kissell, Jansen Kitchens, Skylar Dax Kitchens, Aidan Kite, Matt Kiteley, Vanessa Kitto, KittyTheCat, Allan Kjærgaard, Alex Klaschus, Yvan Klaver, Ken Klavonic, Joshua Klein, Marvin Klein, Ronnie Klein, Uwe Kleinmann, Kara Kleist, Andrew Klemencic, Leon Klempert, Patrik Kleveland, Velin Klisurov, Marnick Kloosterman, Mikołaj Kłos, Alex Klotz, Delon Klotz, Jeff Emil Knak, Jens Knapen, Connor Knapp, Brian Knecht (PicklePeeple1552), Dillon Kneeland, Angelic Knight, Ashley Knight, Daniel Knight, Felix Knight, James Knight, Joe Knight, Lewis Knight, Liam Knight, Michael Knight, Nick Knight, Sam Knight, Thomas Knight, Matt Knights, Matthew Knights, Jack Knoll, Fussel Knopf, Shay Knutson, Joshua Kobes, Dominik Kochta, Zachary Kocken, Andy Kocvara, kodaxmax, Austen Koepke, Robert Koger, Mathias Koh, Christopher Kolar, Brian Kolkka, Sir Kollin, Royal Historian to King Jon the Fat, Ana Komar, Matti Komulainen, Gabriel Konat, Kananart Kongsakon, Tim König, Petra Königstorfer, Tom Konopka, Hercules Konstas, Mehmet Deniz Konuk, Douwe Koopmans, Stephen Kop, Corey Koppelow, Maximilian Korb, Anil Korde, Joey Kordish, Ladislav Kořínek, Ben Kornhaus, Mike Korona, Joris Kortekaas, Kory Fucking Death!, Kai Korzonek, Cezary Kos, Iiro Koskinen, Marvin Kosmider, Wouter Kosse, Angeles Kossio, Henry Koswig, Robin Kottelaar, Matthew Kovacs, Piotr Kowalski, Alexander Kozeniauskas, Tim Kozeniauskas, Sebastian Kozłowski, Simon Kraemer, Daan Kraetzer, Jonathan Kraft, Julian 'Have a Nice Day' Kragset, Ferdi Kramer, Aleksander Kraśnicki, Nicholas Kratzer, Maxime Kraus, Vitezslav Krejci, Jim Kretschmer, Andrew Kriebel, Andrew Krieser, Sander Krijt, KrimzonThief, KrisdaKATT, Kriskke, Jesper Kristensen, Lars Eirik Kristensen, Lasse Kristiansen, Robin Kristiseter, Daniel Kroells, Jacob Krogh, Thomas Krolikowski, Ryan 'The Iceman' Kroon, Sami Kruger, Stephen Kruger, William Kruss, Sebastian Kruzel, Madison Krzciok, Theodore Kuba, Jack Kudryl, Justin Kuemerle, Erin Kugler, Nick Kuhn, Kelso Kuhnel, Deion Kuijpers, Björn Kuiper, Akshay Kulkarni, Harry Kullman, Sampo Kupiainen, Edvin Kuric, Jack Kurtz (ltcmadjack in Dan's streams), Kusalananda, Kacper Kutarnia, Sascha Kutzmann, Toon Kuypers, Kamil Kuzma, Sondre Kvarven, Lukasz Kwasek, Filip Kwasniewski, Aleks Kwiatkowski, Tak Lan Kwong, Piaras Kyne, Nathan Kynett, Rick Kyser, James L, Phoebe L :), Deryn L., La Contessa & MooseAde, Andrew La Mont, Brandon La Violette, Patrick Ari Ekeheien Laakso, Marc Laban, Liam LaBurt, Victor Laevens, Conor LaFlamme, Matti Lahtinen, Caiden Laier, Ross Laing, Scott Laing, Callum Lake, Sarah Lake, Christopher Laker, Sarah Lakke, Christian Lalchan, Max Lalouschek, Alexander Lamb, Phil Lamb, Cailean Lambert, Ed Lambert, Eleanor Lambert, Emily Lambert, Hayley M. Lambert, Jamie Lambert, Luke Lambert, Nicholas Lambert, Tommy Lambert, Sam Lamboo, Lami, LJ Lamie, Karl Laming, Jimi Lamon, John Lamont, Kevin Lamping, Whit Lamport, Harry Lamprey, Ben Land,

Supporters

Jamie Land, Liam Land, Brandon Landry, Aaron Lane, Chris Lane, Tyler Lane, Michael Lanfear, Jake Langdell, Guillaume Langelier, Katherine Langford, Mads Emil Langhoff, Hugh Langridge, Nathan Langston, William Langston, Walter Language, Andrew Lanham, Joshua Lankamp, Alex Larabie, Jonah Laramee, Kevin Larbalestier, Sky Larbalestier, Ben Lardner, McKay Larmer, Micheal Larner, Jalen Laroach, Raymond LaRose, Kirsten Larrison, Benjamin Larsen, David Larsen, Frederik Noah Søndergaard Larsen, Kristoffer Larsen, Rasmus Larsen, Tobias Dahl Larsen, Kaysie Larson, Conny 'Lurid' Larsson, Adrian Laschet, Jeremy Lashinski, Jed Lath, Paul Lauckner, Martin Laugesen, Schweedie Laura, Damien Laurie, Quinn Laurie, Jelle Lauwers, Adam Lavallee, Brett Lavelle, Calum Laverock, Damien Laverty, Vincent LaVigna, Sebas Lavigne, James Lavin, Ariana Law, David Law, Jacob Law, Joel Law, Stephan Law, Philip Lawall, Oliver Lawden, Joseph Lawman, Sam Lawrance, Adam Lawrence, Duncan Lawrence, Mark Lawrence, Michael Lawrence, Taylor Lawrence, Thomas Laws, Bailey Lawson, Cody Lawson, Dean Lawton, Jamie Lawton, Chris Lay, Rob Laycock, Andy Lazar, Melissa Lazaris-O'Toole, Rhys Lazenby, Stefan Lazic, lazycdog, Phuoc Le, Qui Le, Vincent Le, Adam Le Boutillier, Jonathan Le Brocq, Jasmijn Le Roux, Cameron Lea, Katie Leach, Alfie Leadbitter, Benjamin Leader, Jena Leadyi, Joseph Leaf, Samuel Learmouth, Nathan Learnard, Glen Learned, Michael Leask, Erin Leath, Alex Leatherland, Justin Leaton, Marc Lebailly, Dana LeBlanc, Gunnar Leck, Bradley Ledger, Emma Ledoux, Evan Ledoux, Florian Ledreney, Cotton Ledwith, Alex Lee, Benjamin Lee, Harry Lee, Henry (FrazledFish) Lee, Jay Lee, Jacob Lee-Forse, Ben Leedom, Lucillia Leedom, Elliott Leeks, Sam Leeman, Jonas Leenaers, Ben 'Chin' Lees, James Lees, Josh Lees, Matt Lees, Kayne Leeson, Quinn Leeuw, Ethan LeFevre, Nathaniel Leff, Alexsander Lefkort, Martin Legg, Justin Lehman, Stephen Lehr, Manu Lehtonen, Zachary Leib-Perry, Ellie Leigh, Kerry Leigh (BabyLeigh93), Christopher Leighton, Pentti Leino, Tuukka Leino, Patrick Leisk, Jack Leith, Emma Lelek Obenius, Corey Lemelle, Marieke Lemmens, Stijn Lenaerts, Matthew Lenahan, Logan Lenart, Arvid Lengborg, Rúnar Leó, Brandon Leonard, Ryan Leonard, Stephen Leonard, Carson Leonardi-George, Tadas Leonavičius, Justin Leone, Margus Lepik, Arttu Leppälä, Charlie Lerma, Alyssa Lerner, Leroy Lesilolo, Tobias leSquid, Martyn Lester, Damien Letham, David Lever, Luke Levett, David Leviathan, Mitchell Levy, Brandon Lew, James Lewendon, Kevin Lewin, Charlie Lewins, Alex Lewis, Alexander Lewis, Ashur Lewis, Barry Lewis, Carl Lewis, Chris Lewis, Christopher Lewis, Connor Lewis, Dylan Lewis, James Lewis, Jordan Lewis, London Lewis, Lowri Lewis, Lucie Lewis, Matthew Lewis, Owen Lewis, Peter Lewis, Richard Lewis, Sam Lewis, Trent 'Hickstar' Lewis, Zoe Lewis, Glen Leysen, Martin Lezhenin, Adam Li, Christian Liakos, Shawnna Liberty, Johannes Lidberg, Sean Liddiard, Deya Lidster, Dylan Liebgott,

Dominique Liefveld, Jakob Liew, Egidijus Ligeika, John Lighterness, C.J Lightfoot, Evan Lihou, Joakim Liikamaa, Jordy Lijs, Devyne Liles, Fabian Lilje, Duncan Lilly, Annabeth Lim, Nuan Lim, Ryan Lim, Jonatan Linberg, Wille Lindblad, Aron Linde, Craig Linderoth, Cody Lindinger, Ole-Emil Lindkilde, Shawn Lindsay, Oli Linegar, Thomas Lingard, Herman Lingelem, Joshua Lingwood, Harry Link, Matt Linley, LinMac, Joakim Linna, Mikko Lintala, Andrew Linville, Nathan Lions Butcher, Nicholas Lipari, Elias Lipka, LiroLake, Boris Litovski, Oliver Littlefair, Littlefysh, LittleMe, Alex Littlewood, Ben Littlewood, Dominic Littlewood, Martyn Littlewood, Nick Liu, Perry Liu, Alexander Livanos, Nicole Livesey, Yuki Liyanage, Lizard girl, Patrik Ljungbäck, LKPridgeon, James Lloyd, Josh Lloyd, Paris Lloyd, Thomas Lloyd, Tom Lloyd, Alexander Lochore-Ward, Torben Lochow, Jackson Locke, Archie Lockyer, Daniel Loddeke, Alexander Lodge, Sam Lodge, Ray Loerke, Angus Logan, Tobias Logan, Tom Logan, Karol Łojewski, Andrew Loken, Hollie Lomas, Louie Lombardi, Ean Lombardo, Payton Lommers, Daniel Lond, Nathan London, Aerick Long, Daymon Long, Joe Long, Samuel Long, Zach Long, George Longley, Henry Longstaff, Isaac Longworth, René Looge, Dan Looker, Jacob Daniel Loomer, James Loots, Frank Lopes, Brandon Lopez, Connor Lord, Jasmine Lord, Phil Lord, Anders Lorentzon, Alex Loria, Chris Lossie, Robert Loughead, Princess Love, George Loveday, Korben Loveday, Keren Lovie, Andrea Lowe, Matthew Lowe, Jules E Lowes (Foxie), James Lowey, Yas Lowtun, Chris Loxham, Matthew Loynes, The Introverted Procrastinator, Pika Lu, Rachael Lubek, Arran Lucas, David Lucas, Harry Lucas, Lewis Lucas, Steven Lucas, Hannah Lucey, Eliot Luchinsky, Zach Lucia, Vincent Lucia-Tremblay, Ian Mathew Lucken, Karl Lüdecke, Jordan Ludford, Samuel Ludford, Jake Ludlam, Sondre Ludvigsen, Alister Luff, Robert Lumb, Jack Luna, Aaron Lund, Håkon Lund, John Lundy, Thomas Lunn, Juuso Luostarinen, Horatiu Lupsan, Jacob Luther, Justin Luther, Mads Luther Nørlem, Jonathon Lutringer, Maximilian Lux, Mya Lux, Lycopene, Danny Lydiate, Ben Lye-Forster, Zachary Lyman, Adam Lynch, Connor Lynch, Michael Lynch, Tyler Lynch, Dylan Lynn, Mitchell Lynott, Matthew Lyon, Mischa Lyons, Ryan Lyons, Stephen Lyons, Tommy Lyons, Alex Lythall, Davey Lythall, David M, Rowan M, M_Lama, Robert M., M.A.R.K, Seb M'Caw, Janiek Maassen, Joshua Mabbs, Charlie Mabbutt, Preston Maberry, Lorcán Mac an Chrosáin, Rob MacAndrew, Ross MacAskill, Evan Macbean, Sean MacBean, Brandon MacDonald, Connor MacDonald, Ellie Macdonald, Lucas MacDonald, Rhianan MacDonald, Alex Mace, Robin Macer-Wright, Corey Macfarlane, Luke Macfarlane, Ben Macham, Nikki Machell, Robert MacHunter, Matthew MacKarill, Andrew Mackay, Craig Mackay, Jack MacKay, Mackem_Dan, Daniel Mackenzie, Liam Mackenzie, Rowan Mackenzie, Sam Mackenzie, Conor Mackey, Zane Mackey, Siobhan Mackie, Daniel James

MacKinnon, Adam Mackintosh, Kathryn Mackintosh, David MacLachlan, Iain MacLean, James Macleod, Eilidh MacMillan, Sardines MacMillan, Joseph MacMullin, Craig MacNab, Garrett Macomber, Alethea Macphail, Lee Macpherson, Michelle MacRae, Roddy MacRae, Andrew Madden, Katie Maddick, Amy Maddison, Katlin Maddox, Alex Maden, Jakob Nøhr Madsen, Jonathan Maesen, Jed Magee, Eimear Magill, Brady Magner, Josh Magnum, Kassandra Magnusson, Brendan Maguire, Keith Maguire, James Mahar, Molu Maharana, Ian Maher, Lauren Mahony, Michael Mahr, Jeff Mai, James 'Simian' Maiden, Alexander Maidment, Benjamin Main, Devin Main, Rhys Maine, Jordan Mair, Nathan Malaney, Colin Malcolm, Joshua Malcolm, Lawrence Malczak, Dillon and Robbie Malerk, Max Malherbe, Mikko Malinen, Yoan-Daniel Malinov, Nathan Mallalieu, Zachary Mallard, Gemma Mallinson, Sam Malmsten, Sean Malone, David Maloney Jr., Thomas Maltby, Mamlthefool, Christian Manahan, Ross Manby, Devin Mandelbaum, Mark Mandemakers, Eric Mandia, Tomáš Maněna, Dawson Mangels, Elijah Mangnall, Chibi Mango, Manie, Constantine Maniotis, Stephen Manke, McClay Manktelow, Matthew Mann, Zoey Mann, Will Manning, Adam Manning-Davey, Pádraig Mannix, Kyle Mannock, Declan Manock, Ben Mansbridge, Joshua Mansel, Jacob Mansfield, Alex Manton, Georgia Maple, Joseph Maples, Garrett Marchand, Siobhan Marchant, Thomas Marciano, Kacper Marciniak, Riley Marcoux, Elijah Marcum, Kresten Marcussen, Sarah Marcussen, Jane Mardan, Eyad Mardini, Victor Mardon, Hazel Margerison, MargusM, Jacob Marie, Nathan Marino, Peter Marino, Anton Marinski, Jake Marion, Mark, Mark (Whitesonic5748), Matthew Markham, Mihail Markov, Mathieu Marlaire, Alfie Marles, Luke Marley, Jack Marlow, Ben Maron, Justin Marono, Eleanor Marples, Pedro Marquez, Sergio Marquez, Alex Marquis, Noah Marquis, Hannah Marren, Christopher Marrero, Kevin Marriner Jr, Dylan Marriott, Toby Marsden, Luci Marsh, Siani Marsh, Alex Marshall, Austin Marshall, Daniel Leslie Marshall, George Marshall, Glenn Marshall, Jack Marshall, Morgan Marshall, Neil Marshall, Patrick Marshall, Sean Marshall, Tom Marshall, James Marsters, Axel Mårtensson, Aeron Martin, Chad Martin, Daniel Martin, David Martin, Declan Martin, Francis Martin, Jeff Martin, Josh Martin, Lain Martin, Liam Martin, Logan Martin, Maxine Martin, Scott Martin, Sean Martin, Tom Martin, Pete and Sarah Martin, Sue and Owen Pilfold, Luciano Martino, Lou Martofel, Oliver Marven, Marzipan-Albatross, Daniel Masceri, Samantha Maskill, Luke Maslany, Snowy Maslov, Charlie Mason, Digby Mason, Evelyn Mason, Jacob Mason, Joshua Mason, Megan-Rose Mason, Nicholas Mason, Timothy Mason, Wulffe Mason, Zak Mason, Sammy Masri, Caleb Massengill, Julian Massey, Sam Massey, Felix Masters, Kánya Máté, Blake Matheson, Andreas Mathieu, Samuel Mathison, Nicholas A. Matrunich, Matt, Andrew Matthews, Jonathan

Matthews, Kit Matthews, Lloyd Matthews, Phil Matthews, Hayden Matthias, Andrew Mattsen, Natalie Amelia Mattsey, David Maull, Chris Maundrell, William Mavin, Matthew Mawson, Cameron Maxey, Patrick Maxted, Alex May, Cole May, Jacob May, Kali May, Atıf Berk Maya, Andrew Mayer, Ben Mayer-Jones, Zac Maynard, Andre Maynard Seath, Joshua Mayo, Leo Mayr, Brandon Mays, Brian Mc Collum, Sean Mc Court, Shaun McAlister, Andrew McAllister, Kierad McAllister, Lucas McAllister, Andrew McAra, Kieran McArdle, Michael McAteer, Liam McBey, James Mcbride, Aidan McCabe, Joey McCabe, Nicholas McCall, Matthew McCallum, Sam McCalmont, Keenan McCammon, Gage McCann, Billy McCarthy, Christopher McCarthy, Frederick McCarthy, Mathew McCarthy, Ian McCarty, Caleb Mcclain, Matthew McClean, Michael McCloskey, Sean McCloskey, Phillip McCloughan, Owen Mcclurkin, Alexander McColl, Jordan McConnachie, Marc McConnell, Ross McConnell, Stewart McConnell, Finn McCool, Evan McCown, Eoin McCoy, Samuel McCracken, Matthew McCrary, Callum McCreath, Jim McCrory, David McCubbin, Bailye McCue, Jason McCullough, Euan McCutcheon, Nicholas McDaniel, Tom McDee, Darragh McDermott, Brandon McDonald, Joa McDonald, Kaylee McDonald, Kian McDonald, Robert McDonald, Tom McDonald, John Patrick McDonough, Calum McDowell, Scott McElney, Kaylin McElrone, Aidan McFadden, Thomas Mcfadden, Allie McFarland, Lochlainn McGall, John McGarvey, Ross McGarvey, Daniel J McGechie, Jareth McGhee, Olly McGibbon, Chloe McGillivray, Kevin McGinley, Cole McGinnis, Dave McGlashan, Todd McGovern, Niall McGowan, Lewis McGrady, Daniel McGrath, Dylan McGrath, Dylan Basil McGrath, Sam McGrath, Spike McGrath, Ben McGruder, Brenden McGuire, Liam McGuire, Claire McHale, Niall McHale, Cathal 'Bullet Sponge' McHugh, Olivia McHugh, Allister McIlwaine, Baird McIlwraith, James McInnes, Owen J McIntire, Alex McIntyre, Eve McIntyre, Luke McIntyre, Daniel McIver, Lewis McKaig, Miles McKaig, John Aeneas McKay, Reece McKay, Hugh McKean, Andrew Mckechnie, Joshua McKee, Rachel McKelvie, Matthew McKenna, Brock McKenzie, Cameron McKenzie, Richard McKeon, Caoimhe McKeown, John 'Scotsman' McKinlay, Amy McKinley, Sam Mckone/ Jasmine Fogg, Ross McLachlan, Robert McLaren, Cameron Mclaughlin, Callum Mclean, Sammy McLean, James McLeish, Jake McLeman, Helena McLeod, Josh McLeod, Joshua Mcloughlin, James McMahon, Connor McMann, Chad McManus, Liam McManus, Nicholas McManus, Ryan Mcmillan, Peter McMinn, Zachary McMinn, Hayden McMullin, Freya McMurray, Paulo McNab, Dawson McNair, Chris McNally, Cameron Mcnee, Mathew Mcnee, Chris 'Jimmy' McNeil, Kelly Mcneil, George Mcniffe, Jason McPherson, Keiran Mcqueen, Ewan McRobinson, Benny Mcsassy, Troy McVay, Innes McVey, Tauren Mead, Andrew Meadows, Riley Meagher, Ricky Mebarki, Will Meccano-Thomas, TJ Mecone,

Supporters

Tony Medhurst, Mario Medina, Chloe Hannah Medley, Reinis Mednis, David Meechan, Daniel Meek, Alexander Meeks, Sarah Meeks, Roman Meier, Niels Meijer, Jochem Meijers, Louis Meikle, Ronan Meikle, Michael Meinecke, Isaiah Mejia, Keenan Melarkey, Christopher Melendez, Nikolas Melendez, Erik Pilø Melillo, Liam J Mellerup, Josephine Mellor, Timothy Mendelson, Ethen Menendez, Dominik Menke, Markus Menzebach, Andreas Menzel, Charles Mercenit, Doreen Merchant, Joshua Mercik, Martin 'Mez' Meredith, Iikka Meriluoto, Ben Merkett, Michiel Merkx, Simon Mernagh, Christopher Merrell, Jarrad Merrick, Josh 'Merry' Merrick, Phoebe Merrill, Lauren Merriman, Timothy Merriman, Josh Merritt, Kai Merry, Thomas Merry, Nick Mertens, Pepijn Mesie, Carl Mesner Lyons, Kieran Messer, Scott Messina, Melanie Messner, Péter Mészáros, Daniel Metcalfe, Amadeo Meure, James Meyer, Jeremy D. Meyermann, Max Meyers, Gichael Mibson, Matthew Micallef, Steven Michaels, Weronika Michalska, Jarod Michie, Jeshua Mickelson, Adam Middleton, Carl Middleton, Paul D Middleton, Samuel Middleton, Tobin Middleton, Adam Midgley, Iver Midtlyng, Tim Miggelbrink, mightyferret, Nick Mijic, Karlijn Mijnheer, Jo Miklo, Szymon Mikulicz, Andrew Miles, Ben Miles, Cara Miles, Samuel Miles, Tyler Milien, Maroje Miljan, Callum Millan, Jack M Millar, Jonathan Millar, Lewis Millar, Louie Millar, Samantha Millar, Hugh Millard, Ian Millard, Luke 'L78k3' Millard, Thomas Millard, Mike Millea, Adam Miller, Ben Miller, Eilidh Miller, Eli Miller, Isaac Miller, James Miller, Jared Miller, Justine Danielle Miller, Max Miller, Naomi Miller, Raul MIller, Ryan M. Miller, Sam Miller, Toby Miller, Brandon Miller :), Reno Miller (SplodyFace), Michael Millham, Jacob Milligan, Keith Milligan, Lee Milligan, Scott Milligan, Haydn Millington, Ben Mills, Dominic Mills, Nenyi Mills-Robertson, James Millsap, Alexander Milne, Dan Milnes, Jonathan Milord, Ivan Miloslavov, Kiyanni Mims, Minerva & XYmir, MiniBex, Jake Minihan, Ryan Minty, Elliot Mintz, William Mior, KevM8 Mirah, Mathew Miravite, Mirriky, Liam Mischewski, Nathaniel Mischler, Owen Misik, Mark Misset, Niklas Missing, Nanashi Mitame, Aaron Mitchell, Caleb Mitchell, Dakota Mitchell, Davy Mitchell, Dylan Mitchell, Esme Mitchell, Ethan Mitchell, Gregor Mitchell, Harry Mitchell, Henry Mitchell, Jason Mitchell, Lauren Mitchell, Mark Mitchell, Matthew Mitchell, Daniel Mitchelson, Timothy Mitcheson, John Mitchinson, Saurav Mitra, Pepin Mittelhauser, Mitzaru & Jezza, Benjamin R. Mix, Aidan Mobley, Adam Moen, Henry Moerman, Virginia Moffatt, Evan Moffitt, Abo Al-Quassim Mohamad, Ricky Mohl, Callum Moir, Leon Moir, Aaron Mole, Raoul Molenaar, Richard Molitorisz, Chris Molleman, Jacob Paw Møller, Dakota Molloy, Kienan Molloy, Louis Molloy, Jon Molnar, Robert Molnar, Ian Moloney, Brannon Molvik, Tim Monague, Neil Monnery, Thimo Mons, Jay Monson, Michael-Daniel Montalto, Alexander Montalvo, Alexander Montgomery, Ash

Montgomery, George Montgomery, Daniel Monument, Daniel Moody, Dara Moody, Gabriel Moody, Glynn Moody, Logan Moody, Noah Blake Moody, Herman Mooij, mookooy, Ziyaad Moolla, Ian Moon, Mackinley Moon, Aimee Mooney, Fiona Mooney, Ian Mooney, Luca Mooney, Arron Mooneyhan, Angus Moore, Brendan Moore, Clayton Moore, Daniel Moore, Dylan Moore, Hallam Moore, Keith Moore, Louise Moore, Matt Moore, Matthew Moore, Preston Moore, Quinlan 'Sir Quifilous' Moore, Thomas Moore, Tom Moore, Gordon Moores, Will (Wackymonk) Moores, Michael Moorhouse, Erin Moos-Golding, Conor Moran, Nathan 'Tibby_LTP' Moran, Jacob More, Jarrett Moreland, Wesley Moreland, Phoebe Morey, Alex Morgan, Andrew Morgan, Bradley 'bmor' Morgan, David Morgan, David Morgan, Dominic Morgan, Jâc Morgan, Lewis Morgan, Luka Morgan, Matthew Morgan, Oliver Morgan, Paul Morgan, Pete 'Amarielle' Morgan, Jack Morgan (JackMorgan101), Casper Mørkenborg, Louis Morling, Thomas Morningstar, Sam Moron, Chris Morrice, Adam Morris, Aiden Morris, Andrew Morris, Blake Morris, Dominic Morris, Finley Morris, Geoffrey Morris, Harry Morris, James Morris, Louis Morris, Luke Morris, Malcolm Morris, Robbie Morris, Scott Morris, Stan Morris, Tommy Morris, Tristan Morris, Tyler Morris, Zachary Morris, Zackery Morris, Alan Morrison, John Morrissey, Demara Morrow, Colin Morse, Isaac Mort, Philip Mortimer, Samuel Mortimore, Matthew Mortlock, Emma Morton, Tom Morton, Kevin Morum, Garrett Moseke, Kyle Moshinsky, Jake Mosier, Ricky Mosqueda, Jorge Moss, Samuel Moss, João Mota, Philip Mottershead, Lucy Mottram, Lyall Mould, Ollie Moules, Ryan Moulsley, Adam Mountford, Keely Mowatt, Robert Moxon, Jake Moyle, Wyatt Mr, Mr67Steve, MrAndyTF, MrDeathlad, Max Mrjjbob, Niklas Mueller, Howard Charles Mueller V, David Muench, Devon Mugford, Dreni Muhaxheri, Mark Muise, Alex Mulcahy, Ben Mulcahy, Youri Mulder, Stuart Muldrew, Jack Mullen, Marco Müller, Patrick Müller, Sebastian Müller, Matthew Mulligan, Brian Mullin, Casey Mullin, Jacob Mullin, Archie Mullins, Kevin Mulraney, Fiona Mulvey, James Mulvey, Jonas Mumm, Jack Munafo, Hayden Munday, Juan Luis Muñoz Ioannidis, Callum Munro, Dave (Diotior) Munro, Duncan Munro, Connor Murbach, Nickolas Murillo, Albert Murphy, Connor Murphy, Dan Murphy, Ian Murphy, Sam Murphy, Samuel Murphy, Thomas Murphy, Tom Murphy, Dylan Murphy-Castillo, Adam Murray, Ben Murray, Charlie 'Kranitoko' Murray, Christopher Murray, Kirsty Murray, Lewis Murray, Rob Murray, Scott Murray, Simon Murray, Tina Murray, Rhys Murrell, John Murtagh, Maxx Murtaugh, Stefan 'Stuffie' Muscat, Thomas Muse, Daniel Mushrow, Ondra Musil, Sinclair Musiyiwa, Sam Muskovitz, Marvin Müssner, Brad Musson, Nabil Mustafa, Alexander Myagkov, Christopher Myers, Colton Myers, Douglas Myers, Hannah Myers, Jason Myers, Madison Myers, Matthieu Myers, Roald Myers, Samuel

Supporters

Myers, Al Myracle-Martin, Drew N., N², Oscar NA, Eric Nabeta, Nacho Typical Gamer, Daniel Naeb, Will Nagle, Kyle Nagles, Domonkos Nagykaldi, Lewis Naismith, Juan Najera, Kaylen Najera, Noble Namenson, Naree, Linus Närkling, Narski, Jacob David Nash, Jonathan Nash, Gabriel Nathan, Joshua Nathaniel, Jeff Natiuk, Noah Naugler, Matthew Naumann, Javier Navarro Muñoz, Carlo Navato, Lee Navin, Adam Nayler, Jamie Neale, Matthew Neenan, Erik Kristoffer Neerland, Caelan Neil, Cameron Neil, Jack Neilan, Hugh Neill, Ross Neilson, David Nekula, Jonathan Nell, Nelly & Fanny, Sion Nelmes, Robbie Nelms, Emily Nelson, Jared Nelson, Jordan Nelson, Joshua Nelson, Kevin Nelson, Michael Nelson, Robert Nelson, Thomas R. Nelson, Tyler Nelson, Gustaf Nerström, Nerve_Corrosion, Steven Ness, Markus Nesse, Grant Nesvacil, Oliver Netzthaler, Felix Neudecker, Darren Neumann, Mike Neupart, Sam Neville, Tyler Neville, Peter Martin New, Jarrod Newberry, Ian Newborn, Morgan Newell, William Newing, Josh Newman, Myron Newman, Sarah Newman, William (Birdrun) Newman, Adam Newsham, Maxwell Newsom, Alex Newson, Abigail Newton, Dean Newton, Jason Newton, Malcolm Newton, Paul Newton, Wendy Newton, Annie Nguyen, Donovan Nguyen, Mila Nguyen, Ryker Nicandro, Carrie Nichol, Jack Nichol, Oliver Nichol, Jake Nicholas, Charlie Nicholls, Brenden Nichols, J. Brooks Nichols, Lewis Nicholson, Matthew Nicholson, Max Nicholson, Robert Nicholson, Shaun Nicholson, Jason Nickel, David Nickerson, Jacob Nickerson, Billy Nicklin, Michael Nicosia, Andreas Nielsen, Derek Nielsen, Jonatan Nielsen, Nathan Nielsen, Sofie Vang Nielsen, Chase Nielson, Duncan Niess, Joey Niessen, Patrick 'Ekstäzy' Nietzschmann, Drew Niewoehner, Jake NightRaven2365, Ruben Nijveld, Jonathan Nikolaisen, Miles Nikolic, mar nil, Alexander Nilefalk, Johannes Nilson, Joakim Nilsson, Kaj I. Nilsson, Victor Nilsson, Ninjanblue, Aviad Nissel, Kieran Niven, Landi Nix, Eoghan Nixon, Ah No, Angus Noble, Dominic Noble, Kevin Nocito, Daniel Nocket, Edward Noguera, Jake Nolan, Jonny Nolan, Peter Nolan, William Nolan, John Nolden, Jack Nolder, Brian Nolte, Dominique Nolte, Liam Noordanus, Kyle Norburn, Ole Nørby, Anette B. Nordby, Thorstein Buind Nordby, Mathias Nordfjord, Jonas Nordlöf, Archie Norman, Elias Norman, Jayden Norman, Chris Norris, James Norris, Luke Norris, Benjamin Joseph Norris (Borris), Anthony North, Hana North, Casandra Northcutt, Brandon Northrop, Kirk Northrop, Dillan Norton, Erran Norton, Henry Norton, James Norton, Leigh Norton, Rebecca Norton, H L Noss, Ben Nosworthy, Not my real name, Kris Notari, Carsten Nottebohm, Kim Novice, Alexander Noya, William & Lori Noye, Will Nuessle, Adamir Nukić, Thomas Nulty, Luke Nunney, Logan Nunno, Frank Nutter, Bendik Dørum Nygaard, Alexander Nykjær, Selwyn Nypels, Dan O, Diarmaid Ó Braonáin, Naoise Ó Foighil Roantree, Colm Ó hIcí, Dom O., Isaac O' Connor, Mycah O'Brian, Callie O'Brien, Laura O'Brien, Robert O'Callaghan,

William O'Callaghan, Daniel O'Connell, Callum O'connor, Cameron O'Connor, Dylan O'Connor, Ellie O'Daire, Joe O'Donnell, Nathan O'Donnell, Sean O'Donnell, Thomas O'Donnell, Will O'Donnell, Aoife O'Donovan, Joseph O'Donovan, Rory O'Driscoll, Fergus O'Halloran, Stuart O'Hara, Samuel O'Kane, Liam O'Keefe, Conor O'Keeffe, Christopher O'Kelly, Ciaran O'Loughlin, John O'Neal, Daragh O'Neill, Devin O'Neill, Jacob O'Neill, Nick O'Neill, Cian O'Neill-Manning, Caelyn O'Reilly (chutneycubed), Jack O'Rourke, Michael O'Rourke, Jared O'Steen, Donagh O'Sullivan, James O'Sullivan, Michael O'Sullivan, Patrick O'Grady, Matthew O'Hern, Connor O'Reilly, Jon-Ryan Oakes, Thomas Oates, Katrin Obendrauf, Octanas, Travis Odinzoff, Raphael Odukoya, Corrin Offenholley, Corey Ogburn, Bryce Ogle, Paul Ogle, Joshua Ohlsson, John Oke, William Old, Arno Olde Hanter, Nina Olde Keizer, Liam Oldershaw, Jack Oldham, Elz 'Emu' Oldrey, Mark Oldroyd, Anna-Maja Oléhn (Agrajag), Michael Olesen, Victoria Warrer Olesen, Alex Oliver, Beckett Oliver, Dan Oliver, Daniel Oliver, Gary Oliver, Ian Oliver, James Oliver, Joe Oliver, Jonathan Oliver, Luke Oliver, Matthew Oliver, Peter Oliver, Scott Oliver, Juho Ollila, Wyatt Olney, Oskar Olofsson-Dolk, Her royal memejesty Taylor Olsen, Nathaniel Olsen, Ronny Philip Olsen, Sigbjørn 'Sigge300' M Olsen, Stian Olsen, Michael Olson, Christoffer Olsson, Henrik Olsson, Par Olsson, Viktor Ómarsson, Charles Ombler, OMG-BLN, Kelvin 'Hedgehog' On, Kyle Oneal, Eric Ongchango, Kieran Onions, Kjell Oostendorp, Jasper Oosterbroek, Thomas Oosthuyse, John Opatz, Dr Simon Opit, Jamie Orchard, Lee Orchard, Leroy Orel, William Orman, Felix Orme, Elís Orri, Aaron Emanuel Ortega, Luis Ortega, Armando Ortega Cabrera, Christian Ortiz, Philip Orton, Benjamin Osborne, Drew Osborne, Ella-Jay Osborne, Kjell Osborne, Stephen Osborne, Brandon Osier, Olumide Osikomaiya, Hunter Osmera, Asger Hartlev Østerby, Daniel Ostevall, Kristoffer Hegge Østreim, Christopher Ostrom, Daniel Ostrov, Adam Oswalt, Kester Oswick, Jonathan Othelis, Reilly Othoudt, Jesse Otoole, Alexander Ott, Carsten Otte, Morrison Outlaw, Malthe Plenge Overgaard, Officially Overlord, Evan Overly, Etienne Overpelt, Graham Ovington, Alwyn Owen, Charlotte Owen, Jenny Owen, Jonathan Owen, Christopher Owens, Georges Owens, Hugh Owens, Samuel Owens, Matthew Oxborrow, Alastair Oxby, James Oxley, Liam Oxley, Batu Ozer, Cas P, Frank P., P.Lepaffe, Pablo, Joseph Pacitti, Vicky Pacitti, Samantha Pacynko, Samuel Padfield, Simon Paffett, David Pagan, Phil Pagano, Joe Page, Logan Page, Morgan Page, Robert Page, Solomon Page, Taylor Page, Thomas Page, Brendon Paine, Jacob Paisley, Steven Palermo, Issac Palin, Billy Palmer, Callum Palmer, Daniel Palmer, Ethan Palmer, Matthew Palmer, Ryan Palmer, Trevor Palmer, Gunnar Pálsson, Jereld Pan, Leon Pan, Nasos Panagiotopoulos, Sumeet Panchal, Joe Panes, Danny Paniagua-Rodriguez, Joshua 'Mother Ducking' Panic, George Pankhurst, Dominic Panne, Naomi Panter, Anna Panton, Nikitas

Papadopoulos, Connor Pape, Samuel Paplanus, Nick Paquin, Thomas Pare, Amit Parekh, Leigh Parfitt, Ossi Parikka, Jennie Park, Kyoung Tae Park, Adam Parker, Adrian Parker, Alan Parker, Benjamin Parker, Charlie Parker, Charlotte Parker, Chris Parker, Drew Parker, Fred Parker, Jack Parker, Joe Parker, Josh Parker, Sam Parker, Stephen Parker, Steve Parker, Jack Parkin, Natalie Parkin, Jenny Parkins, Brenden Parkinson, Michaela Parkinson, Shyam Parmar, Richard Parnell, Samuel Parnham, Aidan Parr, Chloe Parr, Xian Parr, Alexandra Parris, Charles Parry, Dylan Parry, Heather Parry, Jeremy Parry, Ollie Parry, Callum Parsons, George Parsons, Oli Parsons, Andrea Partner, Eliot Partridge, Josh Partridge, William Partridge, PartyMarty, Almog Pas, Billy Pasciutti, Jordan Pascoe, Matthew Pasierb, Austin Pasquel, Neil Passfield, Temple Pate, Dhruval Patel, Niraj Patel, Pritesh Patel, Sam Patel, Alice Paterson, Andrew Paterson, Jay Paterson, Nicholas Paterson, Tom Paterson-Sylt, Daniel Pates, Jacob Patience, James Patmore, Stevie Patmore, Andrew Paton, Hamish Paton, Samuel Paton, Daniel Patrick, Josh Patrick, Roger Patrick, Justin Patrin, Senn Patteet, David Patten, Kenneth Patterson, Mitchell Patterson, Aiden Pattinson, Kathryn Pattison, Martin Pattison, Alexander Patton, Patton160, Artur Tadeu Paulani Paschoa, Christopher J. Paulbeck, Garrett Pauls, Oak Paws, Lewis Payea, Eleanor Paylor, Jamie Payne, Tim Payne, Josh Payze, Ethan Peace, Roger Peacey, Max Peachey, Andrew Peacock, Edward Peacock, Matt Peacock, Ben Pead, Joseph Peaker, Edward Pearce, Stuart Pearce, David Pearcy, Callum Pearl, David Pearman, Alexia Pearn, Dave Pearson, Jonas Pearson, Robert Pearson, Sean Pearson, Tom Hatton Pearson, Jordan Peart, Kristinn Pease, Spencer Peat, Struan Peat, Traylan Peat, Harry Peate, Alexander Pedersen, Andreas Edal Pedersen, Jørgen Pedersen, Tobias Pedersen, Stuart Pedlar, Lee Pedzisz, Emile Peel, Rob Peerlings, Thomas Peeters, Gabriel Pegram, Adrian Peine, Krista Pekarek, Tanguy Pelado, Charlie Pells, Brady Pemberton-Lloyd, Liana Pena, Noah Pencil, Philip Pender, Gheric Pendley, Craig Penfold, James Penlington, Matthew Penman, Zach Pennell, Toby Penney, Henry Kirk Pennington, Ste Pennington, Brian Penny, Hayley Penny, Holly Penny, Joel Penny, Harry and Jack Penwell, Sean Penxa, Jack Percival, Christian Percy, Daniel Percy, Emily Peregrine, Jade Peregrine, Mark Pereslete, Garrett Peri, Destinea Perkins, George Perkins, Christopher Perman, Taran Perman, Domenic Perna, Zach Perrell-Williams, Jon Alfie Perrett, Vinnie Perrett, Mason Perrin, Zack-orion Thomas James Perrin, Patrick Perring, Adam Perry, Andrew Perry, Daniel Perry, Ethan Perry, Lucy Perry, Nicholas Perry, Thomas Perry, Ciaran Persch, David Mathias Persson, Lovisa Persson, Fokko Perton, Djimy Djack Donovan Pesenti, Holly Petch, Nathan Petch, Bailey Peters, Tim Peters, Tyler Peters, Jacob Petersen, Nikolaj Slumstrup Petersen, Chandler Peterson, Elijah Peterson, Jeff Peterson, Shannon Lynne Peterson, Robert Petrie, Daniel Petrilä, Joseph Pettecrew, Rose Petteway, Adam Pettie, Luke Pettitt, Úlfur 'Wolfy'

Pétursson, Fabio Petza, Daniel Peukert, Matthew Peyton, Felix Pfrang, Nir Phili, Andrew Phillips, Blake Phillips, Caleb Phillips, Caleb Phillips, Callum Phillips, Carl 'Moony' Phillips, Carys Phillips, Charles Phillips, Connor Phillips, Daniel Phillips, Emma Phillips, Lucy Phillips, Luke Phillips, Roy Phillips, Sam Phillips, Tonicha Phillips, Adam Philp, James Philpott, Zac-luc Phipps, Ryan Phipps Kenny, Phoenix 2168, Ryan Piatt, David Picard, Severin Pick, William Pickard, Taylor Pickavance, Nate Pickens, Matthew Pickering, Lewis Pickford, Doctor Picklepuss, Zach Piddock, Arryn Pidwell, Caius Pierard, Devonta Pierce, Eric Clapton Pierce, Michael Pierce, Dustin Pieroelie, Timothy Pieschala, Samuel Pietanza, Pieter Pieterse, Pikachu, Colin Pike, Tegan Pike, David Piles Perea, Peter Pilgaard, Joseph Pilkington, Thomas Pilkington, Lachlan Pinder, Alex Pine, Gina Pine, Mandy Pine, Shaun Pinkerton, Angela Pinkster, Kieran Pinkstone, Robbie Pinnell, Olivia Pinnock, Abigail PinterParsons, Mark Piper, Yanick Pips, Clemens Pitsch, Jack Pittaway, Tim Pittman, Victoria Pittman, Aiden Pitts, Sean Pitty, Evgeny Pivovarskiy, Aaron Place, Jacob Plant, Mike Plant, Logan Platt, Tonie Platten, Pleak, Charlotte Amelia Poe, Poggle566, Henry Pointer, Megan Pointer, Tim Pointer, Andrew Pointon, Sander Pol, Benjamin Polan, Anthony Thomas Poliandro, Robert Polivka, Gabriel Pollard, Justin Pollard, Oliver Pollard, Sean Pollington, Callum Pollock, Ben Polson, Michael Polzin, Talon Pongracz, José Ponte, Lliam Pontifex, Jake Pontin, Jon Pool, Connor Poole, Emily Poole, Andrew Poor, Colton Pope, Connor Pope, Stephen Pope, Oliver Popham, Danny Popkin, Dylan Popovich, Matthias Poppe, Thomas Porada, Gustavs Porietis, Dave Portch, Ross Porteous, Sean Porteous, Aaron Porter, Avery Porter, Ewan Porter, Jacob Porter, Jorden Porter, Keith Porter, Kevin Lynn Porter, Matthew Porter, Thomas Porter, Tobie Porter, Jeremy Porter - Mr Flowers, Owen Portier, Charlie Posey, Roan Post, Angus Postma, Joel Postma, Jorg Pot, Elliott Poteet, Dan Pott, Jack Pottage, Andrew Potter, Ben Potter, Daniel Potter, Elise Potter, Mason Potter, Rachel Potter, Ryan Potter, Timothy Potter, Zac Potter, Carter Potthoff, Joost Potting, Jonathan Potton, Christian Potts, Scarlett Potts, Savana Pouliot, Lasse Poulsen, Benjamin Poulson, Baz Poulton, Alex Povey, Derrick Powell, Hugh Powell, Jordan Powell, LukeMJ Powell, Robin Powell, Taylor Powell, Tom Powell, Matthew Powell-Scarlett, Jamie Power, Aaron Powers, Shane Poynter, Ruth Poynting, Max Prahst, Prasannakalyan (Lanz3lot), Dallin Pratt, Joshua Pratt, Alaysia Prear, Petter Prené, Ben Prentice, Michael Prentice, Matthew Prescott, Zoë Prescott, Michael Presson, Danny Preston, Jennifer Preston, John Preston, Karen Preston, Michael Preston, Philip Preston, Stevie Preston, Joshua Preston-Cooper, Brandon Pretorius, Hywel Price, Jesse Price, Jordan Price, Josh Price, Nicholas Price, Noble Price, Ruby Price, Sam Price, Cameron Pridmore, Hunter Priesol, Rasmus Prim, Sebastian Prim, Jonathan Prince, Willow Pring, Rachel Prinn, Jay Pritchard, Jonathan Pritchard, Dylan Procter,

Supporters

Zachary Proctor, Lucy Micaela Proegler, Jared Profenna, Guy Prosser, Justin Prosser, Matthew prototype654, Frank Provoost, David Prunty, Kevin Pryke, Robert Pryor, psythrone, Jake Puddephatt, Rhys Puddephatt, Nolan Pudimat, Chris Pudney, Rick Pufky, James Pugh, Joshua Tyler Pugh, Samuel Pugh, Matthew Pull, Alexandra Pullen, Lilliam Pumpernickel, Benjamin Punte, Dan Punter, David Punton, George Purchase, Joshua Purdy, Purist, Anthony Purkiss, Juho Purola, Quinn Purtee, Gerwin Puttenstein, Jonjo Pymm, Nur Qatanani, Qdrophenia, Quadstrike, Ariana Quakenbush, Omar Quansah, Dean Quantrill, Pablo Queirolo, Gabriel Quek, Moritz Quester, Gabriel Quick, Sam Quick, Travis Quiding, Eamonn Quigley, Michael Quigley, Oskar Quigley, James Quilliam, Evan Quincy, Ben Quinlan, Brad Quinn, Jamie Quinn, Samantha Quinn, Alex Quirin, A Quite Bitter Being, Aleem Qureshi, Aidan R, Kyle R, Ra_Wolfbane, Joe Raad, Kayam Raaphorst, Kyle Rabin, racenut112, Jordan Rackham, RadagastDM, Duncan Radband, Ty Radcliffe, Greg Rademaekers, Sean Radford, Craig Rae, Steven Rae, Donal Rafferty, Teo Raftopoulos, Michael Raghallaigh, Jared Rahman, Luke Rahman, Moin Rahmani, Harry Rainer, Miko Rajaniemi, Steven Rambo, Brandon Ramirez, Melchor Daniel Ramos, James Ramplin, Martin Ramsay, Jack Ramshaw, Jamie Ramshaw, Sander Ramsrud, Jacob Rand, Connor Rand-Whittlesey, Demian Ranftl, Dario Rangel, Alan Ransome & Erin Greenslade, Emily Rose Ranson, Thomas Ranton, Tony Rapalo, Ryan Raposo, Raptorbricks, Alexander Gabriel Rasch, rashfael, Stewart Rasmusen, Phillip Rasmussen, Nath Raspin, Jack Rathbone, Luke Rathke, Jonathan Rauscher, Rasmus Ravantti, Alexis Raven, Amy Ravenwood, Jakob Ravn, James Rawcliffe, Hollie Rawlings, Stephen Rawlings, Alex Rawlins, Joe Rawlinson, Luke Rawluk, Matt Rawson, Raxa, Dylan Ray, Jordan Ray, Stephen Ray, Rayan, Aidan Rayner, Andrew Rayner, Katie Rayner, Daniel Raynor-Smith, Megan Rea, Amelia Read, Lucas Reade, Cassandra Ream, Ian Reason, Jordie Reason, Alex Rebain, Andreas Redclift, Thomas Redding, Josh Reddy, Molly Reddy, Dalton Rederick, Ben Redfern, Samuel Brian Redfern, Adam Redleaf, Elliot Redshaw, Ben Reed, Charles Reed, Dale Reed, Daniel Martyn Reed, Jack Reed, Jacob Reed, Mathew Reed, Nikolai Reed, Will Reed, Jon Rees, Logan Rees, Nick Rees, Ria Rees, Simon Rees, Sam Reese, Oliver Reeskamp, Matt Reeve, David Reeves, Thomas Reeves, Collin Regalia, Peter Regier, Nikolas Artem Regimbal, Rei and Grace, Parker Reich, Hagan Reichel, Cameron Reid, Christopher Reid, Jacob Reid, Max Reid, Micah Reid, Owen Reid, Phil Reid, Travis Reid, Cornelius Reidy, Jack Reifeis, Lorenzo & Orlando Reijndorp, Addison Reilly, Calum Reilly, Elliott Reilly, Kara Reilly, Xavier Reilly, Olaf Oude Reimer, Steffen Reinbold, Indrek Reinol, Jake Reisen, Matthew Reishman, Josh Reiss, Alexander Reiter, Zachary Reitnauer, Maarten Reitsema, Dani Ren, Anna Renaud, Jacob Reneau, Luke Renik, David Rennie, Kieran

Rennie, Rens Rens, Scott Reszel, Jacob Rettmuller, James Reuben, Adrian Reuling, Blake Revelle, Andrew Reynolds, Daniel Reynolds, Ian Reynolds, Jonathon Reynolds, Mackenzie Reynolds, Mark Reynolds, Matt Reynolds, Cameron Reynolds-Beer, Leon Derek Reynolds-Brown, Terence Rhee, Kyle Rhodeback, Aaron Rhodes, Harrison Rhodes, Kevin Rhodes, Ollie Rhodes, Richard Rhodes, Samuel Rhodes, Thomas Rhodes, Trent Rhodes-Ousley, Jonathan Rhyder, Sherwin Riahi, Cameron Rice, Nicholas Rice, Stewart Rice (Look mum i'm in a book!), Dylan Rich, William Rich, Randy Richard, Alfie Richards, Andrew Richards, Dale Richards, Erik Richards, Sam Richards, Toran Bruce Richards, Tyrese Richards, G Richardson, Jack Richardson, James Richardson, Jamie Richardson, Joe Richardson, Luke Richardson, Nick Richardson, Philip Richardson, Samantha Richardson, Harry Richmond, Zachary Richmond, Cj Richner, Rayne Rickrode, @RickRWard, Liam Ridd, Mackenzie Ridd, Christopher Riddell-Rovira, Emily Ridding, Brett Riddle, Joe Rider, George Riding, Anthony Ridler, Dean Ridley, Vitor Riedel, Aidan Rieger, Claudia Riegger, Trent Riegler, Zane Rietschlin, Dominique Rietveld, Nelleke Rietvink, Daniel Rigby, Alex Riley, Ben Riley, Benjamin Riley, Conor Riley, Jack Riley, Lottie Riley, Oliver Riley, Shaun Riley, Riley-bones, Bailey Rimmer, Rina!, Julian Rind, Jack Riordan, Johan Ripendal, Brian Risinger, RisingFlames, Patrick Risso, Jotte Ristimäki, Peter Kristian Risvik, James Ritchie, Michael Ritchie, Taylor Ritchie, Jonathan Ritson, Harrison Ritter, Richie Ritter, Stephan Ritzdorf, River, Antonio Nicolás Rivero Gómez, Andy Rixon (ToxicNinjaUK), Callum 'BBR' Roach, Matthew Roach, Rob, Adam Robarts, Max Robb, Robert.l, Jarrett Robertazzi, Aaron Roberts, Andrew Roberts, Ashley Roberts, Casey Jay Roberts, Charlie Roberts, Connor Roberts, Danica Roberts, Gareth Roberts, Griff Roberts, Iain 'chumpyman' Roberts, James Roberts, James Roberts, Joanne Roberts, Kai Roberts, Kaleab Roberts, Kelly Roberts, Luke Roberts, Owen Roberts, Patrick Roberts, George Robertson, Joseph 'IrvoL2001' Robertson, Lonny Robertson, Matthew Robertson, Spencer Robertson, Trent Robertson, Cedric Robichaud, Ethan Robichaux, Scott Robins, Adam Robinson, Andrew Robinson, Ashaki Robinson, Christopher Robinson, Isaac Robinson, Jac Robinson, Jude Robinson, Lachlan Robinson, Lawrence Luke Robinson, Lucas Robinson, Martin Robinson, Nicholas Robinson, Paul Robinson, Sam Robinson, Simon Robinson, Steve Robinson, Zachary Robinson, Harry Robson, Louis Robson, Sam Robson, Kaitlan Roby, Stefan Roche, Nathan Rochon, Jevan Rock, Enrico Rockstroh, Erik Rodabaugh, James Rodber, Oliver Roddis, Rob Roddy, Anton Rodenburg, Zander Rodger/Pyromidgit - Frankie Haymer/Piromoth, Billy Rodgers, Jonathan Rodgers, Lewis Rodgers, Rob Rodgers, Samantha Rodgers, Shane Rodgers, Toby 'Zero' Rodgers, Stian Rødland, Matthew Rodrick, William Rodrigues, Christopher Rodriguez, Isaac Rodriguez, Leilani Rodriguez, Zach Rodriguez, Lars